UKRA

Reading: the a b c and Beyond

Proceedings of the Twenty-Fourth Annual Course
and Conference of the United Kingdom Reading
Association,
Cramond Campus,
Moray House College of Education.
Edinburgh, July 1987

Editor: Christine Anderson

 **MACMILLAN EDUCATION**

First published 1988.

Published by
MACMILLAN EDUCATION LTD
Houndmills, Basingstoke, Hampshire RG21 2XS
and London
Companies and representatives
throughout the world

Printed in Great Britain by Richard Clay Ltd. Bungay

British Library Cataloguing in Publication Data

United Kingdom Reading Association.
    Conference (24th : 1987 : Moray House College of Education)
    Reading : the abc and beyond : proceedings of the Twenty
Fourth Annual Course and Conference of the United Kingdom
Reading Association, Cramond Campus, Moray House College
of Education, Edinburgh, July 1987.
    1. Schools. Curriculum subjects : Reading
    I. Title   II. Anderson, Christine
    428.4′071

ISBN 0–333–46724–8

Contents

RESEARCH

Darling!

OVERVIEWS

Acknowledgements

I wish to thank, on behalf of the United Kingdom Reading Association, the following individuals and institutions for their assistance in making it possible for the Twenty-Fourth Annual Conference to take place and hence this book to be compiled:

My family, for their patience and understanding

The Conference Committee –
Ishbel Fraser
William A. Gatherer
Mary Karus
Paquita McMichael
Alex Paulin
Chris Ross
Freda Satow
George Wilson

Cambridge University Press
Holmes McDougall Publishers
Lothian Region
Oliver and Boyd Publishers
Oxford University Press
Rank Xerox
The Scottish Post Office
Ward Lock Educational Publishers

Miranda Carter of Macmillan Education

Christine Anderson
c/o UKRA Administrative Office
Edgehill College of Education
St Helen's Road
Ormskirk
Lancs L39 4QP

Introduction

The theme of the Twenty-Fourth Annual Conference of UKRA held at Cramond Campus of Moray House College of Education, Edinburgh, was:

Reading: the a b c and Beyond

The theme was chosen to emphasise the need to look at reading in the context of all the associated language and communication arts, beyond initial reading, beyond the classroom walls.

Many splendid papers were read and presentations made, from the opening sessions and W. A. Gatherer's rousing address to the eloquent closing speeches of Muriel Spark and Allan Massie. The Association is deeply indebted to everyone who gave so much of their time to share their expertise with us, for no financial reward.

This selection of papers is representative of the scope and diversity of issues covered. For the purpose of this book, the a b c is considered to be the teaching of reading, writing and language. The book, unlike previous Proceedings, is compiled with no marked divisions, though there is grouping, as one aspect of language leads on to another, along with and through yet another – a total ongoing experience. The papers speak for themselves but I should like to make some general observations.

The first papers are those most obviously directed at classroom teaching. Sheila Flower and Betty Stirling set the scene by describing a basic organisation wherein children may enjoy success, purposeful activity and develop confidence in their own learning abilities. Christian Gerhard and Marian Tonjes elaborate on learning to learn, providing theories and ways to enable and model good learning, echoed later in other papers. David Wray continues the theme of purpose and pupil self-help ('Literacy includes the ability to function autonomously') and urges the development of the human skills which no computer possesses.

But all good teachers look beyond the classroom, beyond the a b c. They look to the researches and surveys (some by classroom teachers, some by professional researchers) which influence our methodologies and the theories on which they are based. William Jackson's account of the Foundations of Writing project again stresses the shared learning approach with children given back the 'ownership' of their learning, and with teachers, as well as pupils, benefitting from the experience. He emphasises the quality and variety of purposeful experiences necessary for developing written language and Anne Robinson observes the kind of children's invented spelling/ writing, alluded to by him. Susan Lehr further exhorts us not to underestimate our pupils: they *can* summarise, analyse and generalise from an early age, given a high exposure to literature, and time to verbalise and share views about it.

Beyond again are the experienced practitioners, now in positions from where they can provide overviews of trends and research findings, essential in retaining balance and perspective in all our theories and practice. Margaret Clark bids us heed the danger of certain kinds of assessment impeding the experiences of written language so vital to children's development. Roger Beard puts reading in context, as well as some current issues which have unfortunately become over-simplified. Doug Dennis would promote the teacher as enabler, accommodating and encouraging pupils' considerable learning abilities in a purposeful way. Keith Gardner's reminiscences are invaluable, and his cynical moments are familiar to many of us. Children learn in spite of us? Some do, but he challenges our skills as teachers in the 'Brew XI belt' where they certainly do not become fully literate. And so, having gleaned from all the papers these insights into reading, language and the learning process, and our place as teachers alongside parents and children, the message is clear. We must ensure that we *are* enablers, empowering our pupils to achieve full autonomy in literacy, and consequently in other areas. Our responsibility is heavy.

Beyond, also, are the scholars whose dissertations inform and entertain us. But while we may laugh at some long-gone theories and practices, we must look beyond the amusement and savour the feelings of harmony so engendered. As Ian Michael says, 'more important . . . is the feeling of historical solidarity: that one belongs to a succession of colleagues who even if (like one's present colleagues) they could hold the most extraordinary opinions, were fellow practitioners'.

And beyond all these are the professional writers and poets who have learned in spite of us, who have surmounted all the theories and methodologies. The Muriel Spark Lecture provides a truly delightful finale to this motivating and provocative collection of papers.

Christine Anderson

Chapter 1

Easy as a b c, When You Know How: Meeting the Demands of Today's Curriculum in the Primary School and Classroom

Sheila Flower and Betty Stirling

Are we asking the impossible of today's teachers and headteachers? However enlightened, skilled and committed teachers are, the demands placed on them by recent curriculum development are tremendous. Successful management of the classroom, resources and discipline is the key to fulfilling these demands by making it possible to create a suitable learning and teaching environment with the means at our disposal.

In this paper it is hoped to examine successful strategies for the organisation of resources both within the school and classroom, the management of group teaching and the training of children to be self-disciplined and independent workers.

Introduction

If one examines the two lists (see Table 1.1) compiled by the widely experienced educators who were members of Workshop 1 at the annual UKRA conference at Cramond it will be seen that the reconciliation of today's teachers' needs with desirable experiences for pupils is a daunting objective.

The ways forward being indicated to class teachers by researchers, college-based colleagues, HMIs and Education Departments are compounding the difficulties of the task. Faced with such complex demands it is small wonder there is crisis in the classroom. Unfortunately, in our experience, this state of crisis is not fully realised and sufficient steps are not being taken to train, re-train and support the class teacher in what has developed into a highly complex task – that of providing a suitable learning and teaching environment, with the means available, which meets the needs of today's society. Nursery and infant teachers are more likely to have the necessary materials and to be trained to cope with classes of children, at differing levels of development, engaged in disparate activities simultaneously. However, many primary teachers are still having to rely on methods and organisation that, given the demands, are wasteful of their time and resources.

TABLE 1.1   *Pupils' experiences/Teachers' needs*

Pupils' experiences	Teachers' needs

Free physical activities
Directed physical activities
Free creative activities
Directed creative activities
Individual/group attention
 	
Language skills –
  (reading)
  (writing)
  (listening)
  (talking)
 	
Maths and Science –
  (practical)
  (oral)
  (problem-solving)
  (discovering)
	Job satisfaction
	Time-
	  preparation
	  consultation
	  evaluation (self and
	    pupil)
	  teaching (group, class,
	    individual)
	  liaison (outside services
	    other schools, parents)
	Resources –
	  follow-up materials
	  textbooks
	  A.V. materials (tapes,
	    cassettes, records etc.)
	
	Support –
	  senior staff
	  parents
	  other services
	  auxiliary help

The purpose of this paper is to examine strategies which have been tried and tested and which have proved helpful in overcoming some of the problems facing today's primary schools.

While the strategies will be examined under the headings (a) The Management of Group-teaching, Assignments and Activities, (b) Organisation of Resources and (c) Training in Self-Discipline, these are artificial boundaries created for convenience since these aspects merge and mesh in the primary classroom to create an integrated whole.

The management of group teaching, assignments and activities

Group teaching

Since it is impossible for the class teacher to teach each child separately it is in the small group setting that it *is* possible to teach most effectively towards the ability of the individual. In this setting it is easier to diagnose problems and to assess skills, to draw children out and to assess understanding. Teachers know what they have tried to *teach* and it is in the group setting that they can discover best what has been *learnt*.

Initially teachers may be worried when, in the small group, they discover lack- of understanding of some basic concept or process. However, the sooner such problems are discovered the better for the child since the acquisition of further skills may be hampered by a less than sound foundation. Remedial action can be taken more readily in group situations. So that maximum benefit can be obtained from the periods the pupil spends outside class or group teaching time, it is important that children are trained in independent routines that will give reinforcement and practice of skills taught or opportunities for self-expression through self-chosen or directed tasks.

For this it is essential that each class has *two* timetables – one for the teacher and one for the children, which run concurrently. The teacher's timetable indicates which groups are being taught and when (see Table 1.2). The children's timetable shows the ebb and flow between class, group and individual activities as well as gym, TV and other fixed lessons (see Fig. 1.1).

TABLE 1.2 *Teacher's group teaching timetable*
(Shows 4 ability groups across a composite P1–2)

Monday	Triangles	Circles	Squares	Pandas	Lions
Tuesday	Circles	Squares	Rectangles	Lions	Bears
Wednesday	Squares	Rectangles	Lions	Bears	Tigers
Thursday	Rectangles	Triangles	Bears	Tigers	Pandas
Friday	Triangles	Circles	Tigers	Pandas	

MATHEMATICS GROUPS – Triangles, circles, squares, rectangles.
LANGUAGE GROUPS – Pandas, lions, bears, tigers.
Each of the four groups has three maths. and three language lessons per week in the mornings. These are short and intensive.

Assignments

A programme of group assignments is planned for two main purposes: (i) to offer reinforcement of skills taught and (ii) to give children an opportunity to work independently and responsibly. It also gives the teacher the chance to group teach while other children are busy.

The following questions are designed for the evaluation of assignments and form a framework in which to work.

1. Is the work assigned geared to reinforce the skills taught?
2. Is the language/vocabulary sufficiently easy for a pupil to be able to work independently?
3. Is the standard of worksheet or work card presented to the pupils of the highest order as a good example?

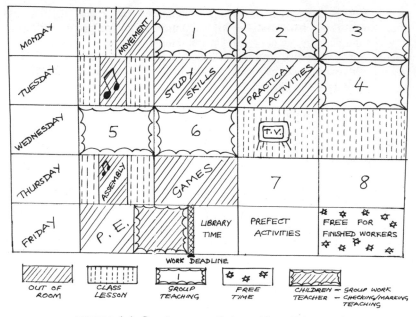

FIGURE 1.1 *Specimen pupil timetable – Primary 6*

FIGURE 1.2 *Primary 1 assignments*

4. Are group programmes displayed clearly? (see Fig. 1.2)
5. Are materials and equipment easily accessible? (see Fig. 1.3)
6. Do assignments cover a variety of skills – reading, drawing, discussion, listening, recording – as well as writing in exercise books?
7. Are children clear about what to do with finished assignments?

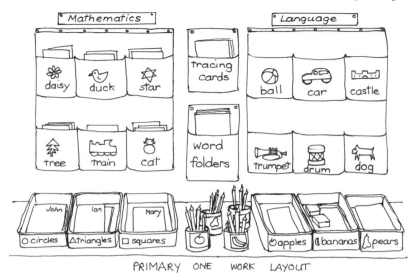

FIGURE 1.3 *Summary of work layout*

8. Are meaningful and educational activities provided for in-between times and for when programmes are completed?
9. How are assignments checked and corrected (as near the time of completion as is possible is recommended)? Recorded?
10. What points are checked if assignments are consistently unfinished?
11. What strategy has been worked out to monitor standards and to deal with badly executed work?
12. At what stage(s) will help be sought from the headteacher or assistant headteacher?

In nursery classes children aged 3–4 are used to a free choice of activities. They are trained to move between these in a very civilised manner. They are able to work at these activities relatively independently and with considerable concentration. They are trained to tidy up behind them and to take responsibility for themselves at an appropriate level. There has to be a continuum of experience. It is, therefore, essential for the succeeding stages in the primary school to build on and develop the experience and practice of previous years.

Self-discipline and responsibility will not grow without opportunities being made to practise them. A group teaching, assignment and activity system provides that opportunity.

Activities

The purpose of setting up workshop/activity areas in the classroom at all stages is (i) to train children in self-discipline and independence, (ii) to give opportunity for the pursuit and development of personal interests, (iii) to give opportunity for self-expression through a variety of media, (iv) to give opportunity for a variety of practice and reinforcement of skills taught, (v) to free the teacher to work undisturbed with other groups of children and (vi) to maximise use of all parts of the classroom.

In planning the organisation of activity areas consideration needs to be given to the following:

1. What learning activities are going to take place?
2. Where is the best place to locate the activity?
3. How many children are going to work at the activity simultaneously?
4. What working space is needed?
5. How will necessary equipment for the activity be labelled and stored for easy access and tidying?
6. What development/progression is being built in to the activity?
7. Is there a balance between direction and free choice?
8. What rules will have to be developed with the children about this area?
9. How will groups be trained to use this area?
10. How will the teacher cope with behavioural problems at the activity?
11. How will a balance of activities for children be achieved? Rota? Timetable? (see Fig. 1.4)

A selection of activities from the following list could be considered.
READING/LANGUAGE – include taped stories, reading games, taping practice

GROUPS	MONDAY	TUESDAY	WEDNESDAY	THURSDAY	FRIDAY
Cats	writer's workshop	games table	library	listening-post	personal project
Fish	personal project	writer's workshop	games table	library	listening-post
Chimps.	listening-post	personal project	writer's workshop	games table	library
Birds	library	listening-post	personal project	writer's workshop	games table
Spiders	games table	library	listening-post	personal project	writers workshop

FIGURE 1.4 *Primary 6 activities form*

for interviews, drama, computer programs, attractive reading material.
WRITING – consider favourite poetry cards, story starters, handwriting
practice cards, variety of paper and pens.
MATHS/SCIENCE – computer programs, maths games and puzzles, maths
extension work, sand, water play etc.
MUSIC/DRAMA – include excerpts from records and tapes to listen to,
creating sound effects for plays, imaginative play/dressing up related to
project.
ART/CRAFT – Painting, model making, clay, collage, plasticine.
GAMES – computer, maths and reading games, constructional materials,
jigsaws etc.
PROJECT AREAS – for display and reference material. Activities are not
'frills' or 'rewards' for work well done, but an essential part of a balanced
curriculum. It is more important that the less able child is given ample
time for these choices and careful attention has to be paid to the tailoring
of assignments so that this can happen.

Organisation of resources

The group teaching/assignment/activities approach has important implications for the management of resources at both class and school levels.

Within the classroom, if children are to work independently at assignments
or selected activities, materials, equipment, books and workcards must be
organised in such a way that children can proceed without teacher
intervention. The teacher requires to devise a system whereby pens, pencils,
paper, paint, exercise and textbooks etc., are readily available and can be
accessed by children without the teaching sessions being interrupted (see
Fig. 1.3).

To a certain extent the lone class teacher can operate this system
satisfactorily. However, in the long run, it is the support of a whole-school
policy which determines its success. The class teacher requires access to a
wide selection of material, equipment and textbooks in order to cater for
the range of ability and variety of activities. Judicious budgeting and
efficient management of resources by the headteacher in consultation with
staff are, therefore, essential.

Whatever the financial circumstances in which a school finds itself,
centralisation of resources, in some form, will enhance its spending power.
Little used, expensive but essential equipment can be shared. Group, rather
than class, sets of textbooks will give far greater choice of text for the same
outlay.

There are, of course, certain issues which must be addressed if the scheme
is to succeed.

1. What resources are to be shared?
2. Where and how will they be stored?
3. What borrowing system will be used?
4. Who will be responsible for maintenance?

Training in self-discipline

In a classroom where the curriculum is interesting and varied and where children, who are learning at their own rate, have opportunities to express themselves in a variety of media behavioural problems are less likely.

Nevertheless, it is by conscious effort on behalf of the teacher that children are encouraged to be self-disciplined. Opportunities have to be made through a programme of assignments and activities as previously described, for children to *practise* self-discipline. However, children have to be *helped* to be aware of such things as (i) acceptable levels of sound for different tasks, (ii) acceptable language of communication within the classroom, (iii) the need to work responsibly and independently at tasks, chosen or set, (iv) when and how it is appropriate to interrupt another person at work (teacher or child) and (v) the necessity of caring for the materials and areas they are using.

Through discussion between pupil and teacher, the need and the reasons for mutually acceptable standards of behaviour will become clear and a few simple and positively couched rules evolved, e.g. 'Come prepared to work', 'Think of other people', 'Behave safely and sensibly'.

The logical consequences of being unable to keep the rules also require to be discussed, e.g. temporary withdrawal from the area where the problem occurred.

If children have been actively involved in formulating the class discipline system then the teacher's training is likely to be more effective.

It is important for the teacher to remember that just as children require a great deal of repetition and practice in order to become literate and numerate so they require the same practice and support to become self-disciplined. Reinforcement in a variety of ways is important.

For those who use a points system to reinforce good behaviour the following guidelines are offered.

1. Give all children a set number with which to begin.
2. Trade these points for privileges such as extra computer time, half an hour's free choice etc.
3. Be fair and consistent.
4. Make it possible for children to win back lost points.
5. Make sure all children have a degree of success and are encouraged to improve on their own performance.
6. If the system fails the child for two weeks in succession think again or investigate.

Conclusion

Providing models has been unpopular practice for many years and so, as the free unstructured classroom failed to meet our needs, the traditional classroom teacher model prevails. Yet, nowadays, in almost every aspect of the curriculum, and particularly in language arts, the techniques required for more effective teaching and learning are practised mainly in the group setting.

The classroom, therefore, requires to become a more structured, but dynamic, place where learning can occur in a variety of ways. We offer our model as a possible means to that end.

Chapter 2

Teaching 10–14 Year Olds a Way to Success

Christian Gerhard

Students need to be active learners able to make independent decisions about processing information, including text. They need to know what to tell themselves in order to be in control. Part of this control is achieved by looking for patterns in all information. These patterns may be rules, such as in spelling, or may be types of relationships such as categories, part-whole, comparison, cause and effect or the way the text is organised. Each of these patterns requires a different type of response. Teachers of 10–14 year olds need to model these responses and provide guided practice.

Introduction

> If you expect people to examine their thoughts, to be mindful about their use of mind, all the evidence points to the fact that they can and will do so.
>
> (Bruner, 1985, p. 607)

There are reasons to be optimistic that teachers of even underachieving and less successful students in the middle years can help them become competent readers in later years. Recent research in neuropsychology and the cognitive sciences as well as in instruction have together drawn a rather clear and convincing picture of the optimal conditions for learning. Successful programmes have shown that teachers, given sufficient leeway, can have a high degree of control over important learning conditions regardless of circumstances outside the classroom. The most important component of successful programmes has been the expectation that all students can learn and that they do so best by being actively involved in their own learning. This is hardly news, but research has produced heavy artillery to support such an approach.

From motivation and brain research we also know that teachers concerned about promoting positive student feelings toward classroom activities are right in believing that this affects not just general behaviour, but also the way information is processed. This knowledge will support their efforts.

Finally, while reading is a special skill, it is now seen as directly affected by thinking, writing, and by acquiring knowledge. This means that every minute of good instruction can contribute to reading progress.

The argument drawn from a wealth of recent research goes like this:
- learning is activated by the individual's goal;
- human beings are pattern seekers and storers;
- students can communicate and learn with language.

Learning is activated by the individual's goal

Learning new information is activated by the *individual's* goal in a task situation. This goal determines what will be attended to and whether task-irrelevant information can be ignored. The goal also determines whether the learner will search for comparable or relevant information in memory and in surrounding items. This must be done so that new information can be incorporated into the *individual's* scheme of things (Roth and Frisby, 1986).

This individual scheme of things – the organisation and later reorganisation of experience into hierarchies and extensive networks of categories – make up what are sometimes called the schemata available for assisting information processing. They make it possible for new information to be quickly assimilated into existing categories, or to create related but new categories. For example, a child familiar with a few birds can assimilate cranes and puffins, but must create a related category such as 'man-made flying objects' when encountering aircraft. New information is not 'learned' until it is thus incorporated. The goal of the learner determines if this process will take place or not. When attention is not paid, NOTHING HAPPENS!

Human beings are pattern seekers and storers

Fortunately, in addition to having memory stored at least partly in the form of a structure of knowledge, human beings are by nature analysers and pattern seekers (Miller, Galanter and Pribram, 1960; Pribram 1981). By creating categories of information, generalisations become available to assist in making the inferences and predictions that are so necessary to mature reading comprehension. This means, for example, that if you learn about the attributes of mammals, you then can infer a great deal of information about any new mammals encountered. Or when you learn about a character in a story, you can predict how that character will react to events.

Students can communicate and learn with language

The third strength teachers can count on is that students have the use of language in varying degrees for communicating with others so that they can learn about other ways of looking at the world and themselves, can gradually distance themselves from immediate experience, and can generalise about relationships of different kinds. That is to say, they can find a resemblance between family trees and hierarchies of ideas, or find conditional connections between 'if you don't clean your room, you will not go to the party' and 'if we don't dispose of hazardous waste properly, we shall suffer dire consequences'.

Goal setting

Before teachers can build upon these three strengths of schemata, pattern seeking, and language, they have to persuade students to have task-relevant goals. Clearly goals are not formulated entirely by cognitive processes. As noted a neurophysiologist as Karl Pribram (1981) writes that after thirty experiments on the function of the frontal cortex to determine the probable effects of lobotomies, he finds that these effects can be couched in such terms as motivation and emotion or decision theory. Emotion and motivation play a key role in setting suitable goals, in persevering, and in taking the risks that are a necessary part of learning.

Both student and teacher expectation of success and failure have repeatedly been shown materially to affect the process and product of classroom activities (Hiebert, Winograd and Danner, 1983; de Charms, 1984; Alvermann and Ratekin, 1982; Brattesani, Weinstein and Marshall, 1984; Brainin, 1985). Once again, since it is the *learner's* goal that activates attention to relevant information and blocks out the irrelevant, all factors affecting this goal must be taken into account (Sigel, 1986).

The teacher's goal is, of course, very important in providing suitable learning opportunities. However, it is not by itself the determinant of learning, even though with young children it may appear to be so. In the early schools years pleasing the teacher and one's parents and feeling competent among school friends often prescribes adopting the teacher's goal. As students reach the middle and upper school years, however, their individual experiences of success and failure colour their self-concept and, therefore, the kind of goal they are likely to choose.

Some students retreat to a defensive position, guarding their fragile egos at all costs and closing off avenues of learning. Establishing patterns of successful goal-setting in the early and middle years is, therefore, at least as important as teaching any individual reading skills. Older students, not to mention those in jobs, must be able to function independently, deciding what to read, when to do it, and how long to take over it, making judgements of what is important or irrelevant and monitoring their own performance. They do not acquire these abilities without having guided practice opportunities in a supportive environment in the formative years.

Developing an interest in learning

Beyond learning to set goals, students also need to have an interest in acquiring information and related processing skills. While there are times when nothing offered seems to interest some older students, taking time to relate the subject matter to their lives often does pay off. Here again, teachers must have leeway to spend more time on introducing material.

Students can also benefit from being given time to read material of their own choice in order to develop a mental representation of reading as something useful and pleasurable (Morrow and Weinstein, 1986). Giving them time to read school materials in the classroom in the higher forms after proper goal setting and introduction can also prevent negative feelings towards reading.

Reading opportunities in school should include a variety of texts and include a discussion of how they and the processing needed differ. An early introduction to interesting informative prose can make the difficult transition from stories to expository text less arduous.

Once students have learned how to set goals and have had opportunities to learn to enjoy reading and to feel competent in dealing with different types of reading, what does an expert reader do?

What does an expert reader do?

Take a problem-solving approach

The expert reader will first of all have a task-relevant goal for reading, distinguishing between reading for fun, reading for facts or directions, for a broad overview, for complex concepts, plot, style, or persuasion. Once the goal for reading is established, the most efficient processing method will be adopted, a number of them being available. In other words, a problem-solving approach is taken: the goal is defined, difficulties assessed, including personal strengths and weaknesses in relation to the task, alternative strategies considered, and results checked. Over the years all this may have become automatic; supraconscious, so to speak. Adaptive organisational skills possessed by all human beings first used unconsciously have become conscious tools and are then used automatically.

Recognises text cues

The expert reader will also recognise text cues in order to activate prior knowledge, or schemata, that will allow the making of inferences and filling of gaps in explicitness every author must leave. Some of the cues noticed will be indicators of top-level structure of text such as cause and effect, comparison, or generalisation and examples (Meyer, 1975). These structural cues will provide an overall guide for the processing of content, setting up slots in which to insert information. This awareness of structure together with situation knowledge needed to provide background for details enables the expert reader to form useful mental representations (Kintsch, 1986).

Identification of the structure of text together with knowledge of the subject (Rissland, 1985) will help the expert reader decide what is important as well as anticipate probable information. This anticipation means that fewer visual cues are needed for recognising words and phrases (Gough, 1984). For example, words like Churchill, Stalin and Roosevelt will be expected in a history of World War II so that only the capital letters and configurations of the words are needed as cues.

Further visual cues to important information such as different sizes or styles or print, spacing, and location on the page also speed up reading for the expert. Even punctuation provides processing cues. A colon followed by several commas will indicate a category, while two widely spaced commas will indicate more than one idea in a sentence (Gerhard, 1984).

Other cues picked up by the expert reader will be to different kinds of relationships within the text. Certain words are used like maths indicators, directing the reader how to think about the other words. *Because* will always signal a cause and effect relationship, *if* a conditional situation, and *but*, or *on the other hand* a comparison or juxtaposition. Other words such as pronouns provide cohesion (Chapman, 1983).

Continuously monitor comprehension

The expert reader will continuously monitor comprehension, albeit perhaps not always consciously (Paris and Myers, 1981). Steps will be taken such as looking for further information, rethinking definitions, and rereading or paraphrasing difficult passages. Writing activities, such as note-taking, outlining, paraphrasing, or summarising, may play a crucial role in the monitoring process as well as in the end product of the reading task. Writing appears to promote more intensive involvement than reading and increase the number of inferences drawn (Langer, 1986).

The expert reader, then, will be a very active problem solver, setting goals, choosing appropriate processing strategies, identifying cues to structure, to important information, to relationships, and to information anticipated because of prior knowledge of the subject and situation. Reading will be relatively swift because well-organised prior knowledge will make this anticipation possible and therefore make recognition of fewer cues necessary. The expert reader, unlike the novice, will be aware when there is a lack of comprehension and take steps to remedy this.

What does the path from novice to expert look like?

One thing is quite certain. There is no straight Roman road. On the contrary, the path is bound to be circuitous and hilly. The traveller will be helped or hindered by a variety of factors. Among these are opportunities to accumulate knowledge of facts and concepts as well as information processing procedures, circumstances of private life such as frequent moves or a death in the family, different reading experiences, and the degree of support from others.

This support may take different forms, but should include being given opportunities for active participation in learning, experiences of meaningful success, encouragement of independence, and help with developing meta-skills such as concentrating on patterns of information.

Active participation

Amidst the uncertainties about learning factors that may help or hinder developing readers, recent neuropsychological and instructional research has reduced some speculation by corroborating the earlier work of Vygotsky, Piaget, Bruner and others. This showed that the single most important stimulus to forward movement in a learning situation beyond the genetic and broader environmental factors is the active participation of the learner and reader in finding and discussing relationships, and in forming images or mental representations of learning situations.

Programmed learning and the division of instructional material into small, discrete steps may be very helpful for reinforcement, but it does not engage the learner in an active manner. This active participation requires, of course, a willingness of students to expose themselves to learning situations. Those who have suffered consistent failure need to be revived by being given meaningful experiences of success; not just being allowed to slip by checkpoints (Herber and Herber, 1984).

Experiences of success

It is here that middle-school teachers are vitally important. While some are discouraged by the difficulties of helping less successful students who have lost their way, and others believe that some students are incapable of acquiring the necessary skills to deal with more abstract material, work has been in progress showing that positive expectations coupled with carefully crafted programmes can make a great difference (Gerhard, 1987).

Striking results were achieved by Feuerstein when he trained teachers to work on thinking processes with disadvantaged and retarded adolescents in Israel, many of whom did not know Hebrew (1979, 1980, 1985). (He is currently running programmes in other countries such as Canada.) While the actual statistical results have been disputed, his programme radically changed the lives of many.

Encouragement of independence

Feuerstein's main goal has been to produce independent learners capable of making their own decisions. He has taught abstract thinking by initially using materials familiar to all students and moving step by step toward the less familiar, paying careful attention to visual presentation at every step. For example, analogies are taught by getting students to name simple relationships of one pair of squares, circles or other basic geometric figures, such as that they are reversed, and applying the resulting knowledge to a second pair. Using the same visual format, he introduces familiar words, demanding a naming of the relationship of the first pair, such as that they are opposites or part of a whole, until students can work alone. Work with analogies is very important because they present opportunities to integrate prior and new information. Feuerstein's success is striking, but many others have also rescued older students who have lost their way.

Help with developing metaskills

Further evidence of the possibility of getting students back on the road to success is found in the work of Anne Brown and her associates in teaching metacognitive skills. That is, they taught students to think about their thinking. They used active group participation in decision making while learning. Most striking have been the results of reciprocal teaching. Teachers model asking questions about and summarising paragraphs, followed by predicting what will come next. Students then take turns being the teacher for a small group and practise following the teacher's example with single paragraphs, posing a question, summarising the information and predicting what is likely to be found in succeeding paragraphs. Teachers coach them to improve the quality of their performance. This method showed dramatic results (Palincsar and Brown, 1984).

Other suggestions of how students can be kept on the path leading to successful reading are to be found in the work of Hart (1983). The author produces strong evidence that the human brain functions through the formation of multitudinous, interconnected relationships and is essentially a pattern-recognition device. Arbitrary divisions between concepts or facts and the memorising of arbitrary lists of disconnected items therefore go against the way the brain works. (This is not an argument against memorising as such, since memorising *patterns* of information would be helpful.) There is nothing new here except very significant reasons for changing some practices.

Gibson and Levin (1975) and other perceptual psychologists have also written of the need for students to look for invariances, or regular patterns in information. Such patterns useful in reading include letter and word patterns, prefixes and suffixes, rules of punctuation, capitalisation and spelling, words indicating relationships, and the basic structure of stories and expository text. When these are automatically processed or used as processing indicators, attention can be given to exceptions and special cases.

How early in reading instruction should relationships be stressed?

The answer is clear. Relationships need to be stressed *before* formal reading begins and should be stressed in terms of events and stories familiar to children rather than by separate exercises. For example, after reading or listening to two or more stories or poems, questions should encourage listeners to say in what way they were similar or different, just as one might compare two leaves or flowers while out walking. Children need to believe from the beginning that they are capable of discriminating and generalising in this way about reading matter, and that they will be rewarded for doing so. They can also create text by comparing their art work or stories with those of other students, learning to express what way they are similar or different (Gerhard, 1982). This method is adaptable to later class work such as having groups organise vocabulary words prior to reading and then comparing their different results.

When formal instruction begins, not only letter patterns, but other kinds of relationships can be investigated. The importance of thinking in terms of relationships can be demonstrated by a very simple sentence. Take, for instance the sentence

The cat sat on the mat.

It will probably not cause great difficulty for most children to see that there are three words with *at*. Beyond that, what relationships and information do they need to comprehend the sentence? They must be able to conjure up images of a cat and a mat that will fit the total situation. That is to say, a wild cat in an attack position and a hanging mat over a door would not do. (Eskimo children might have problems with any cat.) In this situation, the cat must be domesticated and the mat must be on the floor or some flat surface.

Having conjured up these two images, do the children comprehend the sentence? No. They must mentally move the image of the cat onto the mat because of the verb *sat* and the preposition *on*. This one simple sentence shows the need to think in terms of relationships and meaningful related images from the very beginning. A useful definition of meaningful is that it is evaluated by the number of associations a learner can make with information. It is the associations and the recognition of ever-recurring patterns of relationships that enable readers to make inferences such as that the cat is relaxed and friendly and likes to sit on surfaces softer than bare floors.

Students from 10–14 are working on more complex problems than comprehending such a sentence. This means that it is even more important for the stress to be on regularities or patterns, on active roles in observing, comparing, and generalising about new information, and on linking new information to old. Actively learning about basic relationships is a first step in comprehending complex, abstract material.

How can teachers help to prepare the way for future success?

Metacognitive research (reviewed in Garner, 1987) has prepared us to accept the idea that students must learn to think about their own thinking; to be aware of how they are learning and in what ways they need to improve. However, research on teacher thinking (Joyce, 1975; Bamberger *et al.*, 1981; Mandl and Huber, 1982; Gerhard, 1983) indicates that teachers also need to assess their own thinking.

Modelling good reading practices

If teachers are to explain why pattern seeking is so important, why students must themselves seek relationships and form generalisations, they must first be able to model these behaviours. They must know how they themselves learn (Meichenbaum, 1985).

Making inferences

Nowhere is it more important for teachers to think about their thinking than in teaching how to make inferences from text. For many students this is the most difficult reading skill and it is also one that requires searching memory for prior knowledge of subject matter, situations, and the conventions of text.

Gordon (1985) describes a procedure for teachers to help students make inferences. After reading material and thinking about how they process it, teachers can model how to ask an inference question about a paragraph. For example, a paragraph about deep draft boats approaching a sandy shore to attack could evoke a question such as, 'The boats are described as deep draft, which means they require deep water. Why do you think the captain hesitated before attacking?' The reasoning for the correct answer, 'because the men would have to attack in small lifeboats or skiffs and would be an easy target', would then be discussed. This may appear to be very elementary, but learning the process of making inferences should be initiated with simple material.

In the next phase, using new material, the teacher would go as far as giving the correct answer, but then ask the students for the reasoning. They would be required to say what they knew from the text, on the one hand, and from their prior knowledge on the other. In the following phase the students would provide the answer to a question while the teacher would discuss the evidence and the reasoning. Finally, the students would try the entire process on their own.

Teaching vocabulary

Carr (1985) uses a similar ten-step process to train students in establishing a network of relationships among vocabulary words from a text. Students are trained to select, define and study vocabulary, providing themselves with a *personal* cue, and completing an overview by following an overview guide. For example, 'Define the word through the use of context' would include answering questions such as 'What is this passage about?' and 'What do you know about this?'. In the Carr study teachers modelled the process for two sessions, guided students in class over a period of two weeks that included three independent attempts, and taught fifty words. Four weeks later students remembered 80 per cent of the words without a clue and 90 per cent with a clue.

Promoting comprehension

Williams (1984) suggests another activity for promoting comprehension. He evaluated fourth and sixth-year students' ability to identify sentences as appropriate for inclusion in short paragraphs. This involved an inductive process of seeking similarities between sentences wherever there was no topic sentence. Students in the sixth year were able to identify sentences correctly when there were three related sentences even when there was no topic sentence. Fourth-year students were not yet ready. This study suggests a way of teaching subject matter and preparing students for expository text reading.

Using acronyms: IDEAL, MURDER, LETME

Bransford and Stein (1985) offer a useful way of getting students to use a problem-solving approach. The method is called IDEAL with the letters standing for Identify, Define, Explore, Act, and Look Back, or evaluate. Even college students found a brief introduction to this helpful in their studies. Clearly, teachers themselves would have to make frequent use of this approach in teaching for it to be effective.

Dansereau (1985) also has a useful acronym for teaching independent learning strategies called MURDER. These letters stand for Mood, Understanding, Recall, Digest, Expand, and Review. The process is based on two primary strategies of first comprehending and retaining and then retrieving information from text. ('Mood' is explained as studying your mood before a task and undertaking corrective steps to improve it if necessary.) Here, too, teachers would need to explain the value of the approach, model how to do it, provide guided and independent practice and suitable rewards and then keep reminding students about it.

Shenkman (1986) offers a general comprehension strategy to encourage independent reading using the mnemonic LETME. The letters stand for Link, Extract, Transform, Monitor, and Extend. *Link* involves recognising text cues in order to activate prior knowledge. *Extract* is built upon linking and is the process of selecting important information. *Transform* is the crucial act of changing the text to suit the particular reading purpose. It might call for rearranging the order of information, taking notes, outlining only salient ideas, mapping or summarising. *Monitor* requires awareness of one's own particular strengths and weaknesses and constant checking of comprehension. Finally, *Extend* requires in-depth thinking about such things as the significance or usefulness of the material, its association with other material, and its implications.

Using writing to promote independence

One of the best ways to help students become more competent and independent readers is to provide good opportunities for writing. Fulwiler (1982) suggests many ways of using class journals such as reacting to reading, jotting down ideas and arguments derived from text for use in later class discussion, or integrating reading with other sources of information. Having small groups compare their comments and discuss the reasons for agreeing or disagreeing with them based on the text material on the one hand and prior knowledge on the other is another profitable activity. Since these are high-risk activities it is especially important to create a supportive, friendly environment.

Teaching text cue recognition

Systematically teaching students to recognise and use the cues provided in text will also help them become independent readers. A great deal of discussion with familiar materials about different kinds of text structures and standard relationships is necessary before students can be expected to adopt a cue-seeking attitude. For example, the large jump from story structure to expository text structure must be bridged. Younger students are often not aware of single categories in their reading and certainly not of the hierarchies of categories typical of informative text.

Establishing a goal

Finally, the all-important skill of making individual decisions about reading requires years of practice. One way to approach it originally is to require a statement of the ostensible goal of a reading activity as pronounced by the teacher. This means that no reading should ever take place without a well-defined purpose, even if this is just to enjoy it and share this enjoyment with others. The immediate purpose for reading should also be related to a long-term goal which should be the subject of frequent discussion. These steps will help to establish a pattern. Then groups of students can be given choices of how they will accomplish the learning of particular information and be asked to justify the choice. Students who have problems determining their goals can be helped by having them write out contracts for accomplishing a long-term goal in small steps. Constant and consistent emphasis on setting goals and deciding how to reach them needs to occur.

Conclusion

The prospect of helping students in the middle years become competent readers in later years is indeed good if we apply what has been learned about the brain and optimal ways of learning. Opportunities to make use of this knowledge need to be created for subject matter teachers, including adequate class time to carry out activities that will foster independent learning. There is overwhelming evidence in a number of areas to show that learning new ways of processing information, especially with more abstract material, takes time for introducing and modelling them and for providing guided practice.

Finally, teacher expectation about what students can and cannot do plays a major role in whether they become independent readers or not. Bruner said it well: 'If you expect people to examine their thoughts, to be mindful about their use of mind, all evidence points to the fact that they can and will do so.' (1985, p. 607)

References

ALVERMANN, D.E. and RATEKIN, N.H. (1982) 'Metacognitive knowledge about reading proficiency. Its relation to study strategies and task demands', *Journal of Reading Behavior*, 14, pp. 231–41.

BAMBERGER, J., DUCKWORTH, E. and LAMPERT, M. (1981) An experiment in teacher development. National Institute of Education, Washington D.C. Grant #G-78-0219.

BRAININ, S.S. (1985) 'Mediating learning: Pedagogic issues in the improvement of cognitive functioning', E.W. Gordon (ed) *Review of Research in Education*, Vol. 12, Washington D.C. AERA, pp. 121–55.

BRANSFORD, J.D. and STEIN, B. (1984) *The Ideal Problem Solver.* (New York: W.H. Freeman).

BRATTESANI, K., WEINSTEIN, R.S. and MARSHALL, H.H. (1984) 'Student perceptions of differential teacher treatment as moderators of teacher expectation effects', *Journal of Educational Psychology*, 76, pp. 236–47.

BRUNER, J.S. (1985) 'On teaching thinking: An afterthought' in S.F. Chipman, J.W. Segal, and R. Glaser (eds) *Thinking and Learning Skills*, Vol. 2, Hillsdale, N.J., Erlbaum, pp. 597–608.

CARR, E.M. (1985) 'Vocabulary overview guide: A metacognitive strategy to improve vocabulary', *Journal of Reading,* 28, pp. 684–89.

CHAPMAN, J. (1983) *Reading Development and Cohesion* (London: Heinemann).

DANSEREAU, D.F. (1985) 'Learning strategy research', in J.W. Segal, S.F. Chipman, and R. Glaser (eds) *Thinking and Learning Skills*, Vol. 1 (Hillsdale, N.J.: Erlbaum) pp. 209–39.

DE CHARMS, R. (1984) 'Motivation enhancement in educational settings', in R. Ames and C. Ames *Research on Motivation in Education*, Vol. 1 (N.Y.: Academic) pp. 275–310.

FEUERSTEIN, R. (1979) *The Dynamic assessment of Retarded Performers (Baltimore, MD: University Park).*

FEUERSTEIN, R. (1980) *Instrumental Enrichment: An Intervention Program for Cognitive Modifiability* (Baltimore, MD: University Park).

FEUERSTEIN, R., JENSEN, M., HOFFMAN, M.B., and RAND, Y. (1985) 'Instrumental enrichment, an intervention program for structural cognitive modifiability: Theory and practice', in J.W. Segal, S.F. Chipman, and R. Glaser (eds), *Thinking and Learning Skills*, Vol. 1 (Hillsdale, N.J.: Erlbaum), pp. 43–82.

FULWILER, T. (1982) 'The personal connection: Journal writing across the curriculum', in T. Fulwiler and A. Young (eds) *Language Connections: Writing and Reading Across the Curriculum*, National Council of Teachers of English, Champaign, Illinois.

GARNER, R. (1987) *Metacognition and Reading Comprehension*, Norwood (N.J.: Ablex).

GERHARD, C. (1982) 'Improving reading comprehension: Teaching relationships through the arts', in A. Hendry *Teaching Reading: The Key Issues* (London: Heinemann), pp. 62–76.

GERHARD, C. (1983) 'Teacher knowledge about selected aspects of categorizing and their use in the instruction of sixth, seventh and eighth grade students', unpublished doctoral dissertation, George Washington University.

GERHARD, C. (1984) 'Meeting students' needs to understand structure in expository text', in D. Dennis (ed) *Reading: Meeting Children's Special Needs* (London: Heinemann) pp. 76–90.

GERHARD, C. (1987) 'What every educator should know about reading comprehension: Helping students to be successful beyond the early grades', *Research into Practice Digest*, 2,1. (Whole issue).

GIBSON, E.J. and LEVIN, H. (1975) *The Psychology of Reading* (Cambridge, MA: MIT).

GORDON, C.J. (1985) Modeling inference awareness across the curriculum, *Journal of Reading*, 28, pp. 444–447.

GOUGH, P.B. (1984) 'Word recognition', in P.D. Pearson (ed) *Handbook of Reading Research* (N.Y.: Longmans) pp. 225–53.

HART, L.A. (1983) *Human Brain and Human Learning* (N.Y.: Longmans).

HERBER, J.N. and HERBER, H. (1984) 'A positive approach to assessment and correction of reading difficulties in middle and secondary schools', in J. Flood (ed) *Promoting Reading Comprehension* (Newark, DE: IRA).

HIEBERT, E.H., WINOGRAD, P.N., and DANNER, F.D. (1983) 'Children's attributions of failure and success for different aspects of reading.' Paper presented at the annual meeting of AERA, Montreal, Canada.

JOYCE, B. (1975) 'Conceptions of man and their implications for teacher education', in K. Ryan (ed) *Teacher Education*, NSSE, 74th Yearbook Part 2, University of Chicago.

KINTSCH, W. (1986) Learning from text, *Cognition and Instruction* 3, pp. 87–108.

LANGER, J.A. (1986) *Children Reading and Writing: Structures and Strategies* (Norwood, N.J.: Ablex).

MANDL, H. and HUBER, G.L. (1982) 'On teachers' subjective theories: A review of research in West Germany.' Paper presented at the annual meeting of AERA, New York.

MEICHENBAUM, D. (1985) 'Teaching thinking: A cognitive behavioral perspective', in S.F. Chipman, J.W. Segal and R. Glaser (eds) *Thinking and learning skills*, Vol. 2 (Hillsdale, N.J.: Erlbaum) pp. 407–26.

MEYER, B.J.F. (1975) *Organization of Prose and its Effects on Recall* (Amsterdam: North Holland).

MILLER, G.A., GALANTER, E., and PRIBRAM, K.H. (1960) *Plans and the Structure of Behavior* (N.Y.: Holt).

MORROW, L.M. and WEINSTEIN, C.S. (1986) 'Encouraging voluntary reading; The impact of a literature program on children's use of library centers', *Reading Research Quarterly*, 21, pp. 330–46.

NELSON, K. (1986) *Event Knowledge: Structure and Function in Development* (Hillsdale, N.J.: Erlbaum).

PALINCSAR, A.S. and BROWN, A.L. (1984) Reciprocal teaching of comprehension-monitoring activities, *Cognition and Instruction*, 1, pp. 117–175.

PARIS, S.G. and MYERS, M. (1981) Comprehension monitoring, memory, and study strategies of good and poor readers, *Journal of Reading Behavior*, 13, pp. 5–22.

PRIBRAM, K.H. (1981) 'The brain as the locus of cognitive controls on action', in G. d'Ydewalle and W. Lens (eds) *Cognition in Human Motivation and Learning* (Leuven University Press, Belgium, and Hillsdale, N.J.: Erlbaum).

RISSLAND, E.L. (1985) 'The structure of knowledge in complex domains', in S.F. Chipman, J.W. Segal, and R. Glaser (eds) *Thinking and Learning Skills*, Vol. 2 (Hillsdale, N.J.: Erlbaum).

ROTH, I. and FRISBY, J.P. (1986) *Perception and Representation: A Cognitive Approach* (Milton Keynes: Open University Press).

SHENKMAN, H. (1986) 'A theoretical model for a total approach to independent learning from text', *Reading Psychology*, 7, pp. 111–26.

SIGEL, I.E. (1986) 'Cognition-affect: A psychological riddle', in D.J. Bearison and H. Zimiles (eds) *Thought and Emotion: Developmental Perspectives* (Hillsdale, N.J.: Erlbaum).

WILLIAMS, J.P. (1984) 'Categorization, macrostructure, and finding the main idea', *Journal of Educational Psychology*, 76, pp. 874–79.

Chapter 3

Metacognitive Modelling and Glossing: Two Powerful Ways to Teach Self-Responsibility

Marian J. Tonjes

Cognitive psychologists have recently brought to our attention the notion of metacognition, or self-awareness and monitoring of what we do when reading; recognising, without aids, goals, purposes, needs and strategies. Good readers may do this automatically, while poor readers usually need to be shown or reminded of mature readers' insights. This can be accomplished in two ways: through metacognitive modelling, orally sharing our thought processes using a script; or in written form through the technique of glossing, which uses marginal bracketed notations on a separate sheet of paper, inserted partly under the text page for individual, immediate reference. These two powerful strategies can not only help our students but also sharpen our teaching.

Introduction

One of our major aims in teaching is to help our students move towards self-responsibility so that as time goes on they lean on us less and less. As teachers of older children we do an excellent job of explaining facts and concepts, discussing the significance of events, lecturing on the *content*, but do we really stress the *process*, which helps our students to become better at 'learning how to learn'? Our gifted students have usually picked it up intuitively, but what about the less gifted? Have we really shared the mature reader's insights with them? That is exactly what metacognitive script and bracketed gloss can do.

It is my intention here to review briefly, definitions and descriptions of these two powerful, interlinked strategies, showing examples of how they might work and then to make some final observations.

Metacognition and good versus poor readers

Metacognition has become a very popular notion in today's reading literature. As used here it is a process of self-awareness and conscious monitoring of what we do when reading. It means going beyond merely knowing *about* something to being able to appropriately select and use particular strategies. It involves continuous monitoring of our own comprehension and knowing what to do when corrective action is necessary.

I believe that Francis Robinson's Survey, Question, Read, Recite, Review (SQ3R) study strategy would be more in evidence today if students had been shown the true value of taking any combination of the time-consuming steps, if they had been helped to be metacognitively aware of when to use all or part of the strategy, and then only on difficult or uninteresting material when they saw a need for it.

We need to be reminded that good readers have alternatives, not just one rigid way to process print. Good readers may sail through a chapter, readily assimilating major points, following supporting arguments with ease, stopping now and then to reflect, tying into and building upon past experiences, organising information into mental images, wondering about a meaning of a term, skimming forward or backwards to clarify a point. They have a variety of ways to approach a task and a number of fix-up strategies. On the other hand, poor readers often do not know whether they have succeeded in comprehending or not, nor what to do if they have not — except possibly to reread everything over again.

Metacognitive script

Ah, but hope is on the way. We have the tools to help them. With the use of metacognitive script we can read difficult passages to students while they follow along silently with their own copy, and we can model our own thoughts and select strategies as needed. For example, we might say:

1. 'From this title I predict this chapter (section) will tell me about . . . and this will help me focus on the main message.'
2. 'I have a picture of this scene in my mind . . . ', going on to describe it in detail.
3. 'This is similar to the concept we learned last week, in that . . . '
4. 'This doesn't make sense. I had better skim ahead, or reread, or look up that term, or . . . '

In other words, we verbalise for them our mental thoughts, our decisions and our reasons for making those decisions. At the same time we assure them that there are always alternatives, that there is rarely just one way to approach a task or problem.

Let us look now at a brief excerpt (see Table 3.1) from an article on metacognition to show how a script might be developed to help students deal with the process as well as the content. The text has been abbreviated here to only key phrases because of space considerations, but in actual practice students and teacher would be looking at the complete excerpt, while only the teacher would have the script for reference while reading the text orally. Note that the script is divided into two sections, your inner thoughts and then the explanation of what the process is or why it is important for readers.

TABLE 3.1   *Metacognitive script*

Text	Script
Excerpt from Ann L. Brown, *Metacognitive Development and Reading*, Center for the Study of Reading, University of Illinois, Urbana-Champaign (1980) p. 453.	*Thoughts* 'I should think more about this title. What does "Metacognitive" really mean? I know about the cognitive part, why is this more than just knowing?' *Explanation* 'I'm focusing and questioning – getting a mind set for what is to come to help my concentration and comprehension.'
Vygotsky (1962) . . .	*Thoughts* 'Hm-m – this notion has been around for a while – 1962 to 1988 – I recall that he's a Russian researcher and writer.' *Explanation* 'I'm tying this to past experience, what I already know.'
described two phases in the development of knowledge: first, its automatic unconscious acquisition, followed by gradual increases in active conscious control over that knowledge. . .	*Thoughts* 'Two phases – ah, I had better attend carefully to this, make a note or underline these two ("automatic, unconscious acquisition and active conscious control of knowledge").' *Explanation* 'This gives me a foundation for understanding further explanations, therefore it's vital to take time now to ponder and try to understand.'

Glossing

The process of glossing (sometimes referred to as marginal or bracketed gloss), as elaborated by Otto and Associates (1981), has many of the attributes of metacognitive script, but alas, has received much less attention. Whereas in metacognitive script we share orally and informally with students our expert thoughts, predictions, miscues and fix-up strategies, with gloss it is a more formal, written way of helping students become more independent, successful readers. One advantage of gloss is that it is used

TABLE 3.1 *continued*

Text	Script
Metacognition refers to . . .	*Thoughts* 'Ah, a definition! I can tell by the words "refers to".' *Explanation* 'Definitions should always be carefully noted because they can be crucial to understanding.'
In this chapter we attempt to give some idea of . . .	*Thoughts* 'Here's where I find out what the author, Brown, is going to cover. Oh – oops – before that I forgot to check on Brown's credentials. Is she really an authority? The Center at Illinois has great renown, I've read two other articles by her, and I note she has written widely on this subject. So I should be able to rely on what she says.' *Explanation* 'It is normal for even the best of readers to forget at times. The important thing is to realise it and take action. We should always try to be aware of who is giving us the information in expository text, that they have the necessary credentials or authority.'

as an individual, independent study aid which can be ignored by those who do not need it; and because it is in written form it can serve as a handy reference to refer back to when needed.

The original notion of gloss can be seen as marginal illustrations in ancient manuscripts. Later, it became definitions or questions printed in text margins to elaborate or exemplify – to tell readers something. The newer notion uses gloss as a silent teacher peering over readers' shoulders to explain processes, or to describe skills and strategies needed for the task at hand. This provocative procedure uses marginal notations in numbered brackets which direct the reader's attention to specific sections, sentences or keywords *as* they read. Like a type of study guide, gloss serves as a concurrent reading aid.

TABLE 3.2 *Sample gloss: stage one-model*

Slide Paper
Page 176 (left hand page)   in to here   Page 175 (right hand page)

An introduction often is a
preview of what is to come,
a purpose for reading, some   3
background information to
tie this new learning to what   The title of a chapter gives
is already known, and in this   1   us our main focus. Think
case gives suggestions for   about what you already
how to tackle this chapter.   know about this topic, set a
Read it slowly and   purpose for reading and
thoughtfully to get a feel for   predict what you think will
the information to come.   be discussed. This will help
                                     you to better comprehend
                                     and recall later.

                                     The cognitive map for this
                                     chapter shows key concepts
                                     and their interrelationships in
                                 2   a playful format. It is a type
                                     of advanced organiser and
                                     should be studied both prior
This paragraph may help you   4   to reading the chapter and
to better interpret figure 7.1   afterwards as a summary
on the previous page. All   review. Recognising key
graphics are important in a   points keeps you from
text and should not be   getting bogged down in
merely skimmed over. They   unrelated details.
show the information in
another format (e.g., a
picture worth 1,000 words).

Line up with bottom of page   Line up with bottom of page

In terms of the mechanics of developing a specific gloss, it is written on a separate sheet of paper which is partially inserted under the text page, aligned at top and bottom so that the brackets match the section under discussion. Gloss is developed to work in several stages, the first stage, the *model* or *demonstration* stage, being the most difficult to construct because it goes beyond just telling to actually teaching. For example, instead of just telling readers that this is the topic sentence, gloss would delineate the steps in *how* to determine that it is the topic sentence. Gloss explains, gives reasons why, and teaches for transfer to a later task. The second stage *develops* and allows practice of skills and strategies explained in stage one. Finally, we reach the stages of *internalise* and *fade* where only brief reminders need to be given before we bow out to the independent reader.

A sample gloss for the first stage is shown in Table 3.2. Although it was developed here for expository writing (Tonjes and Zintz, 1987), gloss works equally well with all types of literature. The glosser decides what needs attention throughout the chapter or what skills are needed by the students for that class. Note that the brackets are numbered consecutively for future reference if needed. Look at bracket number one, for example. Later on – moving to stage two (Develop and Practice) bracket no. 15 might ask, 'Do you recall what you should be doing with a new title? If not, check back with gloss no. 1.' With no. 2 bracket, stage two might ask, 'What does a cognitive map show you? Check with gloss no. 2 if you are not sure.' Stage three might merely remind – 'Don't forget . . .'

Observations

These are not simple, 'gimmicky' strategies. Since 1982, many of my students, both in-service and pre-service teachers, have initially reacted with doubt or frustration as to whether the time and effort needed to construct them was really worth it. Gradually, with practice, they became grudgingly accepting, and finally, when they received glowing feedback from their students they were happily surprised – even exhilarated.

These strategies do force us as teachers to think more deeply about all aspects surrounding our readers and the text. The process of constructing them can definitely sharpen our instruction. For those students who never before understood why they failed to comprehend adequately, it is reassuring for them to know that now they have some tools for change.

A final word of warning – metacognitive script and bracketed gloss, like other good strategies, should be used in moderation, not overworked. We need to continue to develop other alternatives for helping our students become responsible, independent learners.

References

BAKER, L. (1979) 'Comprehension monitoring: Identifying and coping with text confusions', *Journal of Reading Behaviour*, 11, pp. 365–74.

BAKER, L. and BROWN, A.L. (1984) 'Metacognitive skills and reading', in P.D. Pearson (ed) *Handbook of Reading Research* (New York: Longman) pp. 353–94.

BROWN, A.L. (1980) 'Metacognitive development and reading', in R.J. Spiro, B.C. Bruce and W.F. Brewer (eds) *Theoretical Issues in Reading Comprehension.* (Hillsdale, NJ: Erlbaum) pp. 453–81.

DAVEY, B. (1983) 'Think aloud – Modelling the process of reading comprehension', *Journal of Reading,* 27, 1, pp. 44–7.

OTTO, W. and Associates (1981) *Part I – A Technique for Improving and Understanding of Expository Text: Gloss. Part II – Examples of Gloss Notation.* (Madison, WI: Research Development Center for Individualized Schooling).

RICHGELS, D.J. and HANSEN, R. (1984) 'Gloss: Helping students apply both skills and strategies in reading content texts', *Journal of Reading,* 27, 4, pp. 312–317.

RICHGELS, D.J. and MATEJA, J.A. (1984) 'Gloss II: Integrating content and process for independence', *Journal of Reading,* 27, 5, pp. 424–31.

SMITH, R.J. and DAUER, V.L. (1984) 'A comprehension-monitoring strategy for reading content area materials', *Journal of Reading,* 28, 2, pp. 144–47.

TONJES, M.J. (1985) 'Metacognitive strategies for active reading', *New Mexico Journal of Reading,* 6, 1, pp. 5–8.

TONJES, M.J. and ZINTZ, M.V. (1987) *Teaching Reading/Thinking/Study Skills in Content Classrooms* (2nd ed.) (Dubuque, IA: Wm. C. Brown Publishers).

WAGONER, S.A. (1983) 'Comprehension monitoring: What it is and what we know about it', *Reading Research Quarterly,* 17, pp. 328–46.

Chapter 4

Literacy: The Information Dimension

David Wray

This paper argues that any definition of literacy needs to take into account the need for people to deal effectively with a range of sources of information. The process of handling information is analysed and illustrated, and two essential elements discussed in greater depth; that is the ability to define for oneself a precise purpose for seeking information, and the ability to evaluate the information which is located. The impact of new technologies is discussed. Several points will be raised concerning the ways teachers might approach these areas as part of the process of teaching literacy.

Information handling: an essential skill

Picture the scene. A busy railway station. You have just alighted from a train and know you have to catch a connecting train in a few minutes time. What do you do? Many adults, faced with this situation, would ignore the prominently displayed timetable on which all the information they required could be found, and instead look for someone official to ask. The trouble with this strategy is that by the time they had found someone who knew the timetable accurately off by heart, there would be a fair chance that the train they wanted had already left. Even worse, they might find someone with only a partially accurate knowledge and might catch the wrong train. Another example of information mishandling! Has this never happened to you?

Inability to deal efficiently and confidently with sources of information is not, perhaps, so remarkable. Everyone has problems with things like train timetables, don't they? What it means, though, is that, at best, we are dependent on someone else to do the task for us, and, at worse, we fail at the task. Both these events have major consequences, some obvious, some not, and they apply equally to other information-handling tasks.

Information-handling abilities

Before examining these consequences in more detail, let us look at some of the evidence concerning general levels of information-handling ability in sections of the population. Most of the work done in this area has concerned students at various institutions of further and higher education, and their ability to use information in their studying. Most investigations have found that students, even the most academically gifted, are not generally very proficient at such things as using libraries and books to locate and extract the information they require (Blake, 1956; Irving and Snape, 1979). In the most quoted of these investigations, Perry (1959) managed to find some students at one of the most prestigious universities in the US who, when asked to determine what a particular chapter in a book was roughly about, simply began at the first word and ploughed through a mass of not particularly useful details until they reached the end. When the possibility of reading the chapter in a more circumspect way was pointed out to them their response was, 'Lord, how many times have I been told!' It was not that they did not know about these reading strategies, but rather that they were not aware of when they should apply them. This is a phenomenon which often occurs in studies of information handling, from primary school up to adult level (Lunzer and Gardner, 1979; Neville and Pugh, 1982). Perry calls the performance of these students, 'a demonstration of obedient purposelessness'. This is a phrase to which we shall return.

If we go on to look at the abilities of adults to handle and act on information, we find a similarly bleak picture. The most renowned work here is that done by Murphy (1973) who investigated the abilities of 8,000 American adults to respond to tasks based on everyday reading material. Some of his results make alarming reading. He found, for example, that 15 per cent of his sample could not adequately respond to a task based on the reading of a traffic sign. 62 per cent of the sample had trouble with a magazine subscription form, and a staggering 74 per cent were unable to deal correctly with an income tax form. We may feel this last finding tells us more about the design of the form than it does about the abilities of these adults but we must consider, of course, the consequences of getting the task wrong, which in all these cases can be very significant. Every time we are unable to handle information efficiently there is a 'worst case' consequence of this nature. We pay too much money, we miss trains, we fail to order the goods we want, etc. Almost all adults do something like this at least once in their lifetimes.

These are the obvious consequences of mishandling information. Often, of course, the results are not that drastic. People usually succeed more or less at information-handling tasks, but the price of efficiency shows itself in increased time and effort. When the task is recognised to be of extreme importance, many people, of course, are not prepared to take the risk of getting it wrong, and this leads them to ask for assistance in the task. People with complicated tax affairs employ accountants, people who are nervous of their own abilities ask for other opinions. This is a very common response to information inability with equally important, if more subtle, consequences. By passing on responsibility for the task to someone else, we are in effect putting part of our lives into the control of other people. We have to trust these other people to get the task right and in an important sense we lose personal autonomy.

This is crucial because literacy includes the ability to function autonomously in a literate environment. Literacy is more than simply being able to read the words around us, and it includes knowing when it is appropriate to act upon these words and then being able to decide how to act. Handling information is an essential aspect of literacy and also of autonomy. In a real sense, being able to locate, evaluate and act upon information is linked to having power over our own lives. The phrase 'Information is power' is well known to agencies that seek to control our lives. There are many institutions in our society that seek to preserve their power by monopolising sources of information. As individuals we are rarely in a position to do much about this. Several areas of our lives are so complex that it is unreasonable to expect lay people to have sufficient command of the specialised information necessary to deal with problems themselves. The accountant may be the only person who can deal with complex tax affairs, the solicitor may be the only person who can deal with the complexities of house purchase. However, there are still many areas of our lives which ought to be under our control and which, as literate people, we ought to be able to deal with effectively ourselves. And usually this means being able to locate and use the relevant information.

The information process

Having established that becoming literate involves becoming able to handle information, let us move on to examine more closely what the process of 'handling information' involves.

One useful formulation is that which divides the process into six stages (Winkworth, 1977), each of which has some part to play in any information-handling task. Let us define these stages a little more closely with reference to a particular information task, that is consulting a train timetable.

Stage 1: Define subject and purpose

Obviously when we go to the timetable we have a fairly clear idea of what we want to achieve. We want to find out when the next train leaves to our destination, which platform it leaves from, and perhaps what time it will eventually get us there.

It would be quite unusual for anyone to browse through a timetable. Almost always they will have a clearly defined purpose and this applies to most information tasks. A little later we will look at how this is reflected in the experience we give children of information handling.

Stage 2: Locate information

Obviously before we use information we have firstly to find it. In our particular example this involves finding where the timetable is and then finding particular pieces of information on it. Usually there are particular techniques we can use to speed this up. If we are looking in a book timetable, it will help if we can use the index to find the places we are interested in.

Stage 3: Select information

Once we have found the information, we then have to pick out the precise items that we require; in this case the times of particular trains. We have to evaluate, and to be aware of, a range of possible limiting factors. It is not much use, for example, if we pick out a train to catch, but fail to notice that it only runs on Saturdays.

Stage 4: Organise information

In simple information tasks there may not be much organisation to be done. Sometimes, for example, all we require is one train time, and there are no snags. Often, though, it is more complex. We might have to change trains, and we then have to synchronise several pieces of information. This involves rearranging information into one coherent package and some method of organisation has to be employed. Some people will be able to do this in their heads, but others will need to resort to pen and paper, and take notes. Writing is the basic organisational tool at our disposal.

Stage 5: Evaluate information

The example of the train timetable is not a very good one to illustrate evaluation which should not be necessary in this case. Misprints are possible, but generally we trust to the accuracy of the information on the timetable. There are, however, many important tasks in which evaluation is much more important, as we shall see later.

Stage 6: Communicate results

Most information tasks involve some kind of communication as we relay what we have found to others. Communication may also lead to action as we respond to what we find. In this example we catch our train, either by ourselves, or with others whose knowledge of what they are doing is dependent on our efficiency.

This, then, is the process of handling information and in each information task we follow, more or less, these six stages. We cannot, therefore, really be called literate unless we can perform these stages effectively.

Computers

However, although all six stages are essential components of the information process, it can be argued that, in fact, two of them are more important in the sense of signifying real literacy, which implies personal autonomy. This point can be illustrated by considering briefly the impact of new technologies on definitions of literacy. It is clear that access to a computer can simplify a number of information tasks for us. Processing information is what computers are good at. They can deal with millions of bits of information at very rapid speeds, and, in certain areas, are far more efficient information handlers than we are. So perhaps all this emphasis on people being able to handle information has come too late. Maybe we should just let the computers do it for us, since they are so much more efficient.

This, however, will never be an answer. To see why, let us look at our six stages and assess how a computer can perform at each one of them. There is no doubt that a computer can locate information very efficiently indeed. By tapping my requirements into a computer terminal I can often have access to the precise information I require within seconds. Similarly a computer can select between vast quantities of information and present me with exactly the discrete two or three pieces I require. It can pull together information and organise it into a coherent whole, and it can also, if I tell it, communicate its work to anywhere in the world.

So stages 2, 3, 4 and 6 can be done by computers, usually far more efficiently and quickly than any human could manage. But, of course, the computer can do these things only if it is given precise instructions. What it cannot do is determine a purpose for itself. A computer is a tool and is not capable of more than a limited autonomy. *The ability to define our purpose for information-seeking* is one of the things which sets humans apart from machines in terms of literacy.

The second thing which sets us apart is our *ability to evaluate what we read*. The computer is good at finding information, but poor at evaluating it. This explains why we used to hear tales of people getting bills for £0 or £1 million. These were unfairly put down to computer error, but in fact they were errors made by humans. The computer was only doing what it had been told to do, but was not capable of recognising that a mistake had been made. This still applies. Computers cannot themselves evaluate information they find. Yet the ability to evaluate information is crucial to any real literacy. If we cannot evaluate information, we are at the mercy of what anyone tells us. Again our autonomy is threatened.

Information handling in school

Let us now relate these two crucial elements in information handling to the kind of teaching that may go on in school to develop information skills.

Defining purposes

We argued earlier that adults very rarely enter into information-handling situations without having clearly defined their purpose. It is possible for people to use sources of information in a purposeless way as in, say, browsing through a magazine while in a dentist's waiting room. Nevertheless, in comparison with the myriad of information-finding tasks performed in a week this purposeless approach is of minor importance. The vast majority of times that adults get information from whatever source, they go there with a specific purpose in mind. If this purposefulness tends to characterise adult information handling we ought to expect it to be reflected in the experiences children get of using information in school. Yet, unfortunately, many of children's information handling is characterised by the 'obedient purposelessness' that Perry found in his Harvard students.

The activity in schools in which children do most of their information handling is some form of project work. There is evidence which suggests that their dominant activity in this work is copying out sections from reference books (DES, 1978; Maxwell, 1977). When asked what they are doing they will often say something like, 'I'm finding out about birds, cars etc.'. If asked why, they may ultimately respond with, 'Because teacher told me to'.

There are two points here. The first concerns the difference between the precise purpose an adult will have for seeking information, and the vague and haphazard purpose of the child. What does 'finding out' mean? What it often means is that once children have a topic such as cars, dinosaurs etc. they then have to collect every piece of information they can about it and write it down. It does not really matter whether they understand the information they find – since it is about the topic then it must be relevant. But, of course, this is an impossible task. Finding out about cars could mean finding out everything there is to know about cars. Small wonder that children are so overwhelmed by the task that they simply copy down what the book says. The task is also imprecise since it does not specify what kind of information is required. Everything is relevant, so everything must be written down. This is in contrast to the precise purpose – setting what children will need to do when they enter the adult world of information-finding. No adult will go to a train timetable saying, 'I want to find out about train times', and then proceed to copy them down. Teachers need to move children on from the vague to the precise in terms of purpose setting in project work. It should not be too hard to ask children, 'What do you want to find out about cars, trains etc.?'. In other words, to encourage them to ask specific questions which can then be used as a guide during their information seeking. These questions will demand that they search and sift through a great deal of information before locating the answers.

The second point to make about children's purposes for engaging in information tasks concerns where these come from. For many children their real reason for doing certain activities is because the teacher told them to. Again we have to contrast this with the purposes of adults in pursuing information. Adults will rarely look for information because somebody else has told them to, without seeing the need themselves. Adults have to formulate their own purposes for finding information and cannot rely on someone else doing it for them. There is a need for children to be capable of formulating their own purposes for getting information if they are to be fully literate. In other words, it will not be sufficient to encourage them to be more precise in their purpose-setting if teachers actually do this for them. There is a danger of this happening in materials such as project work cards. Work cards asking children to find specific bits of information avoid the problem of vagueness in setting purposes, but at the same time make the task less real to the children by doing the purpose setting for them.

Negotiated purposes

I have argued elsewhere (Wray, 1985) that the answer to this problem lies in some kind of sharing between teacher and children. Teachers and children need to negotiate to formulate purposes for finding information. In negotiation each of the participants has their special contribution to make. The children contribute desire to learn, while teachers contribute the ability to make purposes more precise and capable of being satisfied. This negotiation can be the key to getting the best of both worlds from the process of purpose setting. Children can be led gradually towards becoming more precise but they need never feel that they are not following *their* interests but their teacher's.

Evaluation of information

The second crucial element in information handling mentioned earlier is the ability to evaluate information. This we need to be able to do to be classed as fully literate, since if we cannot evaluate information we lose our autonomy. There are many occasions in our lives when we are confronted with propaganda, be it blatant or subtle. Blatant propaganda tends to be political and we are at least at an advantage in Britain in that we can choose the propaganda we read. When propaganda is blatant, as in political newspapers, we tend to read it either already sharing its views or with our critical faculties on the alert ready to disbelieve what we read. With more subtle propaganda, however, we need continually to remind ourselves to evaluate the information we are given. One form of this is that found in the publicity material that confronts us daily. This often masquerades as information when it is really designed to be persuasive, and we need, as literate people, to be able to recognise when we are being led to believe and act in certain ways, so that we can assess whether we really want to behave as it is trying to make us. Of course, most of us at times are not good at this, and the whole of the advertising industry is founded on this fact. There would be no point in spending millions of pounds advertising a brand of toothpaste if no extra people bought it afterwards. We do respond to such publicity even if, on the surface, we can recognise the partiality and unreliability of the claim that this toothpaste will lead to 20 per cent fewer fillings and give us a smile with sex appeal.

It is certainly true that we need to sharpen our own critical approach to such information, and even more apparent that we need to give attention to developing such an approach in the children we teach - to make them more able to evaluate the information they come across (Zimet, 1976). Children are perhaps even more inclined than adults to believe that, 'if it says it in print it must be true'. How can we get them beyond this, and how, indeed, can we compensate for the dire effects propaganda, subtle or otherwise, may have upon them?

Coping with bias

One approach to this which has some adherents is that of removing biased materials from the children's reach (Jeffcoate, 1982). This leads many teachers to ban books like *Little Black Sambo* or *Dr Dolittle* from their classrooms on the grounds that they propagate racial stereotypes, and so lead to racism. Many teachers similarly will not want to use books in which gender roles are portrayed in a traditional male-centred way. Other teachers will ban books because they portray family life as something completely removed from that of the children they teach. Nobody responsible for getting books to children can fail to be aware of the growing emphasis on providing non-racist, non-sexist or non-classist books. It is, of course, difficult not to sympathise with the motives of those who take this approach and simply remove the offending books from classrooms, presumably replacing them with books which give desirable messages. This is clearly done with the very best of intentions. It is possible, however, to argue that this approach misses the point. After all, when children leave school they will be confronted with books and other information sources with the same faults of sexism, racism, etc. Some of the classic books in our culture suffer from these faults – *Robinson Crusoe* certainly portrays racial superiority, *The Merchant of Venice* is anti-semitic, and many books can be accused of being sexist in their portrayal of gender roles. The same is true of other sources of information. A brochure from the South African Tourist Board shows only one black face – a Zulu chieftain in traditional costume. Holiday brochures regularly use scantily clad young ladies as a lure to people to take their holidays in particular resorts. It would be inconceivable for us to prevent all this material from being read and used. The point is that when we read this material we need to be alert for the bias and we need to have ways of dealing with it. Children, of course, cannot develop these ways unless they have had practice in applying them.

An alternative response to this problem is the exact opposite of the protective approach taken by those who would ban biased materials from schools. It is possible to argue that what children need is to be confronted with bias, as much as possible, of all different kinds, and then to have the bias brought out into the open. By this means they may begin to realise that much of the information they read is there to persuade them to a certain point of view, and then be able to approach it critically.

Conclusion

This paper began by arguing that any real definition of literacy has to take account of the need for people to deal effectively with a whole range of sources of information. 'Dealing with information' was defined and two crucial stages in the process of information handling were isolated – that of defining for ourselves a precise purpose for seeking information, and that of evaluating the information we do find. Finally some points were made about our approach to developing these two things in the children we teach.

Throughout the paper, one point continually stressed has been the need for literacy to involve autonomy on the part of the literate person, and for children to be led towards this autonomy from the earliest possible stages of the development of their literacy. This may involve a major re-evaluation of the respective roles of teachers and pupils, but the goal of creating independent literates would seem to justify the effort involved in this.

References

BLAKE, W. (1956) 'Do probationary freshmen benefit from compulsory study skills and reading training?', *Journal of Experimental Education*, 25, September, pp. 91–3.

DES (1978) *Primary Education in England* (London: HMSO).

IRVING, A. and SNAPE, W. (1979) *Educating Library Users in Secondary Schools* (London: British Library Research and Development Department).

JEFFCOATE, R. (1982) 'Social values in children's books', in Open University, *Children, Language and Literature* (Milton Keynes: Open University Press).

LUNZER, E. and GARDNER, K. (1979) *The Effective Use of Reading* (London: Heinemann).

MAXWELL, J. (1977) *Reading Progress from 8 to 15* (Windsor: NFER).

MURPHY. R. (1973) *Adults Functional Reading Study, Final Report*, Princeton, New Jersey Educational Testing Service.

NEVILLE, M. and PUGH, A. (1982) *Towards Independent Reading* (London: Heinemann).

PERRY, W. (1959) 'Students' use and misuse of reading skills: a report to a faculty', *Harvard Educational Review*, 29, III.

WINKWORTH, E. (1977) *User Education in Schools* (London: British Library Research and Development Department).

WRAY, D. (1985) *Teaching Information Skills through Project Work* (Sevenoaks: Hodder and Stoughton).

ZIMET, S. (1976) *Print and Prejudice* (Sevenoaks: Hodder and Stoughton).

Chapter 5

Information Abuse and the Teacher

John E. Merritt

This paper argues that teachers in every subject area must play their part in helping children to cope with what we must now recognise as 'information abuse'. This abuse is exercised by all those who have the power to use, manage or control the mass media for their own purposes – purposes which may or may not be consistent with the interests of the majority of readers, listeners, or viewers.

Teachers can only succeed in preparing children to cope with information abuse if the whole school gets to grips with the problem. The best way of doing this, it suggests, is for the school to engage in an information partnership with the community. This paper suggests a practical way of getting started.

We hear a good deal these days about the 'information society'. But perhaps this is a misnomer. Perhaps we should really be talking about the 'dis-information society'. Or is it, perhaps, the 'information-overload society'. Or is it the 'information-deficient society'? Or the 'junk-information society'. Or all of these? And if so, what are the implications for the teacher from the point of view of reading education?

The dis-information society

We all tell lies. Naturally, you and I only tell 'white lies' – lies that do nobody any harm – except, perhaps, ourselves. 'Tell them I'm not in.' That's pretty common. Or we may not even tell a lie. We may simply, to coin a phrase, be 'economical with the truth'.

But let us set aside the question of trivial social lying – convenience lying, if you like. Let us focus, instead, on dis-information that bears directly on our lives in ways that really matter.

By way of example, you will no doubt remember a recent court case in Crocodilia in which the most senior civil servant of the state of Bit-ron tried to get away with a calculated deception by being 'economical with the truth'. The real question in this case, from our point of view, was whether or not a group of out-of-control agents had tried to undermine a democratically elected government. (I am deliberately disguising names so that you will not feel that I am singling out any particular country for criticism.) Even more recently, you may also have noticed reports of an all-time record in dis-information in an enquiry currently being carried out in the United Fates of Dysphasia. This involved covert support for a war in ways which were in direct defiance of the majority vote by those with constitutional responsibility for that particular action. A much longer running saga is also a matter of much debate in Glassnostia. Here, until recently, the writing of politically convenient 'history' was at one time a highly respected activity – although the products tended to have a rather short shelf-life.

The point I wish to make here is that any government of any country is quite likely to dis-inform its own citizens on many important issues. We used to think this was simply something that happened in nasty dictatorships. Now we know that it is more or less standard practice even in 'democratic' countries. Governments do not hesitate to issue grossly misleading information. They do not hesitate to pack 'independent' committees with their own partisans, or people with a vested interest in particular outcomes. And when the reports of their own committees are 'unhelpful', that is implicitly critical of their own policies and practices, they have no hesitation in ensuring that they are suitably doctored before release – or even suppressed altogether.

Why does this happen? It could be that politicians are simply corrupt and that they are trying to defend the indefensible. If we are charitable, however, we may think that they are doing all this 'for our own good' – the 'nanny knows best' syndrome. But this is clearly not democracy for *democracy cannot exist if people do not have the information they need in order to make their own judgements.* These judgements may not always be wise – but the alternatives to truly democratic, that is properly informed, decision making are almost invariably worse.

What are the implications for us as educators? Should we provide children with the kinds of experiences necessary for citizens to protect themselves against what I think we must now term 'information abuse'. Or should we leave them to the tender mercies of the dis-informers acting for whatever government happens to be in power at any particular time?

You cannot simply opt out of this issue. You cannot play Pontius Pilate – or use the 'Nuremberg defence'. That is to say, you cannot protest that you are simply obeying orders if you choose to evade this particular responsibility. Education is not 'value free'. Education means helping people to *be* free, that is to be independent, responsible human beings. This is the responsibility of every teacher. Whether we are teaching reading, science, history or mathematics we are contributing to a curriculum, part hidden and part explicit, which is either supporting the democratic process or undermining it – deliberately or by neglect.

Unfortunately, it is not just in politics that we find ourselves up against disinformation techniques. Public institutions, private firms, pressure groups, trade unions – and even professional associations – can be found engaging in similar practices. And, of course, we can always rely on 'news'papers such as the Sludge of the Week and the Morning Twinkle Stinkle to add to the pollution in our information channels with detritus of their own creation.

In all of this we are up against dis-informers of outstanding calibre – people who are highly trained in dissemble-speak by those masters of the art – the ad-men. You will have noticed, for example, how rarely politicians answer questions that are put to them at interviews. They answer questions that were not asked with 'replies' to points that are simply not at issue. You will also have noticed how often their tone of voice suggests that they have in fact given a more than satisfactory answer, however thin their answer really was – or their tone suggests that the interviewer should really have known better than to ask that particular question! Captains of industry, trade union leaders, pressure groups and the rest have not achieved the high standards of information abuse achieved by the successful politician – but they are on target and closing fast.

If it is simply a matter of being persuaded to buy this or that soap powder we may not be unduly concerned. If, on the other hand, we or our children are likely to be exposed to excessive nuclear radiation, polluted water supplies, injurious food ingredients – or a debilitated education system – then we have every right, as individual citizens, to reject the freedom to dis-inform. As educators, it is clearly an essential part of our professional responsibility to ensure that children are thoroughly educated in ways of coping with information abuse.

An information-overload society

There is so much printed material on any given subject that we simply cannot afford to read it all. As a teacher, you just do not have time to read even a well-selected sample of all the relevant information. It is extremely difficult to keep abreast even in a single specialist area. But as human beings, rather than specialists, the whole world of knowledge is our oyster. Even if we try to keep our reading to a bare minimum we cannot cope with everything that comes thumping through the letter box, never mind the material we would like to be familiar with if only we had the time. The school, therefore, must provide a much more realistic training in the skills of identifying information priorities.

An information-deficient society

Amidst all this mass of information, paradoxically, we find, time and time again, that we are short of the very information we most need. The doctor does not tell us how long to go on taking the tablets and neither does the label on the bottle; we want to know which parts are most likely to need repair most often on a television set or a new car and the likely costs; or we want to know if this hotel is really as well located as the travel brochure implies. There is certainly a role here for education– and, as I shall shortly argue, partly as provider.

A junk-information society

We have junk information just as we have junk food. Typical of this genre are the large packages of unsolicited advertising literature that seem to arrive almost every day in life. These contain hundreds of words telling us what we didn't want to know – usually in a thoroughly misleading way – and all of this verbiage makes it extremely difficult to find the tiny bit of information that is, for us, of most interest or importance. If the money spent on the junk information sent to doctors each week were to be used on health and fitness we should all be running sub-four minute miles – those of us who want to! This is also an area in which, as educators, we might do more – and do it better.

An interim summary

To summarise thus far, we may say that information abuse can serve one of two purposes. On the one hand, the general intention might be to take advantage of you in some way. On the other hand, the intention might be to protect you. Either way, your own personal freedom is restricted without your consent. This may sometimes be inevitable: a 'cure' can sometimes be worse than the disease. But you do need to understand the problem – and have enough information to make up your own mind on each separate kind of issue. Otherwise, you are at the mercy of any fanatical under-cover agent who chooses to do it his way. You are at the mercy of any devious politician who regards the electorate as so many sheep to be herded to suit his or her own vainglorious theories. And you are at the mercy of any criminal who is prepared to fortify your wine with anti-freeze to increase his or her own profits.

I would suggest that it is our inescapable responsibility to help our pupils to learn how to set about making their own decisions on such issues. If we simply teach them to abide by our decisions – or those of anyone else – we are guilty of indoctrination. But if we *fail* to teach them how to decide for themselves on the basis of careful analysis and sound argument then, as I said earlier, we are in serious breach of our responsibilities as educators.

So much for the problem – impressionistic as this treatment has necessarily been. What can we actually do about it that is down to earth and practical?

A possible way forward

The first thing we have to recognise is that if we want anyone to learn anything at all they have to have the necessary practical experience on which to build their abstractions. This is true whether we are helping very young children to acquire basic number concepts or training constructional engineers at university level. Piagetian principles hold at every stage of learning – and at every age. If, therefore, we want children to learn how to handle information and cope with information abuse then they must have experience that is, from their point of view, 'for real'. Is this a problem – given the sheltered, over-protected life of the school? Not at all. We simply have to come out of the ivory castle and enter the real world.

How? Simple. We begin to develop each and every school as an information centre for its own community. Any school can gather information that is of short-term interest or value to the community and constantly update it. It can also gather information that is of longer term importance and review and revise this also as often as may be necessary. In addition, where a school can get hold of information that may be of particular interest or value to other communities, or schools, this too can be gathered and stored – sometimes on demand and sometimes in anticipation of probable needs.

We can do all of this today by making use of the computer in setting up data bases to handle all the relevant information and administration with maximum ease and efficiency. Tomorrow, given the amazing speed of development of computer power and computer memory, it will be even easier.

What would be the gains? Frankly, there are so many that it is only worthwhile listing the more obvious:

(1) Children gain direct experience:

- in identifying the wide range of real information needs and priorities of individuals in their own and other communities
- in identifying, locating and gaining access to relevant sources
- in evaluating sources in relation to specified purposes
- in selecting, abstracting and editing for specific purposes and audiences
- in organising information into formats that are most appropriate for realistic purposes
- in storing information so that it can be retrieved with maximum efficiency according to the different kinds of purpose that might be anticipated
- in reviewing and evaluating the quality of their own data in the light of their own growing awareness and broadening experience
- in making such additional enquiries – scientific, technical, historical, geographical, economic, etc. – as may be necessary to supplement the information obtained from printed sources.

(2) Teachers gain experience:

- in all of the above – learning with, and from, the children and from the sources they access
- in negotiating with people in each of the various sectors of the community and in developing a better relationship with those to whom they are ultimately responsible

(3) Parents gain experience:

- in acting as a resource for the school and, in turn, taking advantage of the school as a community resource
- in identifying the practical needs of children as future citizens and bringing a much better informed view to a curriculum debate that must keep in continuous touch with the ever-changing needs of the community.

Added to this, the community gains directly from the resources provided by the school – at little or no extra cost. What is much more important, however, is gains in the quality of thinking that goes into every aspect of community decision making and community action.

Those of you who have read that most chastening of all books on education, *The Saber-Tooth Curriculum* (Peddiwell, 1939), will be well aware that much of what we teach, and how we teach, owes more to outdated traditions than to any realistic appraisal of what is needed by way of apprenticeship for life in the twentieth century, much less the twenty-first century. The current emphasis on testing could easily make matters worse by driving us all back to the bad old days – the days when children were brought up on a diet of examination-passing techniques.

If our legislators are so ignorant of education as to allow that to happen we only have ourselves to blame. We must blame ourselves for failing to break out of our own narrow mould and failing to communicate adequately with that wider public to whom we are professionally responsible. We have, by default, brought our present troubles upon ourselves.

The strategy that I have suggested today is one that addresses these professional problems. In addition, I would suggest, it can help our pupils to move towards a more relevant use of curriculum time and, at the same time, a higher standard of all-round achievement even in traditional terms.

But let us conclude by reminding ourselves about the role of technology. Many people still do not realise just how fundamentally our lives are changing as powerful computers become more readily available for use in the home. As we become more dependent on computer sources we shall run the risk of becoming more and more like battery hens. We shall find ourselves imprisoned in a dis-information cage – a cage that is cunningly designed by people for whom 'presentation' is a legitimate device which they can use, quite arbitrarily, to control what we think and how we think.

Alternatively, we can learn to make intelligent use of public data bases and contribute to the development of a wide range of private data bases. We can learn to use these intelligently and skilfully to check the extravagant claims and misleading statements of pedlars, 'presstitutes', and politicians. We can learn to share ideas and information networks so that we develop a quality of judgement that is far superior to that which we achieve in isolation. Information technology provides us with our seven-league boots. Let us help our pupils to discover how to use them – before someone else steals them.

References

PEDDIWELL, J. ABNER (pseudonym for Benjamin, H.) (1939) *The Saber-Tooth Curriculum,* (New York: McGraw Hill).

Chapter 6

Moving Shadows: Teaching a Film

Joyce Kilpatrick

It is no accident that one of the very best of the thousands of books which deal with film *is called 'How To* Read *A Film'. This paper examines some approaches as to how to* teach *a film as a piece of classroom material.*

The paper also considers aspects of the language of film, the philosophy of the film as an art form, and the relationship between the film and the book. In essence the central focus is the teaching of English through the moving picture.

What are the purposes of teaching English?

James Thurber criticised *his* English teacher, one Miss Groby, because she brought 'the fierce light of identification' to the study of literature:

> She was forever climbing up the margins of books and crawling between the lines, hunting for the little gold phrase, making marks with a pencil. As Palimodes hunted the Questing Beast, she hunted Figures of Speech. She hunted them through the clangorous halls of Shakespeare and through the green forests of Scott, as if she were hunting for TIGERS.
>
> Night after night, for homework, Miss Groby set us searching in Ivanhoe and Julius Caesar for metaphors, similies, metonymies, apostrophes, personifications, and all the rest. It got so the figures of speech jumped out of the pages at you . . . '

Consider the perceived purposes of teaching English in our secondary schools. It is to nurture and improve and renew language skills and literary appreciation. It is to develop pupil competence in the four modes of reading, writing, listening and talking. It is above all the education of the intellect and sensibility – beyond identification towards understanding, and enrichment.

A choice of film

A fine example of a film rich in teaching material is *The Prime of Miss Jean Brodie*, released in 1969, and adapted from Muriel Spark's classic novel. The author herself agreed to return to Edinburgh to speak to the

UKRA Conference in 1987. She remarked to me that she thought the film version of her novel 'quite delightful'. Doubtless she would have expanded this view had I not retreated, overcome by that strange mixture of untypical timidity and justifiable awe that one first experienced, all too long ago, on first meeting a *real* Santa as a small child at Christmas time. Perhaps at times our teaching of English fails to inculcate much awe, or wonder.

'Tigers'

Here are some of the 'Tigers' to be found in this particular film, tigers to be identified, but also to provide many opportunities for profitable study – indeed, for enrichment:

Action and Reaction	Metaphor
Acting	Monosyllable
Allegory	Music
Alliteration	Narrative
Casting	Pace
Characterisation	Parallelism
Cross-cutting	Perspective
Dialogue	Point of view
Dramatisation	Script
Dub-over	Setting
Euphemism	Sequencing
Irony	Simile
Kinetics (movement and gesture)	Spectator positioning
Light and Shade	Symbolism

Moving shadows

Consider the word 'shadow'. We might hold the word in our hands, and turn it over, and admire its facets. There are no less than sixteen definitions of the word shadow in the Oxford English Dictionary, and many more shades of meaning. A shadow can mean comparative darkness, or gloom, or unhappiness, or the darkness of night, or the shadows of Hell. A shadow can be something fleeting or ephemeral, or a reflected image, or a form from which the substance has departed. A shadow can be a creature from a magical world – in *A Midsummer Night's Dream* Oberon is 'King of Shadows'. And of course a shadow can be a stage player. Puck tells the audience:

> If we *shadows* have offended,
> Think but this, and all is mended:
> That you have but slumber'd here,
> While these visions did appear.

It was Shakespeare's marvellous metaphor for life itself:

> Life's but a walking shadow,
> A poor player who struts and frets
> His hour upon the stage . . .

And so, to examine the players in *their* 'hour' upon the stage. To observe the moving shadows of the world of the film.

Assignments

Study of a film can produce a wide variety of assignments, and the teacher might wish to have a class tackle all of them, or simply to select one or two. The aim of the study is to encourage close listening and viewing, and to develop those perceptual skills inherent in *visual literacy*; the purposes and tasks designed to develop pupil competence in the four modes of reading, writing, listening and talking. The assignments would require outcomes which can be assessed according to grade related criteria. Pupil responses can involve discussion, scripting and taping, storyboarding and a wide variety of written assignments. There would be some conscious analysis of film and acting techniques. The complete study would demonstrate the riches to be found in a good film, the multi-facets of the moving picture as an art form.

Character sketches

Dialogue is very important in any film. What the characters say tells us important things about them, and their relationships with other people. In the character sketch assignment in Fig. 6.1 pupils are given some twenty short pieces of dialogue which relate to the character of Jean Brodie. They are asked to discuss how these extracts reveal various aspects of her personality, and contribute to the rest of the film.

Consider the line, 'Hugh fell like an autumn leaf'. It is spoken by Jean Brodie, referring to her former boyfriend, who has been killed in the First World War. Note the euphemistic 'fell', to cover all the horror of death in war. Admire, if you will, the simple Keatsian simile, which gives power to the pastiche of the eccentric schoolteacher, seeming to confuse melodrama with tragedy. For Jean Brodie, in that line, confirms a generation of loss.

Another example is the word 'assassin'. It is the hyperbole of a 'ridiculous woman' who has lost to the young girl, Sandy. And as Maggie Smith calls out 'assassin' to Sandy's retreating back, the camera zooms into the girl's shoulder blades, and back and in, as if the word were a spear. To make the effect quite complete, the word is allowed to echo, and we can almost see the spear quiver and settle.

Each line of dialogue selected for the character sketch page is rich in significant meaning. As an extension exercise, pupils might be asked to

Character Sketch

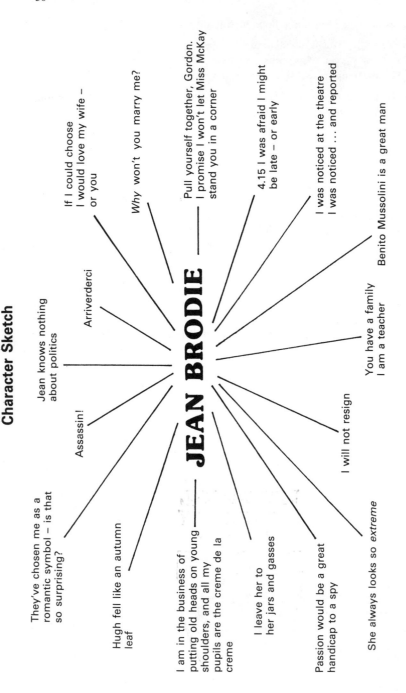

FIGURE 6.1 *Character sketch assignment*

choose one other character from the film, and to make up a character sketch for him or her, using this example as a pattern.

Interpretative questions and assignments

This type of work provides the structure of the narrative for the pupil. Questions highlight some of the central incidents in the film, and provide a built-in memory bank, to avoid heavy reliance on recall as opposed to understanding and critical appreciation. The questions might begin by establishing the type of school Marcia Blane's appears to be, and reinforcing the 'status quo' of the classical narrative pattern which the film follows. One particular assignment might require students to 'climb into' the character of Mary McGregor in her early days at Marcia Blane, by writing a letter from her to her remarkable brother. Another assignment might simply ask that students identify one scene or incident where there is clever use of comedy, or music.

The camera

In a film we see the world from behind the camera. The visual impressions we receive are influenced by thoughtful use of the camera lens, which becomes our eyes. 'Spectator-positioning' and point of view is quite crucial to the impressions we receive, the arrangement of the picture, the use of light and shade, the setting. In the camera assignment, pupils could be given descriptions of eight pictures from the film, eight fast-freezes in words if you like, for discussion.

Consider, for example, the scene looking down on Jean Brodie, as she hands apples from the tree to Mr Lowther. The sun is shining; these are halcyon days. Symbolically they are the golden apples of the sun, and she is Eve while he is Adam. Another example is the camera shot where we as spectators look in the mirror with Sandy. It is a subtle use of action and reaction to further dramatise this moment in the film, where Sandy's dual life is becoming so central to the denouement of the narrative. Like the notorious Dorian Gray she is leading a double life, and as she looks in the mirror at that moment we see, with her, her 'other self'.

A central scene

A practical criticism assignment might focus on the scene where Miss McKay sends for Jean Brodie and Gordon Lowther. The headmistress reads the incriminating letter aloud, and the scene requires skilled acting, to exploit to the full all its comi/tragic elements.

A short extract from the letter is given, and then ten questions and assignments. Lowther is virtually silent throughout the entire scene, and pupils are asked to discuss that. The tone of voice adopted by Miss McKay is explored, as are the wide range of emotional reactions required to be displayed by Maggie Smith as Jean Brodie. Comic farce and cliches, the kinetics of movement and gesture, monosyllabic lines in a tense moment are highlighted. As an extension assignment, students might write their own script for this scene in a storyboard form, or give choices of camera shots they might use to gain most dramatic effect.

Some other assignments

Space would not truly accommodate too exhaustive a coverage of every possible approach to a film. A word interpolation can efficiently reinforce the plot. A newspaper facsimile with the headline 'Marcia Blane in Fascist Storm', where pupils are asked to write the article, given a word limit, of course, is another rewarding approach. Or imagine that Jean Brodie has found a time-warp to the Terry Wogan Show – after her dismissal, of course. Pupils can be asked to script, tape, or even video the interview which results.

This film followed a successful stage production of the novel, and has several very good exit lines. One assignment might give five of these exit lines, and ask pupils to discuss each one, and consider such dramatic effects as tone, meaning, purpose and delivery. The opening and closing sequences of the film could be the subject of another assignment, where such aspects as irony, anticipation, the school motto, the first line and the final dub-over are examined.

Poetry and shadows

In the moving shadows of this film the pivotal scene occurs at the end of the first time sequence, under the sunshine of light and hope. The child asks, 'What shall I recite, Miss Brodie?' And she replies, 'Something of magic'. The child, in a *deliberately* childish voice, recites four lines from *The Lady of Shalott*, comes to the word 'curse', and the Brodie girls giggle at the *double entendre*. And, of course, this allows the great change in *tone* as Jean Brodie takes over, to recite the marvellous Tennysonian lines:

> But in her web she still delights
> To weave the mirror's magic sights,
> For often thro' the silent nights
> A funeral, with plumes and lights
>   And music, went to Camelot:
> Or when the moon was overhead,
> Came two young lovers lately wed;
> 'I am half sick of shadows,' said
>   The Lady of Shalott.

The Lady of Shalott, you will recall, saw life only in a mirror . . . and when she turned to partake of real life, her world was destroyed. Like the lady of the poem, Jean Brodie lives in a world of shadows, a world of comparative darkness. The scene anticipates the gloom and unhappiness of her future. Perhaps it reminds her, too, of that something fleeting and ephemeral, that happiness which has begun to leave her. For in some ways this parallelism with the Lady of Shalott, forever excluded from the lights and music of Camelot, becomes an allegory on Jean Brodie's isolation. A further comparison can be made with the Liz Lochhead poem, which is a modern parody of Tennyson's classic.

The novel

Muriel Spark's novel is essentially much more complex and subtle than the film. A further assignment might require that pupils examine some important differences between the novel and the film. For example, in the novel Miss McKay is younger than Jean Brodie – yet the visual impact of the older woman, the stereotype of a head of school, lends authenticity and authority to the screen portrayal. In the novel we gain the retrospective quality of elastic time, as Muriel Spark weaves past and present and future together in a most sophisticated web. We see Jean Brodie at the end of her life 'as she sat, shrivelled and betrayed'. Sandy becomes a nun, and an extremely interesting study of guilt. Teddy's wife Deirdre is actualised into a character of some complexity. One of the Brodie set visits Edinburgh years later, and suggests to her husband that they go to visit Miss Brodie's grave. 'Who was Miss Brodie?', he asks. And the reply can only hint at the artistry of the novel:

> A teacher of mine, she was full of culture.
> She was an Edinburgh Festival all on her own.

Beyond the a b c

The world of the film offers a wealth of riches. A good film, like a fine novel, or a stimulating play, or a thoughtful poem, is a piece of literature, an art form. It can take us 'beyond the abc' towards rewarding enhancement of the intellect and the sensibility. Consider these words of Alexander Solzhenitsyn on the nature of art:

> They were wrong, and they will always be wrong, those prophets who say Art will degenerate, will exhaust all conceivable forms, will die. It is we who will die; Art will remain. And shall we, before we perish, manage to understand all its facets and all its purposes?
> Not everything has a name. Some things lead us into a realm beyond words. Art thaws even the frozen, darkened soul, opening it to lofty spiritual experience. Through Art we are sometimes sent – indistinctly, briefly – revelations not to be achieved by rational thought.
> It is like that small mirror in the fairy tales – you glance in it and what you see is not yourself; for an instance you glimpse the Inaccessible, where no horse or magic carpet can take you. And the soul cries out for it . . .'

References

ARNHEIM, R. (1958) *Film as Art* (London: Faber and Faber).

BALAZS, B. (1952) *Theory of the Film* (London: Dobson).

HALLIWELL, L. (1985) *Halliwell's Film Guide* (London: Granada).

KILPATRICK, J. (1987) *The Prime of Miss Jean Brodie* (Film Teaching Package) (West Lothian: Inveralmond Community High School).

LOCHHEAD, L. (1977) *The Sense of Belonging: Six Scottish Poets of the Seventies* (Glasgow and London: Blackie).

MILLAR, R. and CURRIE, I. (1970) *The Language of Poetry* (London and Edinburgh: Heinemann).

MONACO, J. (1981) *How to Read A Film* (New York: Oxford University Press).

SOLZHENITSYN, A. (1972) *One Word of Truth* (London: The Bodley Head).

SPARK, M. (1965) *The Prime of Miss Jean Brodie* (London: Penguin).

TENNYSON, A. (1968) *Poems of 1842* (London and Glasgow: Collins).

Chapter 7

The Use of Music, Songs and Lyrics in Reading Instruction

Rona F. Flippo

A thorough review of the research and literature relevant to investigating the use of music, songs, and lyrics to enhance reading and comprehension abilities is presented here. The review focuses on research and literature pertinent to the use of music, songs, and lyrics in reading and reading-related instruction, and the suggested uses of these materials. While the research and literature review reveals that the use of music, songs, and lyrics in reading instruction is far from new, it also reveals that there is relatively little research in the area, and there is a need to do this research systematically. The literature also reveals that the use of music, songs, and lyrics could be beneficial for use by reading teachers. *

Review of the literature

The literature review indicates that historically reading was in the hands of the Church (Martin, 1981), and music and songs were very much part of this reading. Hymnals were often considered a textbook for reading instruction. Songs from these books would be sung in various parts of the church service and used in class to be read and analysed. The hymns were not altered or varied from the original form in instruction. Yet, students had the benefit of hearing and singing them in addition to reading (Farresh, 1978).

Music and songs lend themselves to repetition. Students learn lyrics through this immersion or repeated exposure. Using the idea of repeated exposure to lyrics, Chomsky (1976) devised a programme where children were repeatedly exposed to taped books until they were memorised.

Use of music, songs, and lyrics can be a natural part of learning to read. There have been many articles published in support of their use. However, the majority of these publications tend to be testimonials (Sullivan, 1979) rather than reported research. Many cite use of music and lyrics as pleasing, interesting, and a strong motivational vehicle for teaching reading and the

---

*The initial review of the literature and research was carried out by Laurie P. Wright (1984), one of my graduate students, who carried out the review under my guidance and direction. Special recognition and thanks are expressed to Laurie Wright for her diligent comprehensive work.

language arts (Smith, 1981; Wright, 1977; McKenna, 1977; Kuhmerker, 1969). Others have particularly cited use of lyrics from rock, country, pop, and current hit music for reading instruction (Larrick, 1971; Nelson, 1979; Newsom, 1979; Reeves, 1978; Wulffson, 1970; Smith, 1981; Martin, 1981).

Larrick (1971) found that by using music, the students' enjoyment of reading class increased attendance and performance in her class. Reluctant readers were more apt to read lyrics that they enjoyed and were familiar with. Discussion time increased and Larrick found oral expression skills were also being strengthened.

Nelson (1979) worked with albums on specific themes. By pulling out vocabulary words from the lyrics and having students try out definitions for these words, he found an increase in vocabulary test scores as well as an increase in motivation. Smith (1981) indicates that lyrics can also be used to teach literal comprehension as well as the higher-level comprehension skills.

Some educational publishing companies have developed teaching materials to capitalise on use of taped popular music and lyrics. However, Newsom (1979) and Chomsky (1976) and others have found some disadvantages in using these commercial materials. The tapes move too quickly for many students and often become frustrating for them. Also, by the time tapes are made by commercial companies a song may no longer be a hit. Due to these and other reasons, it is suggested that teachers make their own tapes. Teacher-made tapes can be current, paced for the needs of individual students, and divided appropriately for the teachers' use and purposes.

Another related and highly motivating source of material is musical television commercials. Students can often be heard humming, singing or making puns with the latest jingles on the television. Hirst and O'Such (1979) put together what they identified as a successful reading programme based on musical television commercials.

Music is also examined as to its usefulness in developing reading readiness and other facilitative skills. Many mention the important part music can play in developing listening skills and building attention spans (Lloyd, 1978; McDonald, 1975; Rietz, 1976); auditory discrimination skills (Cohen, 1974; McDonald, 1975); auditory acuity (Uhl, 1969); syllabication (McDonald, 1975; Yaakob, 1973; Uhl, 1969); pronunciation and accent (McKenna, 1977); phrasing and syntax (Wright, 1979; McDonald, 1975); articulation (Blanton, 1962); vocabulary (Smith, 1981; McDonald, 1975; Mateja, 1982); perceptual skills (Cohen, 1974; Berman, 1976; Movsesian, 1969); and visual skills (Lloyd, 1978). Cardarelli (1979) reviews many activities utilising music, songs, and lyrics, that have been supported in the literature, which can be used to build reading and reading-related skills.

Songs can also provide experience with common phrase structures and syntax patterns (McDonald, 1975). A favourite song can be used to help students develop a 'feel' for sentence structure and phrasing. For example, 'Mary Had a Little Lamb' can serve as the text from which students can fit other words into specified slots or positions to develop whole new phrases. 'Mary had a big red ball' can be made from 'slot filling'. Questions can then be asked to generate additional response verses to the song. Whole sentence structure would be used to encourage the use of correct writing forms. Singing conversations can be used in a similar fashion. Singing conversations follow the idea that, 'What can be said can also be sung, and often pitch and rhythm can provide a vividness to the experience which may not be easily provided otherwise'. (McDonald, 1975, p. 874).

The literature also supports use of music, songs, and lyrics in specific content areas (Tucker, 1981; Johnson, 1969; Larrick, 1971; Ritt, 1974; Lamme, 1979). Johnson (1969) indicates that the use of folk songs and ballads in teaching history, geography, economics, and literature provide an opportunity to show children that all aspects of life are interdependent. Use of music enhances reading in various content areas. Some specific uses are cited from the literature as follows:

1. Use titles of songs as topic headlines for reports (Larrick, 1971).
2. Play the records or sing songs on a particular topic to present atmosphere (Ritt, 1974).
3. Music and singing used during the lesson can help to illustrate specific points (Ritt, 1974).
4. Music and singing used at the end of a lesson help to summarise the learning that has taken place (Ritt, 1974).
5. Examine and discuss the customs and language of the people represented in the songs (Ritt, 1974; Johnson, 1969).
6. Play the songs over and over to establish 'a feel' for the music (Ritt, 1974).
7. Provide copies of the lyrics for students to follow (Ritt, 1974).
8. Skimming songs about a certain topic and using the SQ3R technique can also be beneficial (Ritt, 1974).

The drama portrayed in songs provides additional opportunity. Monson (1982) indicates that knowing that a composer has captured the drama of a story in musical form helps to reinforce the notion of a dramatic response to literature. The drama in songs and music also alludes to the emotions that are expressed. The lyrics can be examined by students to find the mood that a composer is trying to establish.

Nash (1974) states, 'Singing is defined as an extension of speech where more emotions can be expressed'. Children can invent melodic rhythms to match a situation or an experience. Music lends itself to experimentation and discovery which leads to expression. This expression and feeling for the written word, for lyrics, opens doors to children. It lets them discover that reading can be more than a mundane exercise; it can actually be an expression of one's self. Moffett (1973) continues this line of thought through his statement that, 'Music offers stimuli which children can interpret through body movements and inner feelings. Music suggests moods, actions, and will encourage individual invention, and spontaneous interpretation. Music can make reading multi-sensory, it can make reading real.' (p. 93)

The idea of writing musicals for the classroom, which develops skills related to writing and oral language, as well as reading, are outlined by Dwyer (1982, p. 729).

1. Find songs that the children enjoy. Bring in many records to provide a varied musical experience.
2. Duplicate and hand out lyrics of well-liked songs.
3. Select approximately five songs that are particular favourites.
4. Write a play around those five songs. Use the ideas contained in the songs and add character and events.
5. A basic piano arrangement seems to work better than complex musical arrangements. A tape can be made to make the singing easier.
6. Have many characters with little dialogue rather than a few main characters. Assign every student a speaking part.
7. Avoid scene changes which involve pauses in the action. The play should have one fast-moving scene which lasts about twenty minutes.

Choral reading and singing is another dramatic area that music can bring to reading instructions. Choral speaking works on many important reading skills as an individual learns to use his voice effectively. The concepts and pitch, stress, juncture, etc. and the possibilities in meanings based on the use of these become apparent through dramatic reading. Choral reading emphasises the art rather than the skill of reading (Stewig, 1981). In a study of choral reading and singing, Bassett (1979), presented students with a series of song lyrics which were in a sequential order of syntactic complexity. He found that the choral reading and singing treatment group made significant gains over the control group.

To determine if the addition of music and sound effects to recorded stories increased comprehension and retention of information, Mann (1979), conducted a study with fourth-grade students. The results indicate that the use of music and sound effects in conjunction with stories seems to help both long-term and short-term memory. Four hypotheses are suggested by Mann:

1. Music and sound effects may draw attention to specific information.
2. Music and sound effects mask out other distinctions.
3. Music and sound effects may help to create a mental image.
4. Music and sound effects may provide for more enjoyment of stories.

Summary

In summary, the reviewed literature indicates that songs and the lyrics in songs and in the media are a good source of reading instructional materials, providing a multi-sensory experience, variety and pleasure, and reducing what could otherwise be monotonous drills. It is suggested that a vast amount and variety of recorded material be available, and that the lyrics be printed and available for students to follow.

Additionally, the literature abounds with suggestions and ideas for using songs, lyrics, and music in reading and reading-related skill instruction. Unfortunately, relatively few research studies have been conducted to measure the success of these ideas. However, the literature tends to indicate that teachers and students have found the use of music, songs, and lyrics enjoyable and beneficial. It might be because as Wulffson (1970) points out, 'The success of a learning activity depends more than anything else upon its effectiveness in involving the student' (p. 180). Nevertheless, music, songs, and lyrics are potentially wonderful teaching materials, materials that can be used, expanded on, altered, and instructionally implemented in countless ways. Implementation using these materials can be of benefit to reading teachers and their students. This is a relatively unexplored, yet highly potential, area that needs systematic research and exploration. Those of us in reading education who enjoy music, song and lyrics are called upon to carry through this needed research.

References

BASSETT, R.K. (1979) *An investigation of the effects of choral reading and sensory on language achievement, reading achievement and oral development of 6th grade students* (The University of Tennessee: ERIC Document Reproduction Service No. ED 181 489).

BERMAN, J.R. (1976) *The use of music for a non-verbal reading prototype: An investigation of auditory-visual processing in poor and good readers* (Atlanta, Georgia: ERIC Document Reproduction Service No. ED 120 699).

BLANTON, W.L. (1962) *An experimental application of language theory, learning theory, and personality theory to evaluate the influence of music in language learning.* Doctoral Dissertation, University of Texas at Austin. (ERIC Document Reproduction Service No. ED 250 609).

CARDARELLI, A.F. (1979) *Twenty-one ways to use music in teaching the language arts.* (Indiana State University: ERIC Document Reproduction Service No. ED 176 268).

CHOMSKY, C. (1976) 'After decoding what?', *Language Arts*, 53 (3), pp. 288–96, 314.

COHEN, M. (1974) 'Move him into reading with music', *Instructor*, 83 (6), pp. 60–62.

DWYER, E.J. (1982) 'Writing musicals in the classroom', *The Reading Teacher*, 35 (6), p. 729.

FARRESH, B. (Ed.) (1978) *A Music teachers' primer to reading. Supplemental material for RDG 467, RDG 480, RDG 507, and RDG 544* (Arizona State University: ERIC Document Reproduction Service No. ED 225 983).

HIRST, L.T. and O'SUCH, T. (1979) 'Using musical television commercials to teach reading', *Teaching Exceptional Children*, 11 (2), pp. 80–81.

JOHNSON, P. (1969) 'The use of folk songs in education: Some examples of the use of folk songs in the teaching of history, geography, economics, and English literature', *The Vocational Aspect of Education*, 21, pp. 91–109.

KUHMERKER, L. (1969) 'Music in the beginning reading program', *Young Children*, 24 (3), pp. 157–163.

LAMME, L. (1979) 'Song Picture Books – A maturing genre of children's literature', *Language Arts*, 56 (4), pp. 400–407.

LARRICK, N. (1971) 'Pop-Rock Lyrics, Poetry Reading', *Journal of Reading*, 15 (3), pp. 184–90.

LLOYD, M.J. (1978) 'Teach music to aid beginning readers', *The Reading Teacher*, 32 (3), pp. 323–27.

MANN, R. (1979) *The effect of music and sound effects on the listening comprehension of 4th grade students* (North Texas State University: ERIC Document Reproduction No. ED 172 738).

MARTIN, R.J. (1981) 'Folk songs in developmental literature', *Language Arts*, 58 (3), pp. 326–29.

MATEJA, J. (1982) 'Musical cloze: Background purpose and sample', *The Reading Teacher*, 35 (4), pp. 444–48.

MCDONALD, D. (1975) 'Music and reading readiness', *Language Arts*, 52 (6), pp. 872–76.

MCKENNA, M. (1977) 'Songs for language study', *Audiovisual Instructor*, 22 (4), pp. 42–3.

MOFFETT, J.A. (1973) *A student centered Language Arts Curriculum Grades K-6: A Handbook for Teachers* (Boston: Houghton-Mifflin).

MONSON, D. (1982) The literature program and the arts. *Language Arts*, 59 (3), pp. 254–58.

MOVSESIAN, E.A. (1969) 'Reading music and reading words', *Today's Education*, 58 (1), pp. 42–3.

NASH, G.C. (1974) *Creative Approaches to Child Development with Music Language and Movement* (New York: Alfred Publishing Company).

NELSON, M. (1979) 'The orchestrated classroom', *English Journal*, 69 (7), pp. 41–2.

NEWSOM, S.D. (1979) 'Rock n' Roll n' Reading', *Journal of Reading*, 22 (8), pp. 726–30.

REEVES, H. (1978) 'Building basic skills with music', *Music Educators Journal*, 65, pp. 75–9.

RIETZ, S.A. (1976) *Using childen's folksongs to transition beginning readers from the familiar structure of oral language to the structure of written language* (Anaheim, California: Paper presented at Annual Meeting of the IRA, ERIC Document Reproduction Service No. ED 142 983).

RITT, S.L. (1974) 'Using music to teach reading skills in social studies', *The Reading Teacher*, 27 (6), pp. 224–25.

SMITH, C.F. Jr (1981) 'Motivating the reluctant reader through the top twenty', in A. Ciani (Ed.) *Motivating reluctant readers* (Newark, Delaware: International Reading Association).

STEWIG, J.W. (1981) 'Choral speaking: Who has the time? Why take the time?', *Childhood Education*, 58 (1), pp. 25–9.

SULLIVAN, E.P. (1979) *Using music to teach reading: State of the art review* (San Antonio, Texas: ERIC Document Reproduction Service No. ED 184 109).

TUCKER, A (1981) 'Music and the teaching of reading: A review of the literature', *Reading Improvement*, 18 (1), pp. 14–19.

UHL, G.C. (1969) 'Singing helps children learn how to read', *Music Educational Journal*, 56 (4), pp. 45–6.

WRIGHT, L.P. (1984) 'Music, song, lyrics, and the enhancement of reading', unpublished paper.

WRIGHT, S.G. (1977) *Music: A vehicle for teaching certain aspects of the elementary language arts* (New York, New York: ERIC Document Reproduction Service No. ED 150 599).

WRIGHT, S.G. (1979) *Music, songs and literature* (San Francisco, California: ERIC Document Reproduction Service No. ED 181 480).

WULFFSON, D.L. (1970) 'Music to teach reading', *Journal of Reading*, 14 (3), pp. 179–82.

YAAKOB, P.M. (1973) 'Music and reading', *Elementary English, 50 (4), pp. 578–89.*

Chapter 8

Children's Literature: The Strategic Connection

Carol and John Butzow

The purpose of this work is to suggest an alternative approach to the teaching of primary school science, through the utilisation of well-selected, conceptually and factually correct works of fictional children's literature. This method is most easily applied with children at the first school or elementary level of education. These literature books should not be used solely for motivation or to provide background information for the science class. Nor are they intended to be a means of clarifying concepts which have been presented by other methods.

Fictional literature can be used as the foundation of science instruction. Because literature has a story line, children may find it easier to follow the ideas that are part of a plot, than to comprehend facts as presented in a textbook. Science is very abstract for youngsters. It must be seen as part of the youngster's own personal world if it is to be understood and remembered. The story does this by putting facts and concepts into a form which encourages children to build a hypothesis, predict events, and see if their ideas are correct. In this way, the lesson becomes relevant and conceptually in tune with the child's abilities.

This method can be used as a means of integrating reading, writing and language arts, as well as maths, humanities, physical activities and the creative arts into a single unit or lesson. The strategies employed in 'learning to read' and 'learning science' are very similar; for example, observing, comparing, measuring, seeking relationships, interpreting, communicating, predicting outcomes, making judgements, and evaluating. This paper presents strategies to accomplish this integration of science and reading-language arts instruction and provides sample activities based on selected children's books.

Introduction

At the present time, parallel events are occurring in the fields of reading instruction and science instruction. Reading is no longer seen as a series of subskills which, when 'mastered', can be equated with the ability to comprehend. Reading is an active process of simultaneously combining several strategies. The numerous subskills which have traditionally been taught in segregated fashion have merely enabled children to perform isolated skills. No single thought process can be performed without overlapping others. To draw conclusions, for example, one must have knowledge of the main idea and details of the selection and also be able to make predictions and inferences. Many experts indicate there are only three basic elements which children must possess to become proficient readers: word knowledge, relationships and reasoning.

In science, the memorisation of facts and vocabulary words is somewhat akin to working with skills in isolation in the reading class. It is an experience which lends itself to mental activity, but it does not necessarily provide an increase in knowledge or facilitate the ability to reason and see relationships. While it is necessary to acquire factual knowledge, it is more important that children understand the conceptual framework which relates these facts to each other and to the world in which they live. Since the amount of knowledge upon which we draw is doubling every few years, reliance on factual memory is insufficient for producing students who will understand the role and use of science in a technological world.

Both science and reading are processes which must be partially constructed by the learner, by combining the child's pre-knowledge with new information. Children must experience learning and be allowed to build meanings and relationships for themselves. Only then will they have learned to read, not decode, and to understand concepts, not to memorise.

For the child in the first or primary school, the use of children's literature in the classroom can serve as a link and catalyst between these needs. By breaking down the artificial barriers of subjects as individual units locked into specific time frames, strategies and processes which are basic to science and reading can be employed to facilitate learning in both areas.

Approach

The major thrust of this work is to exemplify a method by which children's literature books, which are strong in scientific facts and concepts, can be used to teach science as well as the language arts. It is necessary to help children realise that science is not a technical 'school subject' but it is all encompassing. Science should be a study of the familiar, and educators must facilitate the learning of science as it relates to the child's world. As science is learned, knowledge in the language arts and other areas of communication are also being developed and reinforced.

Using non-fictional books with young children is often ineffective, for the books are not written in the context of the child's world, and are a mere compilation of information. Many teachers are reticent to use non-fictional books because these works do not excite children, and do not appear to be effective teaching tools. Children's fictional literature, on the other hand, is very appealing and fascinating for primary children and may be a more efficient means of teaching. Students' interest is sustained and the story schema helps them to comprehend and draw relationships. For example, trees are a common sight for most children. A non-fictional book or chapter dealing with trees and their uses can become totally objective, abstract, and stripped of its relevance to the child's world. It might be more appropriate to use a fictional work such as Janice Urdy's *A Tree is Nice* or Shel Silverstein's *The Giving Tree* which explains the concepts in terms of the effect on the child's reality. Teaching elementary school science is not the same as teaching secondary-level students, yet often the approach is basically the same. Only the difficulty of the material or the amount covered may be of significant difference. To work successfully with young children, we must look at the learning process through the mind of the child and realise that the child's world is conceptually very different from that of the older learner or adult. Piaget tells us that before the age of eight, children are in a pre-operational stage. This has serious implications in establishing instructional curricula for elementary science. For example:

1.   Children have not developed the ability to think logically or abstractly; reasoning is unsystematic and does not lead to generalisations.
2.   Children can focus only on the beginning or end state of a transformation, not the transformation itself.
3.   Children are not able to recognise the invariance of a number of objects when their spatial relationship is transformed.
4.   Children are egocentric and view the world from their own perspective.

Therefore, scientific cause and effect have no relevance to these youngsters who still live in a world of *animism* (all objects act voluntarily) and *artificialism* (everything is fashioned by man or some being). Anything which cannot be explained in these terms is *magic*. If we try to be completely realistic at too early an age, the child is left confused by the adult's abstract reasoning. Therefore, we need to teach in terms of their existing conceptual view of the world.

The fictional books which are utilised in this method should be of high literary quality, appropriately illustrated to correspond to the text, and have an interest level relative to first school/primary-aged children. The plot of the book should be fresh and plausible, and should logically build to a climax through a series of cause and effect events. A specific setting should be indicated as well as a theme. Characters ought to develop during the story, but must be believable, especially if anthropomorphism is employed. Above all, the work must be accurate, realistic, relative to the world of the student, and should stimulate a learning experience.

Use of whole language

To integrate the teaching of reading and the teaching of science, it is best that one subscribes to some, or all, of the tenets of the 'whole language' approach to learning. By 'whole language' we mean that children should learn to read for information, ideas, insights and entertainment, all at the same time. Meaning is not to be found in isolated words, but in the entire context of the sentence, paragraph, or selection. We no longer segregate skills into separate little boxes, but reach across subject areas to create a total learning experience. Just as children have learned to speak from interacting with the language heard around them, so, too, do they learn to read by being placed in a literate, natural environment. Several characteristics of whole language learning are listed below.

Whole-language elements	Strategies for instruction
Use of children's literature	Read daily
Sustained silent reading	Encourage risk taking
Sustained writing	Skills in context
'Big Books'	Purpose of language
Free spelling for beginners	Relevancy
Study skills	Self correction
Editing of own writing	Construct meaning
Key word vocabulary	Whole to part
Personal dictionary	Predict and integrate
Predictive books	Interrelate skills
Words in context	Question content
Total meaning of print	Limit use of phonics

Use of science

The goals of the whole-language approach and scientific method are very similar and warrant close comparison. In both cases, the child looks at the entire passage and then builds generalisations. By using story books, children can question at an age when they are too young to design and carry out experiments with formal logic, and draw conclusions from them. For early childhood instruction in science, a more right-brain oriented, concrete, creative method can assist children to organise their experiences and observations into meaningful learnings. In the following insert, traditionally used methodology which emphasises recall of specific information is described as 'fact science' in contrast to a more conceptually based approach which corresponds to the whole language philosophy.

Whole science	Fact science
Conceptually oriented	Recall of specific vocabulary
Technology is science	Applications not emphasised
Problem solving	Preparation for later learning
Explanations invented as learned	Explanations are provided
Activities lead	Activities to follow
Motivation is paramount	Motivation not essential

The lesson begins by sharing the book with the class as a group, then using several, varied hands-on activities. These may be performed by individuals, small groups or the entire class, depending on the intended purpose. To carry out the task of teaching with the whole-language approach in mind, several generalised activities might be utilised. These include:

Read to children everyday
Have sustained silent reading for children
Read books by the same author, or other books on the same topic
Writing workshop or other formal writing instruction
Have children read and edit each other's writings
Write stories, including language experience stories
Keep journals
Draw maps, charts and diagrams which are labelled
Write letters to each other, authors, characters, etc.
Sequence events
Turn stories into radio dramas, plays, TV programmes
Publish newspapers
Formulate interview questions
Write from the viewpoint of another character in the book
Keep key word dictionaries
Write summaries
Learn to write out directions, e.g. animal and plant care
Write up scientific observations and results
Make time lines
Put written signs on items in room
Message boards – to teacher and to other students
Weather board
Collage of concepts and/or events (labelled)
Competitive board games (include questions on vocabulary, events, characters, sequences, higher level thinking)
Choral reading – by large groups or sections
Improvise or role play – conflict, other endings, scientific happenings, etc.

Example

The basis of science is to learn to solve problems. Children are facilitated in exploring, evaluating and discovering by specific skills apropos of the scientific method: measurement, observation, inference, classification and hypothesisation. In this process of learning to solve problems, children are not so much instructed in specific tasks but rather given opportunities to make first-hand observations and inferences and communicate about them in a variety of interesting ways. They need to be allowed to make mistakes and further predict possible outcomes to truly comprehend. They are not being trained merely to repeat information, but rather are learning to restate ideas from their own manipulating of objects as well as words, in terms that make sense in their world.

The major purpose of the whole-language approach and scientific learning experiences should be to guide children to question, doubt, investigate and invent. The known facts of the books should not be ignored, but one should not be satisfied with just learning facts and stopping instruction at that point. *The Bad Tempered Ladybird* by Eric Carle, is a good example of these ideas. The book tells the story of a day in the life of a ladybird. The ladybird wakes up hungry and tries to usurp another ladybird's breakfast of aphids. The bad tempered ladybird then proceeds to attack a different animal every hour of the day. The animals successfully ward off the ladybird's aggressiveness by employing one of their special adaptations. The lobster has pinching claws, the whale has its size, the gorilla is extremely strong, etc. Finally, at day's end, the hungry ladybird returns to its home leaf ready to share. Fig. 8.1 shows the content of *The Bad Tempered Ladybird* depicted as a concept map. Several important, scientifically relevant ideas are identified from the book.

Two activities will serve as examples of how the major concept of *adaptation* can be used as the focus of an exciting lesson. They are called 'The Matching Game' and 'Invent a Grouch'.

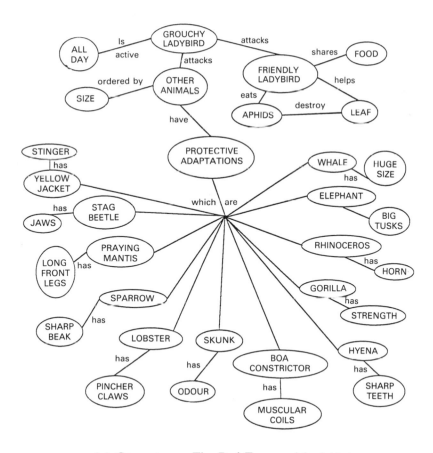

FIGURE 8.1 *Concept map:* The Bad Tempered Ladybird

The matching game

This activity is intended to help players learn some of the special characteristics of the animals in the book. Each player draws a random card which contains a statement describing one characteristic of one animal from the book. Players then read their card and hunt for three other players whose cards also describe their animal. When the game is completed, players who think they all have the same animal, group together and defend their choice. This presents a good opportunity to compare the animals with each other for patterns of appearance or behaviour. The statements provided below are intended as examples which describe some of the twelve animals in the book. The number of cards distributed to the players should be controlled so that each player has only one card, and each animal is described on three cards.

YELLOW JACKET

> Despite my average length of 1.5 centimetres, my protective defence can cause great discomfort, or even death, to humans.

> I do not have two or four legs and am very essential to the reproduction of many species of the plant kingdom.

BOA CONSTRICTOR

> Forty to sixty species of this animal, found mainly in warm regions, do not depend on legs or feet for locomotion.

> My young are born alive, not from eggs, and can grow to a length of 25 feet.

SKUNK

> I am a member of the weasel family and prefer to eat rodents, rats and birds, although I will eat plant material.

> My foul-smelling defensive device can reach up to 4 metres.

LOBSTER

> My flipper tail helps me navigate as I scavage for dead matter. I also feed on seaweed and live animals.

> My visibility is good because my eyes are located at the end of movable stalks.

Invent a grouch

As a second follow-up to *The Bad Tempered Ladybird*, you might ask groups of children to express their creativity by designing a yet undiscovered animal with very special adaptations for survival. Creativity is especially tested if the animals are created from an assortment of odd bits of cloth, wood, coloured paper and packing materials which are glued to a stiff sheet of paper.

> *List of Adaptations*
> 1. Invent a grouchy animal that rips its food apart before swallowing it.

2. Invent a grouchy animal that squeezes its enemies to death.
3. Invent a grouchy animal that can hide anywhere without being seen.
4. Invent a grouchy animal that can live in the cracks of walks.
5. Invent a grouchy animal that has skin 'harder than nails'.
6. Invent a grouchy animal that can poison its enemies quicker than they can blink their eyes.

Activities for The Bad Tempered

Science Activities

1. Study the pictures of a ladybird. Paint a ladybird on an easel-sized sheet of paper or use felt pieces to construct one on a flannel board. Label body parts and functions.
2. Set up a sundial on the playground and mark the shadow length to correspond to the clock faces in the book.
3. Sweep net an area to collect insects for study in the classroom.
4. What wild animals are native to your country? How do they protect themselves? Does the government protect them?
5. Catalogue and chart animals in the book:
   e.g. protection devices
   classification of animal (mammal, insect, etc.)
   natural habitat
   type of food eaten
   use to mankind

Language Activities

1. Before finishing the book, predict the ending. When you are through write some new endings.
2. List the different words the author uses for 'meet'. Look in a thesaurus for more words which mean encounter.
3. Practise the proper form of introducing people. Write them down to show use of 'quotation' marks.
4. Write poems about the bad tempered ladybird and the nice ladybird. Show contrasting adjectives.
5. Use figurative language to describe the ladybird, especially similes.
6. Research each animal and make a descriptive card about it, showing size, habitat, cating habits, etc.
7. Make your own personal time line showing where you are or what you are doing at each time shown on the clocks in the book.
8. Write a paragraph about why the ladybird changed her attitude.
9. Read other Eric Carle books for more science/language lessons.

Maths Activities

1. How many hours does the book cover? Is that a whole day?
2. Work with simple fractions: half an hour, quarter of an hour, etc.

Art Activities

1. Have each child make thum print ladybirds or 'pet rock' ladybirds.
2. Invent an animal with any combination of materials and indicate how it protects itself.
3. Make containers to hold insects while you study them in the classroom.

Outdoor/Movement Activities

1. Select an animal and mime how it protects itself.
2. Make an animal which adapts through camouflage. Hide it outside the school and see if others can find it.
3. To show comparative size, find other objects about the same size as each animal in the book. For larger animals, make outlines on the playground to show size. On a smaller scale, make a mobile of the various animals.

Rhythm and music

1. Listen to recordings of whale songs; try to reproduce them.
2. Research the different sounds made by animals in the book.
3. Can you find songs to sing about any of these animals?

Humanities

1. View films from the Nature Conservancy on topics such as the balance of nature.
2. On a world map, locate the natural habitats of these animals.

It is possible, and even preferable, to combine several activities instead of treating them as separate subject areas, since integration is a major focus of this work. As one example, the children may wish to make a video of The Bad Tempered Ladybird. This would involve making masks or costumes, finding out how the animal moves and sounds, making sets which resemble the native habitat, choral or individual reading, music selection, etc.

Summary

Taken to its ultimate end, the teaching of science and reading could touch every area of the school curriculum: reading, language arts, humanities, art, music, health, physical education. While it is not possible or even desirable to do this with every book used, it does indicate the many avenues that can be taken when teaching from a children's literature basis. A major connection has been emphasised between science and reading/language arts, which enables students to derive meaning from children's literature and follow-up activities.

Fictional literature offers a wide range of considerations and does not extol single concepts in isolation. It does not limit our learning to a list of scientific phenomenon, but is rich in application and nuances. This will help us lead our students so that they will become thinking, communicative citizens.

(An extensive bibliography of American Children's Literature, suitable for use in the above manner, is available from the Authors. See list of contributors for address.)

Chapter 9

Bring Back Grammar (or 'Metalinguistics' if you must)

Peter Brinton and Sue Palmer

These days the subject of grammar teaching can arouse some very fierce emotions. When the 1984 HMI document English 5–16, *for instance, suggested certain aspects of language and literacy which should be covered by children at various stages in their education, it was the recommendation that elements of grammatical knowledge be taught which drew all the flak, and which the Inspectorate later withdrew in the face of such a hostile reception. Many educators seem to regard the teaching of English grammar as a kind of heresy against child-centred education. On the other hand, there are those who would regard it (along with the multiplication tables and a selection of dates and capital cities) as the solution to all education's present woes.*

We do not espouse either of these views, particularly not the latter. We do, however, believe that there is a place for some teaching about the English language in our schools (particularly primary schools, which is the area of education with which we are concerned), and we hope today to put forward our case for this, and for the way it might be taught. But to begin with, we are going to look at the case AGAINST grammar, to review the reasons why so many people connect teaching of this subject with all that is worst in education.

The case for the abolition of grammar

Grammar first swung out of fashion in the Plowden years. There had been mumblings and murmurings against it before then, but nothing substantial enough to make a national impression. It was in the late '60s and early '70s that schools began to discard it, as massive changes in educational attitudes and methodologies got under way. Plowden popularisd the concepts of 'child-centred education' and active 'discovery' learning; and the emphasis moved from class teaching to the individual development of each child, and from 'getting the right answer' to creative, open-ended learning.

The old-fashioned grammar exercise did not fit this new bill at all. It was clearly intended for class teaching; it was boring and repetitive, inhibiting rather than encouraging of creativity; it was decontextualised and meaningless to the children, and therefore highly unmotivating; and it was designed to teach specific grammatical facts rather than to encourage active learning of the language. In all the best schools, therefore, it was consigned to the dustbin.

Research findings were available to confirm the inefficiency of the grammar exercise. Among others, Cawley (1958) had found that many children could not learn the parts of speech despite repeated teaching – so what was the point of teaching them? – and Harris (1962, had shown that, of two groups, one of which took grammar lessons over a school year while the other took extra writing practice, the latter showed the greater gain in writing ability. It seemed that analytic study of the language was unnecessary to the achievement of proficiency in its use.

The belief that children would best learn to use language by using language, not by completing endless exercises about it, moved into the national educational consciousness. The dictum of post-Plowden generations has been: talk, listen, write, read – in meaningful motivating contexts. In the early years, the criterion for many in pursuing these activities was 'creativity', and 'correctness' became irrelevant. Another nail in the coffin of grammar teaching.

There was, perhaps, a further reason that the idea of grammar became anathema to those committed to child-centred education – an irrational reason, but potent, and one which should be mentioned. 'Grammar', the very word itself, is redolent of the old system. It smacks of traditional methods of teaching ('Latin grammar', 'grammar books'), of the eleven-plus and elitism in education ('grammar schools'), of analytic methods and pedantry ('grammarian', 'grammatical error'). There are many associations with the word which are rooted in those pre-Plowden days. Grammar, like mortarboards and gowns, rote learning, and desks in 'serried ranks', was to many a symbol of the bad old days before teachers discovered that children were people. As far as many educators in the post-Plowden days were concerned, it had to be put up against the wall, and shot.

The status quo

Twenty years have now passed since the Plowden Report, and child-centred education has become the norm. Educators have also learned a great deal more about how children acquire the skills and motivation necessary for success in the language arts. In the area of writing, the drive for 'creativity' has been tempered with common sense, and functional writing has assumed an importance in the curriculum as great as that afforded to self-expressive, developmental writing. Teachers have begun to recognise the importance of audience, of contexts for writing, of opportunities for children's own drafting and editing of their work.

'Correctness' – that is, attention to the accepted conventions of written language – has once again become acceptable, as the need for explicitness, coherence and clarity in written English is acknowledged. It is recognised, however, that the learning of the conventions of written English should not be an end in itself, nor should obsessive concern for correctness be allowed to inhibit the act of writing. It is generally agreed, and we would not in any way wish to disagree, that the best way to learn to write in the English language is to write in the English language, for a variety of purposes and audiences, and in a meaningful motivating context. Nor would we disagree that the best means of improving each pupil's command of written English is by mutual evaluation of that pupil's work in discussion between teacher and individual pupil.

What we would disagree with, however, is that there is no place for 'grammar' in all this. We believe that some acquaintance with grammatical terms, some opportunities to reflect on the ways in which the English language works, some understanding of the system by which our written conventions work, are important constituents of literacy. We believe that 'grammar' is a baby which, because of its associations with archaic teaching methods and other elements of traditional education, was thrown out with the post-Plowden bath water.

The case for the restitution of grammar

The case *against* grammar was, briefly, threefold:

1. teaching it doesn't help improve children's writing;
2. the methods by which it was taught were fundamentally unsound;
3. it has associations with a bygone (and in most cases unmourned) era of education.

(1) Teaching grammar does not improve children's writing:

The first argument against grammar teaching was based on research in which grammar was taught to children and proved ineffective. However, the methods by which it was taught were those same unsound methods which crop up in reason two. Perhaps if it had been taught more effectively the findings would have been different – we shall look later at possible ways of improving grammar teaching.

Leaving aside the research, therefore, let us look at the question of the possible effects of grammar teaching on children's written work – indeed, on their language work as a whole. Much of what is known as 'grammar' is, in fact, technical vocabulary: it is the language by which we talk about language (which is known in linguistic circles as 'metalanguage', and its study as 'metalinguistics'). For instance, we categorise words by their functions and label them as 'nouns', 'verbs' and so on; we employ certain technical terms for elements of punctuation ('comma', 'full stop', etc.); and we identify the main parts of a sentence as 'subject', 'object', etc. In the primary stages, the learning of grammar is merely the learning of these technical terms and the linguistic concepts which underlie them.

It would seem that, if one is to talk about language (as when teacher and pupil are discussing a piece of that pupil's written work), it would be helpful to have access to some shared technical vocabulary. Otherwise discussion will be very limited, and teacher and pupil may find themselves discussing at cross-purposes. The need for specialised vocabulary is readily accepted in other areas of the curriculum. No teacher, for example, would be at pains in a maths lesson to avoid talking about 'multiplication' or 'rectangles' or 'ratios', and s/he would consider it essential to the pupils' learning that they understood these terms and used them correctly. It therefore seems inconsistent to deny the pupil access to specialised vocabulary when learning how to use their own language.

As long as it is still agreed, therefore, that the pupils' purposeful language work across the curriculum is of primary importance, and that grammatical knowledge is to be taught as an aid to this purposeful language work (and not as an end in itself), it seems likely that grammar teaching would enhance pupils' language work, by providing them with the vocabulary with which to discuss it. It could also make them more aware of the rules by which language is governed and the conventions by which it is written. The methods employed to teach grammar would be of importance, of course, and these will be discussed shortly. However, it does seem possible that new research, undertaken in the light of new developments in teaching, would find that some knowledge of grammar is an asset to pupils.

There is a growing body of research which indicates that knowledge about language, awareness of and interest in its rule-based nature, and, above all, awareness of the major differences between its spoken and written forms, is of great importance in improving children's performances not only in written English, nor indeed in other areas of literacy, but in education in general.

While schools have been abandoning specific language teaching over the last twenty years, there has been an explosion of interest and excitement in the study of linguistics in the higher echelons of education. New approaches to grammar have been discovered, which have revolutionised thought in the psychological sciences; new disciplines have been spawned – sociolinguistics, psycholinguistics – each adding hugely to the information base on which educational advance depends; new theories, rooted in the study of language, have rocked the world – Bernstein's theory of 'restricted and elaborated codes', for instance, and the theory that sexism and racism are incorporated in the language we speak.

But the most important development from our point of view is the suggestion by many of our foremost thinkers in education that language awareness is the first step along the path to objective thought. Olson's 1975 paper 'From Utterance to Text' suggests that a command of *written* language forms is essential to rational argument, that literacy – and awareness of what constitutes that literacy – is, therefore, the precursor of objective thought. Margaret Donaldson takes a similar line in *Children's Minds*. She suggests that it is by children's increasing capacity to *disembed* language from an everyday context (that is, basically, to conceptualise the differences between spoken and written language), and to become aware of it as a symbolic system which can be manipulated to give shape to their own thoughts, that they can eventually achieve intellectual autonomy. Michael Stubbs (1980) has suggested that the old 'restricted and elaborated codes' may, in fact, amount to spoken and written language forms – awareness and, through that awareness, command of the structures of the written form makes a person an 'elaborated code' speaker, and thus gives him or her the passport to educational success.

If these theories are accepted, then it is essential that schools should do their utmost to increase children's language awareness. Children must be taught to think about language, to gain control of it, to notice how the language of speech differs from the language of writing. In this case some 'metalanguage' is a necessity, and so is the opportunity to *look* at language as well as using it. The teaching of grammar may be more vitally important than any of us have hitherto realised.

(2) The methods by which grammar was taught were fundamentally unsound:

We accept absolutely that the traditional grammar exercise is an unacceptable way of teaching grammar. Apart from the ideological objections to it which arise from a child-centred view of education, there are sound pedagogical reasons that a subject should not be taught in this way. However, the fact that previous teaching methods were inadequate, inefficient or just plain bad is not an argument against the subject-matter itself. Teaching methods in mathematics in the bad old days were often similarly uninspired, yet no one suggests that we should abandon teaching addition, subtraction and so on. What was suggested in the post-Plowden years, was that maths teaching should take account of how children learn – of their need to learn through meaningful activity, dealing with concrete materials; of their need to conceptualise; of the variations in children's learning speeds, abilities and strategies.

For some reason, no one thought to apply these criteria to teaching about the elements of language. And yet, developmental linguistics shows that children teach themselves a great deal about language by something very like activity methods. Young children 'play' with language – they make up silly rhymes and rhythmic chants, they experiment with nonsense words and syllables, they make up silly sentences and (frequently incomprehensible) jokes. By the age of eight or nine they delight in puns and other semantic games (the most popular children's comics all abound in such linguistic playfulness). There seems no reason why this natural inclination to 'manipulate' language should not be developed through teaching. Learning about grammar does not have to be a dull, repetitive, receptive occupation. It can be an interesting, participative *activity*, in which children 'discover' rules about language for themselves.

When activities are devised for teaching elements of grammar to primary children, we believe the first criterion should be that pupils are involved in *active mental processing* of the subject matter. They should meet situations where they have to think about language, and consider it objectively, becoming increasingly aware of language as they learn the very elements which will *contribute to their further awareness.*

The second criterion should be that, wherever possible, they are encouraged to *manipulate* language – to 'pick it up and play around with it'.

The third criterion – perhaps, as pupils' interest and thus their learning depends on this, the most important – is that the activities should be *fun*, and should draw on that natural interest in the language which seems to be common to all children. Plowden couldn't quibble with that!

Naturally, such activities cannot take place when children are reading and writing for their own purposes – which, we stress again is the main means by which we believe they should develop their literacy skills – nor when they are discussing their individual written work with their teacher and improving upon its effectiveness. But if language awareness activities are given a separate place in the curriculum, the linguistic concepts and generally increased level of awareness acquired there would inform and perhaps enhance those 'real' literacy activities. They would also ensure that suitable vocabulary was available for useful teacher/pupil discussion of written work.

Moreover, if theories of the importance of linguistic awareness (outlined in the last section) are accepted, lessons specifically devoted to the study of language in this way would be the ideal means of promoting such awareness. They would require children to consider, to conceptualise, and to manipulate language in the very ways that the authorities we have quoted suggest.

(3) Grammar has associations with a bygone era of education:

The final reason we found for the abandonment of grammar was that the word itself had strong associations with what many people consider the bad old days of education. Perhaps if everyone could look rationally and objectively at the question, these associations would be of no importance, and this objection to the teaching of grammar could be brushed aside. Unfortunately, education is as riven with prejudice as any other area of life, so this seems unlikely. It would therefore perhaps be sensible to follow the lead of the government when a name or word is displeasing to the populace, and change it. We needn't call it 'grammar' any more; we could call it anything – 'Sam', 'Harry', 'Sellafield', 'language awareness' – 'metalinguistics' if you must.

We were reluctant to do this renaming trick, because it makes it sound as though we're talking about something new, and there's nothing new about nouns and verbs and sentences. Neither is there anything new about teaching children grammar by interesting, child-centred methods – many good teachers with a particular interest in language have been doing so (often covertly) throughout the last twenty years, and we acknowledge our debt to them. All that is new is the plea that these teaching methods be made available and recommended to other teachers, the ones who do not have a special interest in language, and who do not therefore feel competent to teach it at all. Many of them have come through the education system fairly recently, and have been taught little about language themselves. They know that 'old-fahioned grammar' is out but, so far, they have been given nothing with which to replace it, and they can feel the void.

They feel it when they are trying to explain spelling rules without being able to refer to particular parts of speech; or when they are helping a child to punctuate his work; or when they are attempting to explain, without any linguistic vocabulary, the need for consistency of tenses in a piece of writing, or agreement between subject and verb; or when they are trying to help a child find the main message of a piece of writing by identifying the main clause; or, in trumps, when they come to teach a second language.

Their pupils feel it too, because it is difficult to learn how to use something well if you are unable to talk about it coherently, if you are being kept in the dark about the mechanics by which it works. We have often heard the argument against language teaching that 'you can't make a gazelle run faster by telling it how its muscles work; thus you cannot make a child use language better by telling it about nouns and verbs and adjectives'. But children are not gazelles and language is not merely a physical activity. Language is the means by which we think, and the more we know about it, the more we understand it, the better we will be able to control our use of it.

Our message then is simple: it doesn't matter what you decide to call it, but – Bring Back Grammar – call it what you will!

References

CAWLEY. F. (1958) 'The Difficulty of English Grammar for Pupils of Secondary School Age', *British Journal of Educational Psychology*, 28.

DONALDSON. M. (1978) *Children's Minds* (London: Fontana).

HARRIS. R.J. (1962) 'An Experimental Enquiry into the functions and value of formal grammar in the teaching of English, with special reference to the teaching of correct written English to children aged 12 to 14', unpublished Ph D.

HMI (1984) *English from 5 to 16* (London: HMSO).

OLSON (1975) 'From Utterance to Text: The Bias of Language in Speech and Writing', *Harvard Educational Review*, 47, 3.

PALMER. S. and BRINTON. P. (198●) *Mind Your Language* (Edinburgh: Oliver and Boyd).

PLOWDEN. *et al.* (1967) *Children and Their Primary Schools* (London: HMSO).

STUBBS. M. (1980) *Language and Literacy – The Sociolinguistics of Reading and Writing* (London: Routledge and Kegan Paul).

Chapter 10

Throwing More Light on LITE (The 'What' of Linguistics in Teacher Education)

Joy A. Leitch

In our education system the teaching/learning activity depends almost exclusively on language – spoken, written and non-verbal. The HMI document English from 5 to 16, *lists a great many objectives which teachers may be expected to implement in the near future. What do teachers need to know about the language of their pupils in order to help them become proficient speakers, readers and writers of English? In attempting to answer the question this paper briefly describes the linguistic diversity in British schools today.*

It then focuses on West Indian English in Britain (WIEB), the language spoken by some pupils of Caribbean origin, some aspects of which may cause problems for the speakers in the areas of reading and comprehension. Implications for teachers and teacher education are considered and proposals for a language awareness course offered.

Linguistic diversity in schools today

I have become increasingly aware of and concerned about the difficult task ordinary classroom teachers face when they attempt to cope with the range of linguistic diversity in their classes.

In many of our schools classes may be comprised of pupils drawn from three identifiable linguistic groups. First, there are those for whom English is the mother tongue, but in many cases the variety used may not be that acceptable to the school. Second, there are those for whom English is a second language, the first language being Urdu or Bengali, Punjabi, Tagalog or Cantonese, or any one of a number of other languages (Rosen and Burgess, 1980). Finally, there are those pupils whose language is influenced by a Caribbean dialect, that is speakers of West Indian English in Britain (WIEB).

I carried out a small study among teachers who were neither language nor reading specialists in order to find out their perception of the linguistic diversity in their schools and the implications for them as teachers. All the teachers appeared to be confident that they would have no difficulty in dealing with the first group, since much has been written about regional and social class dialects of English (for example, Trudgill, 1975, 1978, 1982,

1983; Bernstein, 1973) and much of which they claimed to have read. The view was expressed that most English-speaking teachers would be fairly familiar with the features which mark these dialects as different from each other and from the standard dialect. Also the differences in grammar, phonology and lexical items tend, on the whole, not to be very great.

With regards to the second group, the tendency has been to depend on the 'experts' like the E2L teacher, the language support teacher, the bilingual teacher and in some cases, the remedial department. Subject specialists (other than English) and classroom teachers in the primary sector apparently do not see a role for themselves here.

Where the third group is concerned, however, many teachers express an interest and confess to some measure of confusion. The latter is not surprising since there is little agreement among educationists and linguists as to the nature, the incidence of usage of WIEB, or about implications for classroom teaching.

The language of pupils of Caribbean origin

In thinking about this issue I set myself the task of exploring the following questions:

   (i) Can the language of all pupils of Caribbean origin be defined as English?
  (ii) Is WIEB different from the language of 'other English-speaking pupils' in our schools?
 (iii) If it is, how does it differ, and are the differences significant?
  (iv) Does the written language of speakers of WIEB reflect their spoken language?
   (v) How, if at all, does WIEB affect pupils' reading, that is learning to read from standard English texts in the early stages and comprehension in later stages?
  (vi) What are the implications for teachers and teacher education?

Researchers and students of language have come to conflicting conclusions regarding WIEB. It has been suggested by some (for example ILEA 'Reading Through Understanding' project, 1974–78; J. Wight, 1976; Rosen and Burgess, 1980; Rampton/Swann Committee, 1985; Wallace, 1986) that most pupils of Caribbean origin speak British English. It is also suggested that the incidence of WIEB is insignificant and any differences unproblematical.

That the mother tongue of the majority of pupils of Caribbean origin is English is debatable. There is evidence that many speak a language which differs not only from British standard English, but also from its non-standard varieties on phonological, grammatical and lexical levels to such an extent that what emerges can hardly be said to be English, but rather a derivative of a Caribbean Atlantic English Creole (Carrington and Borely, 1977). There is also evidence to suggest that interference from WIEB may be experienced in both *reception* and *production* of standard English, even for some pupils who are second, third, and fourth generation. Not only in their spoken language, but also in their written communication, features which are recognisably Caribbean in origin can be identified.

Viv Edwards (1979, 1983, 1986) suggests that WIEB interference may become an important factor in later stages of reading, particularly in the area of comprehension tasks. This view is supported by Sutcliffe (1978, 1982), and by data gathered from my own M.Ed and DPSE students and Teacher Fellows over the past five years.

Phonological differences

In an excellent analysis of WIEB, Loreto Todd (Todd, 1984) found that British speakers of Caribbean origin tend to use *twelve vowel sounds* as follows:

(a) *five short monopthongs* – *i,e,a,o,u*, as in

k*i*l (BSE – kill)
d*e*m (BSE – them)
m*a*da (BSE – mother)
*o*p (BSE – up)
p*u*t (BSE – put)

(b) *three long monopthongs* – *ii, aa, and uu*, as in

tr*ii* (BSE – three)
j*aa* (BSE – jaw)
d*uu* (BSE – do)

(c) *four dipthongs* – *ie, ai, ou, and uo*, as in

b*ie*sin (BSE – basin)
bl*ai*n (BSE – blind)
r*ou*n (BSE – round)
*uo*l (BSE – old)

The vowel *uo* is the sound used in words like 'don't', 'go', 'know' and 'home'. So that for the following BSE sentence

The boys don't know if they must go home.

a speaker of WIEB may produce

De bwai dem *duon nuo* if dem mus *guo huom*.

Another phonological feature common among speakers of WIEB is frequent palatalisation after 'g' and 'k'. So that 'girl' is likely to be pronounced 'gyaal' and 'car', 'kyar'.

Non-actualisation of final 't' and 'd' is likely to result in 'san' for 'sand', 'pas' for 'past' and/or 'passed', and 'ole' for 'old'.

Todd also found that Caribbean speakers of English in Britain tend to utilise only *33* of the 44 sounds used in received pronunciation (R.P.).

Caribbean speakers tend to make fewer vocalic and consonantal distinctions than speakers of some other varieties of British English. This means that the word 'rat' could be produced to represent either 'rot' or 'rat', and 'tai' for either 'toy' or 'tie'.

Implications for reading and writing

The view seems to be held by some teachers and educationists that linguistics of the kind dealt with in this paper, has no relevance for reading and the teaching of reading. This seems to me quite ludicrous, since in my view reading implies language and a grasp of language.

Teachers need to have a knowledge of their pupils' language in order to make informed decisions about methods for teaching reading in the early stages. How appropriate or effective would phonics be for pupils who use a phonological system as that outlined above? How appropriate would ITA be? From the pupils' perspective, spelling difficulties may occur like these examples taken from the writing of a nine year old:

> My sister give me *tree* sweets.
> I did not come to school *lass* week I had a *mile coal*.

Both these examples reflect the WIEB phonology.

Finally, the new secondary examinations with their oracy requirements could put some pupils at a great disadvantage if they were unable to or had difficulty in producing standard English pronunciations. Teachers would need to be familiar with the pupils' sound system if they are not to penalise them unduly during assessments.

Grammatical differences

There are a number of differences between the grammar of WIEB and that of BSE. In a paper of this length it is possible to deal with only a few of these.

Nouns
WIEB does not usually mark plural nouns with an 's' as in BSE.
For example, an eight-year-old pupil writes

> The headlight are thing you put on at night to look out for thing like dog or cat.

> Plurality is often indicated by use of the determiner 'de' and 'dem'.

Verbs
There is usually no concord between subject and verb.
Hence:

> They was fighting with one another.

The main verb is usually unmarked for tense and voice:
For example,

>He take the money to the lady last week.

The verb 'to be' is largely redundant in WIEB.
Hence:

>This food nice.

Possession

WIEB shows possession not with the genitive marker 's' as in BSE, but by the relative positions of possessor and possessed. For example,

>My sister name Doris.

>(8 year old)

or in the case of speakers of Jamaican origin,

>di book a fi John.

Passives

WIEB expresses Passive meaning but does not employ BSE structures. For example,

>All the food eat.

>(WIEB)

for

>All the food has been eaten.

>(BSE)

The following examples are taken from the writing of a nine-year-old in an Inner city school. One can identify features which show evidence of creole interference.

>(*i*) '. . .we did see'
>(*ii*) '. . .they did get'
>(*iii*) 'bees did always'
>(*iv*) 'My dad does go to work in the night.'

This pupil, who was born in England of parents also born in England, persistently produced features of this sort in all her writing.

Post-creole continuum in Britain

The West Indian language situation in Britain today can best be described in terms of a continuum (Fig. 10.1, p. 84), with speakers operating along various spans.

Where a pupil operates on the continuum would tend to be influenced by one or more of the following factors:

WIEB	WIEB	BLENDS	BSE
(Jamaican dialect influence)	(Other Caribbean dialect influence)	with dialects of BE	

FIGURE 10.1 *Post-creole continuum in Britain*

(*i*)   Where in the Caribbean their family comes from.
(*ii*) The social background of the family.
(*iii*) The proportion of people with whom they associate who speak WIEB.
(*iv*) The extent to which they identify with Caribbean or British culture.

Research evidence (Edwards, 1986; Sutcliffe, 1982; Sebba and Le Pagel, 1983; Leitch, 1984) suggests that language use is influenced by:

(*i*)   Parents' language
(*ii*) Peer group language.
(*iii*) Language of the school and media
(*iv*) London Jamaican.
(*v*)   Rastafarian terminology.

Some pupils of Caribbean origin in our schools may be experiencing difficulties in any or all three of the following areas:

(*i*)   *difficulties of hearing*: in the sense that their framework of reference for the sounds which strike their ears is one of perception according to WIEB patterns, and not according to BSE patterns. This, of course, would have implications for both reading and writing in BSE, as suggested above.

(*ii*) *difficulties of understanding*; even if they hear the words correctly, some of the lexical items and grammatical constructions may have vastly different meanings for them. There are implications here for comprehension tasks.

(*iii*) *difficulties of expressing themselves*; inhibition may arise because the teacher does not understand the language in which the pupil is fluent nor is sympathetic to the pupil's particular needs. The pupil whose language is influenced by WIEB may find it inhibiting to use the teacher's language, both orally and in writing.

My concern is with teachers who are non-language specialists. How can they be helped to cope with the complex linguistic situation they face? One of the first steps would be to identify those areas in which pupils persistently make errors in their written work. To facilitate this a Diagnostic Schedule

Plurals omitted	Subject/ verb agreement	Present tense used for past	Verb to be omitted	Active voice used for passive	Different sentence structure	Words used differently	WIEB spellings	Other differences	

FIGURE 10.2 *Diagnostic schedule*

modelled on a schedule devised by Viv Edwards is offered in Fig. 10.2. Originally designed for use with pupils of Caribbean origin, this schedule could be used for logging *any* use of language which is unconventional or non-English, that is areas in which the pupil/student may need to be helped to acquire standard English forms.

The contribution of teacher education

Below I offer a proposal for a language awareness course which I hope would stimulate some discussion not only among teacher educators, but also among colleagues in both the language and reading fields.

Target Student Population:

(a) B.Ed; PGCE; (initial Professional Training)
(b) Various forms of INSET
   (i) School based
   (ii) College based short course
   (iii) College diploma.
   (iv) Award bearing courses, for example DPSE and M.Ed.

Aims

1. To make students aware of the diversity of forms of communication and language.
2. To make students aware of different aspects of language, language teaching and language learning.
3. To make students aware of the fundamental need for, and shared purpose of, communication.
4. To make students aware of those features common to all languages and forms of communication.

5. To give students an insight into the processes of language learning and development.
6. To enable students to appreciate the importance of the communication process and communication skills in all teaching/learning situations across the curriculum.

Possible content to include

1. Non-verbal communication.
2. Placing languages in their world-wide context.
3. Elements common to all languages, for example grammar. Concepts to include register, dialect, accent etc.
4. Language variation and change.
5. Language diversity – general issues, debates, implications for teaching.
6. Spoken and written language.
7. Bilingualism
8. WIEB   } Special studies
9. E2L issues for non specialists.
10. The language skills (*listening, speaking, reading, writing*)
11. Language acquisition and learning.

Teachers on completion of a course such as this would, in my view, be well equipped not only to cope with the range of linguistic diversity in their classes, but also to guide their pupils into an awareness of their own language, and those of their peers.

Linguistics-informed teachers and pupils could only lead to better and more efficient users of language and more competent readers.

References

BERNSTEIN, B. (1973) *Class, Codes and Control* (London: Routledge and Kegan Paul).

CARRINGTON, L. and BORELY, M. (Eds) (1977) *The Language Arts Syllabus, 1975: Comment and Countercomment* (University of the West Indies, St. Augustine, Trinidad).

DES (1983) *West Indian Children in Our Schools* – (London: HMSO).

DES (1985) *Education for All – The Swann Report* (London: HMSO).

EDWARDS, V. K. (1979) *The West Indian Language Issue in British Schools – Challenges and Responses* (London: Routledge and Kegan Paul).

EDWARDS, V. (1983) *Language in Multicultural Classrooms* (London: Batsford).

EDWARDS, V. (1986) *Language in A Black Community* (Clevedon, Avon: Multilingual Matters Ltd.).

LEITCH, J. (1984) M.A. Dissertation, University of London Institute of Education (unpublished).

ROSEN, H. and BURGESS, T. (1980) *Languages and Dialects of London School Children* (London: Ward Lock).

SEBBA, M. and LE PAGE, R. (1983) *Transplanted parents, indigenous children: the linguistic symptoms of fresh cultural groupings,* Paper presented at the Society for Caribbean Linguistics Annual Meeting.

SUTCLIFFE, D. (1978) *The Language of First and Second Generation West Indian Children in Bedfordshire,* M.Ed thesis, University of Leicester.

SUTCLIFFE, D. (1982) *British Black English* (Oxford: Blackwell).

TODD, L. (1984)*Modern Englishes (Pidgins and Creoles)* (Oxford: Blackwell).

TRUDGILL, P. (1975) *Accent, Dialect and the School* (London: Edward Arnold).

TRUDGILL, P. (1978) *Sociolinguistic Patterns in British English* (London: Edward Arnold).

TRUDGILL, P. (1982) *On Dialect – Social and Geographical Perspectives* (Oxford: Basil Blackwell).

TRUDGILL, P. (Ed) (1983) *Language in the British Isles* (Cambridge: Cambridge University Press).

WALLACE, C. (1986) *Learning to Read in a Multicultural Society* (Oxford: Pergamon).

WIGHT, J. (1976) 'How Much Interference?', *Times Educational Supplement* 14 May.

Chapter 11

The Loneliness of the Long Distance Writer

William Jackson

The Foundations of Writing *project was designed to develop strategies and materials to support the development of writing skills. The important factors appear to be the teacher's assumptions about writing, the maximising of support for the solitary writer from other writers and the provision of rich writing contexts. Improvement was not confined to writing but was reported in most curricular areas and in the child's 'ownership' of learning. This seemed to depend on the relationship between the written language and cognitive functioning.*

Introduction

The Foundations of Writing project originated in the Scottish Committee on the Language Arts (SCOLA) publication *Hand in your Writing* (COPE, 1982). The Committee in its discussion of the teaching of writing in Scottish primary schools expressed certain doubts about the quality of writing in the large sample of children's work that it had examined. The Committee accepted that most primary children learned to write in the narrowest definition of the word, but this writing seemed inadequate to express their experiences or imaginings. There was a 'cloned' quality, a dull uniformity, about the writing. There was little sense of involvement and little evidence of 'the eye of childhood'. The writing represented the minimal response to the demands of school as identified by the children. SCOLA believed that the origins of this inadequate work lay in the way in which writing was taught throughout the school and that it did not simply emerge in the later stages. SCOLA recommended to the Committee on Primary Education (COPE) the setting up of a project to examine the teaching of writing in the first three years of primary education. This was not a research project; its remit was to develop strategies and materials to support the development of writing skills in P1 to P3. The project is described in *Foundations of Writing* (Jackson and Michael, 1986).

Who teaches what?

Children learn to write from others who can write – including other children in the home and at school, the authors of books read and eventually from themselves as self-conscious writers. However, the main responsibility for the development of literacy falls on the schools. For many children writing is what the school says it is. Project teachers had to contemplate the possibility that inadequate writers had been conscientiously taught to be inadequate writers. Preliminary discussions with project teachers demonstrated that many saw writing as speech written down and defined their role as the teaching of handwriting skills. The teachers saw other competences in writing as 'a gift', as 'something that just happened' or as something determined by home influences. Alternatively teachers might argue that their task was to teach the mechanics of writing; teachers in later stages would show children how to put these to use.

Teachers were asked to consider the possibility that although speech and writing had much in common the written language differed from speech in important respects and that writing had uses and possibilities which differed from those of speech. They were asked to consider the contexts within which speech and writing took place. Speech takes place in a physical and human context where many of the communication choices speakers have to make are made for them. Topic and purpose may be defined and audience need, interests and level of understanding may be indicated through immediate feedback. The digressions and repetitions of speech, necessary to clarify meaning for both speaker and listeners, would be unacceptable in writing. Talk relies on this collaborative interchange and there is a kind of minimal verbalisation in talk where writing has to be more explicit. Above all talk takes place in a sharing context which may be pleasurable and stimulating and where satisfaction or resolution may be immediate.

Now think of the solitary writer sitting at a desk and confronting a blank sheet of paper – 'the loneliness of the long distance writer'. Writing is much more context independent than talk. Fewer communication choices are made for writers; there is not the same sense of contact with the audience and there may be little immediate helpful or encouraging feedback. Writers have to draw more on their own resources; hence the project's ultimate goal of producing the 'autonomous writer'. The lack of immediate audience feedback to signal relevance or comprehensibility demands that writing has a greater degree of explicitness and coherence than speech. However, the context independence of writing permits a degree of reflectiveness which encourages a more deliberate choice of structures and words and which allows for a planning and for a revision and expansion which the impermanence of the spoken word does not readily afford. Writing allows writers to hold their meanings before them, to contemplate these and to develop more complex and more precisely defined meanings.

As teachers began to contemplate the various skills and awarenesses that children had to bring to writing it became apparent that those aspects of writing which had dominated their teaching – the secretarial skills of letter formation, spelling and punctuation etc. – represented the tip of an iceberg and that beneath this was a complex of compositional skills that they had taken for granted. Children were being left to tackle the demands of written communication with the awarenesses of speech. In speech speakers could assume that their listeners had possession of 'given information' about the events being discussed and this meant that significant data could be omitted – after all listeners could always ask if they didn't understand. The writing samples in *Hand in your Writing* had indicated a reliance on a simple narrative which did not always communicate the writer's perception of components of the recalled experience that readers might be interested in or would need to know if the nature of the recalled or imagined events or their significance were to be understood. In addition, the carrying over into writing of those accretive structures common to much talk, and acceptable within it, or the digressiveness of much talk, could produce a slackness in writing which might generate, at the best, tedium, and at the worst, incomprehensibility.

Children seemed to make little use of the reflective possibilities of writing. There was a minimum of pre-planning and children seemed reluctant to redraft or modify texts beyond simple editing.

The establishing of criteria

Although children inhabit a world of ambient print and are surrounded by the end-products of written communication they may not have seen many people actually producing writing. Within many homes the experience of writing will be limited. The questioning of groups of children about what was expected of them when they wrote indicated that teachers had not succeeded in sharing either their expectations or criteria with children (Graves, 1983; Nicholls, 1985). However, children cannot be left in a non-learning situation and it was obvious that they had striven to make sense of writing tasks. They built up criteria derived from comments made by teachers and as a result children saw 'good writing' as being characterised by such things as neatness and correctness. Beyond these there might be vague criteria like using 'good words' or 'putting down what you think' or 'saying everything that happened'. Inevitably there were some children who saw good writing as being 'long enough'!

If children had to become competent writers then teachers had to become more explicit in their expression of their expectations when children wrote; children had to be helped to define their purposes when writing and helped in the construction of their own criteria. The teacher's response had to be more than the sniffing out of error or the awarding of vaguely encouraging ticks and stars. Responses from teachers should be consistent and should refer to items that children understand. Within the project young children could understand that the meaning of their writing could be affected if they left out significant details or if the sequence of events was confused. These consistent responses help children develop that explicitness and coherence that are characteristic of written language.

What do children bring to writing?

Many of the project teachers related to children as if they had little to contribute to their learning to write, but children are strongly motivated to master language and the ability to read and write represent 'grown up' skills and are an ability equally prized by most parents.

Children bring to school certain mechanisms for the acquisition of language and these are as relevant for writing as they are for speech.

Children learn to write actively by writing within contexts which provide a variety of purposes for writing and which provide meaningful feedback.

Children acquire writing skills systematically by using and responding to a variety of written forms which provide data for their internalising of rules for the generation of written language forms.

Children acquire competence in writing skills creatively by moving through a series of approximations to the emulative (adult) model (Harris and Wilkinson, 1986).

Children also bring to school certain awarenesses about the written language. Surrounded as they are by print and probably with some experience of being read to it is unlikely that they do not strive to make some sense of all this. Children entering the project demonstrated that they realised that print may carry meanings which relate to experiences outside the print although these meanings are not yet consistent or universal. For many children print was already seen as a source of pleasure and information.

Children have experience of narrative – from stories told or read to them, from comic books and from television. They bring some awareness of story, they tell of events in time, they say something about human character and motivation, they have a number of formal items – 'once upon a time' – which identify them as stories. This awareness will provide a structure for children's organisation of experience (Applebee, 1978).

The incorporation of 'writing' in many children's games – letters, lists, menus, etc. – indicate that some children understand what writing can do, as do their requests to teachers to scribe the stories they tell.

All children are not completely illiterate when they come to school.

Children and the 'ownership' of learning

Most of the project teachers subscribed to a child-centred approach. Their classrooms gave evidence of active, creative and experientially based learning yet their teaching of basic literacy skills denied this approach, being teacher dominated and, in the case of writing, being whole-class teaching involving copying, tracing and the filling-in of blanks. In their teaching of letter formation teachers normally presented children with an adult system of written symbols, the alphabet, which children mastered through copying and repetition. Letter formation was normally taught as a decontextualised activity and was not related to the expression of meaning. Teachers did not use 'natural' or 'scribble' writing where children communicate their meanings through their own 'writing' system with a gradual movement towards a universal and consistent system through feedback and the children's wider experience of reading (Chomsky, 1971, 1973; Clay, 1975; Ferreiro and Teberosky, 1979; Graves, 1983). (The project's rejection of such approaches in favour of a teacher-initiated, albeit highly effective, letter formation kit, is one of its most serious inconsistencies.)

The early writing of children in classes visited had little to do with meaning. Children were set to write stories which drew on themes and vocabulary from their reading books or which presented few spelling problems. Children wrote in order to learn how to write. The activity satisfied the arcane demands of school but not children's need to express and share things meaningful to them. (For a fuller examination of this see Jackson and Michael, 1986.) Teachers' responses to these 'stories' were generally encouraging with the only specific comments being about neatness or correctness. Even 'non-writing', stories which were meaningless in themselves, was accepted provided it was neatly written. The stories were usually one-off and there was little sign of their being continued or redrafted no matter how desirable this might have been. Children were not learning that their writing could be modified in the light of their own second thoughts or feedback from readers.

The themes on which children were set to write were curiously mundane. They might draw on domestic activities that children would know about, but to know about is not necessarily to value. Children soon 'graduated' to the ubiquitous 'newstime' or 'diary'. There was a wide ignoring of the difficulties involved in some of the writing tasks set – the problems of selection posed by 'newstime' or the difficulties for children in expanding on the short declarative sentences in the present tense which were common. Content was frequently subordinated to the needs of letter formation or spelling. Almost from the first days in writing one could see an anticipation of the dull uniformity of later writing. For both teacher and pupil inadequacy was becoming normalcy.

The skills and awareness that children brought with them to school were too often abandoned at the classroom door and children might find themselves involved in activities which could have little or no meaning for them. The activities might be purposeful and the processes logical from an adult point of view, but children must often have inhabited a Kafkaesque world.

Children had little ownership of their learning in the basic skills of literacy. What they learned, how they learned, even those experiences on which they might draw, were tightly controlled by the teacher.

This was a measure of the importance which the school placed on literacy.

What did children have to learn?

From discussions with project teachers and from participation in the work of their classrooms certain significant areas began to emerge.

Writing is one form of communication. Children had to be helped to find satisfaction in the expressing and sharing of their experiences and imaginings. Teachers had to demonstrate that they took these communications seriously and valued them. Children had to be helped to take pride in their own expertise.

Project teachers now appreciated that children would learn to form letters, but that many would never become competent writers. The teachers now saw the composing skills as the most significant.

Children had to be helped to appreciate that in their own experiences and imaginings there was much that others would wish to share.

Children had to realise that their readers might not have experienced those things the children were writing about and that there was a responsibility on them to give sufficient information.

Children would have to consider what their readers might be interested in. They might not be interested in the recording of commonplace events unless these were recorded in an interesting way.

In writing factual pieces children would have to consider what their readers might need to be told. Children had to consider the purpose of their writing.

Since narrative provided the base for most writing children had to be helped to construct well-ordered sequences of events. They had to appreciate that disordered sequences might not be understood by their readers.

Children had to appreciate that anything they made – drawing, model, story – could be modified in the light of their second thoughts or audience feedback.

Children had to be helped to develop a form of language, the written language, which might differ in certain respects from spoken language.

Children had to learn certain motor skills, particularly fine control and the making of a continuous line, which would help them become fast and legible writers.

Children had to appreciate that their readers might have certain expectations as to how they would write and that there were certain writing conventions that had to be observed.

How were these things taught?

Writing is sometimes described as a unique activity, but effectiveness in writing depends to a certain extent on awarenesses and sensitivities which may find expression in other activities. When project children entered school they were involved in a number of activities which they enjoyed and which employed skills they already had, for example telling stories, drawing, modelmaking, plasticine work, sand and water play, etc. Most of the activities had some of the characteristics of writing, having a degree of permanence and being capable of modification. Many of these activities were already in the classroom, but observation suggested that they were not taken seriously and were often regarded as time-fillers. These activities were individualised and modified to demand greater involvement on the part of the children. Many of the skills listed above could be developed through these activities, finding things to communicate to others and modifying constructions in the light of feedback, telling or dictating stories derived from these activities, developing motor skills through drawing with fine instruments, supporting narratives with lines which can record movement through space and time, storyboards, magnetised backgrounds and figures. The teachers' responses encouraged the incorporation of significant data and the telling or dictating of stories with an explicitness and a coherence appropriate to the written language. A wide variety of activities were used and are described in the project report (Jackson and Michael, 1986).

Writing took place in contexts which ranged from backgrounds depicting familiar or stimulating backgrounds to theme contexts which involved children over a lengthy period of time with a variety of different writing tasks.

The basic writing unit was the group and not the individual child. This provided some of that support that children found in conversational groups. Children shared their work, discussed and criticised, helped others in difficulties. From this collaborative interchange came an increased awareness of what one does when one writes. The continuing feedback from readers helped in the construction of criteria. Out of collaboration would come autonomy.

Project teachers redefined their roles in the development of writing skills. They no longer stimulated children to write – the contexts did that – nor did they simply conduct *post mortems* on work in which the child no longer was much interested. Teachers saw themselves as master craftsmen passing on the tricks of the trade to apprentice writers. Project teachers were agreed that they most helped children by helping them shape, in a way appropriate to writing, what it was the children wished to share. This meant working with the children during the actual process of composing. By acting both as reader and commentator the teacher was able to participate in that interpretative summarising through which writers could judge the effectiveness of their communication. The project had sought to give children ownership of their learning and the teachers volunteered that their new awareness of what had to be learned in writing, what children brought to this and their own awareness of how they might best help children meant that they now taught with an authority which they admitted had not been there before.

The assessment of children's writing

Teachers appreciated that they had to concern themselves with the meanings that children's writing conveyed. Meaning is found not in things but in the relations between things and, in writing, these relations exist within the text – what is being written now relates to what has been, or will be, written. Teachers were less concerned now with the gist of a message or with it correctness; they were more concerned with what was going on inside it and their interest in this helped make children more self-conscious as writers.

There were three markers which teachers found helpful.

The first was children's articulation of the relationship between events – time, place and causality. Much of the teacher's discussion had been directed towards this and many of the activities were specifically designed to encourage such articulation. Many of the project children demonstrated that they were capable of quite sophisticated relationships and there was less dependence on simple connectives.

Another useful marker was the degree of 'disembeddedness' in the writing, how far children had moved away from a simple time-related and self-centred organisation of experience (Donaldson, 1978). Over the three years children showed an ability to comment on their own experiences, inhabit the experiences of others and deal speculatively with future possibility.

A final marker was the overall organisation that the child imposed on experiences, the way in which he ordered his world so as to make sense of it. The basic and continuing organisation was chronological as in narrative. Children had to report on experiences, observations and reflections which were not time-related. This created a need for logical organisations. From their reading or viewing some children developed 'literary' organisations, like flashback or contrast. All of these organisations were found by the P3 stage – but not in all children. One of the tasks of the teacher was to help children build up a repertoire of relationships and organisations through which they might find meaning in their experiences.

These markers not only helped teachers say where particular children were at a particular time, they helped teachers anticipate and prepare for future developments.

Conclusions

All project teachers were agreed that there had been an improvement in the children's writing ability – in some cases this was substantial.

Improvement seemed to depend on the following:
- the teacher's ability to conceptualise the teaching of reading;
- the provision of a rich environment with a variety of writing purposes;
- the maximising of encouragement and help from other writers;
- the development of autonomy and self-consciousness in writers.

Improvement was not confined to writing. Teachers reported improvement in all curricular areas and in the way children tackled problems and 'managed' their learning. Teachers volunteered that they had underestimated the potential of children.

The main reason for this appears to be the relationship between written language and cognitive functioning. Children were developing a language more able to deal with relationships, generalisations, theorising and problem solving.

References

APPLEBEE, A. N. (1978) *The Child's Concept of Story* (Illinois: University of Chicago Press).

CHOMSKY, C. (1971) 'Write first, read later', *Childhood Education*, 47, No. 6. March 1971.

CHOMSKY, C. (1973) *Beginning writing through invented spelling; selected papers from 1973 Kindergarten Papers* (Cambridge, Mass.: Lesley College).

CLAY, M. M. (1975) *What did I write?* (Auckland: Heinemann Books).

COMMITTEE ON PRIMARY EDUCATION (1982) *Hand in your writing* (Edinburgh: Scottish Curriculum Development Service).

DONALDSON, M. (1978) *Children's Minds* (Glasgow: Collins).

FERREIRO, E., and TEBEROSKY, A. (1979) *Literacy before school* (New York: Heinemann).

GRAVES, D. (1983) *Writing* (London: Heinemann).

HARRIS, J. and WILKINSON, J. (1986) *Reading Children's Writing* (London: Allen and Unwin).

JACKSON, W. J. and MICHAEL, B. (1986) *Foundations of Writing* (Edinburgh: Scottish Curriculum Development Service).

NICHOLLS, J. (Ed.) (1985) *Learning to write and teaching writing* (Norwich: University of East Anglia).

Chapter 12

Observations on 5–6 Year Olds' Use of Invented Spelling

Anne Robinson

This paper, which is intended for those to whom the term 'invented' spelling is new, considers the evidence for children's developing abilities to generate their own rule-bound spellings. It demonstrates how initially the non-standard spellings are based on children's auditory perceptions of speech. Samples of children's work are used to show the kinds of developmental changes that can occur as an awareness of written language, influenced by reading, takes effect. The work of Read (1986) and Henderson (1980) in the USA has created interest in children's early attempts at spelling. If teachers can be encouraged to look at children's own attempts in a positive way (similar to miscue analysis in reading), then it may provide them with a useful diagnostic strategy.

On re-entering the classroom

After two weeks of term a second-year infant child voiced an opinion of me. 'You are cruel,' he said. The reason I appeared so heartless was, 'Because you don't tell us the words'. Another indignant child explained the role of the teacher: 'You are supposed to write it down so I can copy it'.

Returning to the classroom to renew my experience after twelve years of reading and lecturing about the development of literacy, I did not agree with the children. My apparent cruelty arose from the fact that I was challenging the children's constructs about reading and writing, as well as the role of the teacher. For them, a full year in school had established the world of literacy in their minds. They *knew* what was required. Yet here was a teacher who did not want children to draw first and then write about the picture; who did not sit down with them and transcribe their spoken words; who did not approve of the 'rubber'; who insisted that they 'had a go' themselves; and who expected them to take responsibility for their own written work. Moreover, the children were not the only ones who felt threatened. The behaviour of this new, temporary, teacher challenged many of the beliefs of other members of staff and probably of the parents as well.

The copy writing produced on the first day of term had indicated that almost every one of the thirty children had good pencil control and was aware of letter shapes and word spacing. Informal phonic activities had shown that all of them were aware of basic alphabet sounds. However, the children's own writing was to reveal quite a different picture.

The attempts that children make when writing unaided are seldom seen by many teachers or parents. The sequence of events which runs from letter patterns, over writing, under writing, and copying from work cards or the board, produces conventional writing. It may not always be correct, but the errors arise from the problems of copying. To be faced with writing in the 'raw', with marks and spellings which to the unpractised eye seem bizarre, can be very disturbing for adults. Furthermore, the acceptance of this kind of writing with all its distinct qualities seems almost heretical. Surely errors must be corrected at once or bad habits will ensue?

Attitudes to children's early writing are traditionally quite different to those we hold for learning to walk, talk, or draw, where acceptance of the child's attempt is usually the rule. As Sowers (1982) reminds us, we don't worry when we see a child's early drawings of people. They may not be 'correct', but we accept them; we do not force repetition or expect them slavishly to copy our own efforts. Why should our response to children's writing be so different, particularly as Goodman's (1982) work on miscue analysis in reading is so widely accepted as a means of gaining insight into children's understanding of the reading process? Knowing that children's spelling errors display logic and consistency and follow a pattern of sequential development may help teachers to approach children's writing from a similarly positive perspective.

Read's (1971) early work with American pre-school children has provided the basis for many studies of children's creative spelling. He showed that children's errors did not happen by chance. He was the first to note that short vowel errors followed a consistent pattern which could be explained with reference to the pronunciation of Old English. While still cautious about the idea of a precise developmental sequence, he is prepared to suggest a general outline of spelling development (Read, 1986). Henderson and Beers (1980), reporting on extensions of Read's work, are confident in identifying characteristics in children's spelling which they relate to discernible conceptual stages. These stages seem to hold with great stability across varying methods of teaching and even different languages. It was these stages that I began to search for when I re-entered the classroom. Table 12.1 provides a brief description of them.

On observing children's own writing

The 'pre-literate' stage

Because I was working with only one age group (5y.0m. to 5y.11m. in September 1986), I did not expect to find representatives of every level of understanding, but since the children's copy writing had implied a class of similar levels of competence, I was eager to see if this was confirmed in their own writing. All my children had already made what I consider to be a major cognitive shift: they understood that special shapes are required for writing. Patricia's (5y.7m) (Fig. 12.1) work appeared to be representative of the most immature level of understanding within this class. She was simply producing strings of letters, but she had no hesitation in telling me what her writing 'said'. On the surface, Justin (5y.0m) (Fig. 12.2) seemed to be very similar. When he tried to read his story about 'Jaws', however, he began by trying to sound out the letters.

Over a period of some weeks Justin seemed very puzzled that he could not read his writing back to me. He would look at his work and say, 'I meant to write. . .', or 'It should say. . .'. Both these children had letter sound knowledge; neither of them, however, reflected it in their writing. It seemed significant that both of them understood that *reading* could make use of sound/symbol relationships but that neither of them transferred this knowledge to writing. For them, writing had only to do with producing the visual shapes they could recall.

Robert (5y.1m.) (Fig. 12.3) had progressed further. He demonstrated a clear example of the use of initial letters to symbolise words. For him, the dots 'show you where the words are'. Using initials in this way is fairly commonplace and it seems worthwhile considering the relationship between this device and the teaching of letter sounds through the use of alphabet books. How often do we say, for example, ' "a" is *for* apple'; ' "b" is *for* ball'? Is it surprising that children might assume that the letter can *stand for* the word? Certainly adults employ this idea when using initials and acronyms. Robert, in my opinion, had made another major shift in understanding. He was aware that writing involved sound/symbol relationships and, while he may have been able or inclined to represent only the first sound, his writing differed markedly from that of Patricia and Justin. He used letters in a relevant sequence to represent the flow of speech.

As children's skill in representing sounds in words increases they use more letters, often strings of consonants with missing vowels (Table 12.1). Although no child in my class used this strategy as a general rule, it is worth examining an example of such writing taken from the reception class later in the year (Fig. 12.4).

In speculating why children use this kind of representation it is important to remember that consonants do provide critical information in words and it is possible to read words without vowels relatively easily. In some circumstances, for instance, written Hebrew dispenses not only with vowels but also with vowel markers and yet remains readable. It is also well known that in teaching the pronunciation of consonants it is almost impossible to avoid the addition of some vowel sound. In consequence, it is at least possible that children may assume the representation of the vowel sounds when using just consonants. These anyway tend to be over-emphasised when analysing words for spelling. This development may be regarded as a refining of the ability to represent the sound sequences in words rather than a major shift in word knowledge.

TABLE 12.1 *Conceptual stages in spelling development*

Names of stages		Characteristics	Changes in understanding
Compiled from Henderson & Beers (1980)	Henderson (1985)		
Pre-literate Pre-phonetic		Child makes marks which he calls writing and which he differentiates from pictures, scribble developing into use of letter-like shapes	Writing is not drawing
		Uses letters for writing	Major shift? Any old shape will not do
	Pre-literate Stage 1	Child associates letters with sounds, uses initial letters	Major shift? Letters represent sounds
Pre-literate Phonetic		Child uses sequences of consonants to represent words, often develops as first, then first and last, then adds some middle sounds	Refining ability to capture sound in print?

Letter name Stage 2	Introduction of vowels, short vowel errors may use nearest letter name strategy, long vowel sounds may use letter name substitute. Overall characteristic is attempt to match letters to phonetic elements in consistent direction	Refining ability to capture sound in print?
Vowel Transition Stage 3	Short vowels corrected, long vowels represented using vowel markers, indicating awareness that sound matching is no longer the only consideration	Major shift? Sound is not all there is to spelling
Syllable juncture Stage 4	Doubling consonants – which may be over-generalised	Refining?
Derivational constancies Stage 5	Awareness of how 'root' word may influence spelling	Refining?

Letter name

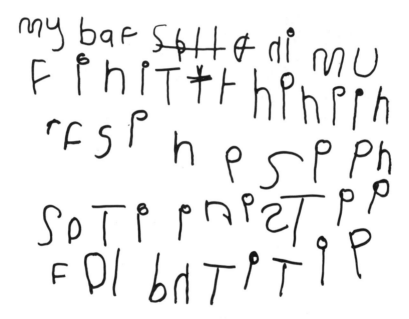

FIGURE 12.1

Patricia 5y.7m.
'The fire was burning, the firemen came.'

FIGURE 12.2

Justin 5y.0m.
A story about Jaws.

The 'letter name' stage

The developments discussed so far all fall within a single stage, that is the pre-literate stage, according to Henderson (1985). Stage two is the 'letter name stage' and some characteristics of this level of understanding were

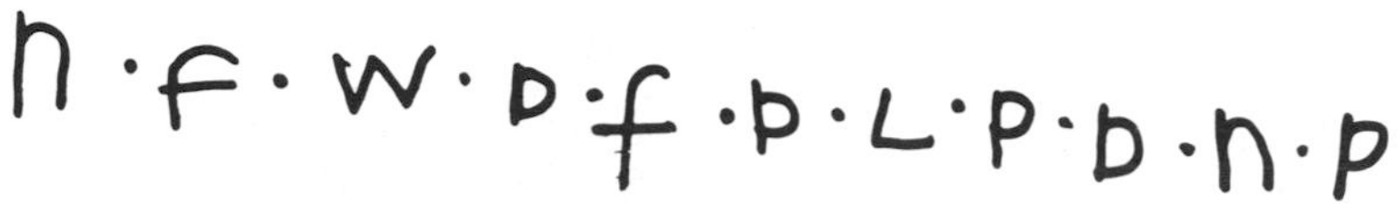

П ·Ϝ· W ·ᴅϝ ·ᴅ ·ᴌ·ᴘ·ᴅ ·П·ᴘ

FIGURE 12.3

Robert 5y.1m.
'N fireengine with a fire and lots of people and 'n dog.'

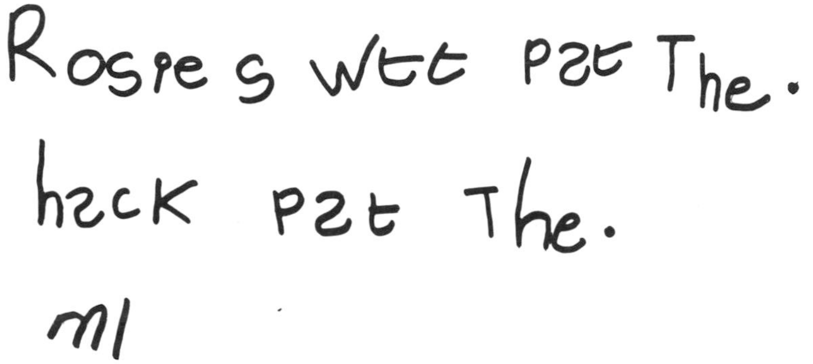

Rosᴘe ꞛ wᴇᴇ ᴘᴈᴛ Tₕₑ.

hᴢcK ᴘᴈᴛ Tₕₑ.

ₘl

FIGURE 12.4

Sarah 5y.3m.
'Rosie went past the haystack past the mill.'

shown by approximately half the class. Although Read (1986) suggests that, 'In the United States, Canada and Great Britain, letter names receive much attention' (p. 76), in my experience there is no tradition of using letter names with young infant children in England. Certainly, the previous teacher of my class had tried to minimise confusion by avoiding their use, and the children looked puzzled by my own occasional reference to them. Remembering this was to become increasingly important in my analysis of the children's work. The underlying characteristic of this stage is the remarkable ability to analyse and represent the sounds of words as they are spoken. In doing so, the children present spellings which appear bizarre yet may be closer to the real sounds in speech than our conventional spelling. This skill demonstrates itself in a variety of ways. For example, words ending in 'ed' may be recorded as 'noct' for 'knocked', 'patid' for 'painted', 'muvd' for 'moved', and so on. Similarly, the spelling of 'king' as 'kig' or 'jump' as 'jup', rather than merely indicating careless errors, may show the logic of economy. Thus, in normal speech, nasal consonants are hardly formed at all; the mouth is already getting ready to make the final 'p' as it is moving from the initial 'ju' sound in 'jump'. These omissions by the children may actually reflect a keen awareness of the real sound of the word.

Other symptoms of the letter name stage are those which give the stage its name. They are those discussed first by Read (1971) and noted by many others when writing about invented spelling (Henderson and Beers, 1980; Bissex, 1980; Walshe, 1981; Graves, 1983; Henderson, 1985). They all refer to the fact that children make spelling errors with short vowel sounds and often use the letter name to represent long vowels at this stage. I was searching for short vowel errors which followed a consistent pattern, where children would regularly choose the vowel whose *name* was closest in sound to the one they were trying to represent. Typical errors would use b*a*t for b*e*t, p*e*n for p*i*n, c*i*t for c*o*t, b*o*t for b*u*t, reflecting the sound pairs originally used in Old English before the 'great vowel shift' clearly described by Henderson (1986). I was soon to realise, however, that my children, while clearly trying to represent the sound pattern in words, were making very few short vowel errors and, except for very rare examples, these did not follow the nearest letter name strategy. In addition, their long vowel errors almost never used the expected letter name.

Of course, it was possible that this group of children had developed beyond the letter name stage and made a further cognitive shift to understand that spelling was more than matching sounds. Samples of their work and discussions with the children, however, belied this. Their major consideration was still the sound of the word. Typical examples are the work of Adrian, Tom and Victoria (Figs. 12.5, 12.6, 12.7).

Some examples of long vowel sound errors collected from various children's work are worth further consideration. Table 12.2 exemplifies the very frequent use of the letter 'y' which at first confused my analysis of long vowel sound errors. At this point, however, I remembered the lack of letter name knowledge. A child who knows the name of letter 'a' can use this information to spell 'play' as 'pla', or 'they' as 'tha'. The child without this information, though, does not have this option. He can only

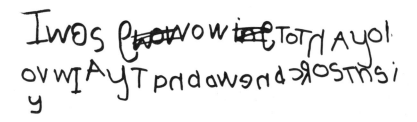

FIGURE 12.5

Adrian   6y.0m.
   'I was going to the Isle of Wight and I went across the sea.'

use letter sound knowledge. Knowing 'e' as in 'egg' and 'y' as in 'yet', the choice of 'ey' in 'geym' (game) is most reasonable. Similarly, the use of 'ay' in 'taym' (time) indicates good phonic awareness. What at first seemed to be the introduction of vowel markers, common at the next higher stage of development, seems to be nothing more than the refining of the ability to represent the sounds as heard.

The inconsistency of short vowel errors seems equally likely to be based on the lack of letter name knowledge. My children did not have the 'next best option' available to others, American children for example. It is not easy to explain why children, who were not yet at the vowel transition stage, made so few short vowel errors. One might speculate that the local accent of the area – on the Lancashire/Yorkshire border – produces such clearly distinguished flat vowels that confusion is rare. Certainly children in the new reception class who were encouraged to write freely towards the end of the school year, also demonstrated a similar lack of errors and the use of 'y' to spell the sound of some long vowels.

Whatever the reason, the letter name stage seems to be a misnomer in the case of these children. They displayed the basic characteristic of the stage, namely keen phonic awareness and the ability to represent accurately the sounds of words; they had not yet developed an awareness that spelling might require more than this. It still needs to be asked, however, whether children at this 'stage' display a significant advance in their concept of spelling over children using strings of consonants.

If we compare Robert's initial letter writing (Fig. 12.3) with Paul's (5y.5m.) story about Christmas (Fig. 12.8), we can see an obvious difference between them. But does this reflect different knowledge about words? Consider what is involved in writing a word. We have the word in our mind; we must say it to ourselves or even out loud; we hold the sound pattern in our mind while we search for the symbols which could be used to represent the sounds. We may also recall a visual image of the word, and knowing what the word means may also help us. Motor movement, too, can play a part in capturing the whole on paper. Children in the early stages of development, however, rarely have well-established or extensive visual models to check against. As Graves (1983) says, 'The ear for sound dominates invention' (p. 184). The child's handwriting proficiency will be of little use either as the habitual formation of common letter sequences will not be well established, particularly when spelling words not written before. The beginner, therefore, is dependent to an excessive degree on auditory analysis. While every child who learns to speak demonstrates ability in this area, the fact remains that children do not learn to talk by building up words from their consituent parts. Even when a child knows that spelling involves representing sounds, lots of practice is required in perfecting this new skill. I would argue that Robert and Paul represent different levels of skill development, but the same basic level of understanding. I find it difficult to accept that the 'letter name stage' constitutes a distinct conceptual level.

Wons opanpon ter wos tree litnl piez ter mut pie
Seb two musb litlv homm onb bilb o woo howm

but teeyc cer ter bie bob wu f bue nobow t nr homr
bown tee2 Seb ter fsb (say) litul pie ten tee ten set of
on ter teu tee mee a man wit sum soter set of
ten fsb litulpig pig pus elv mu sum soter teg

Ses ter man heer ts eur serer ses ten man
bee ot ter frsb hows by seer ten wulf
wot to bow ten hi hob I wil see litpje woz t iteig
mit kum in onb hi bid litupi iet

s litpies pow on teu on tee certot ter wulf
connet ces us .

'Within word pattern' stage

The third stage reported in the literature (Table 12.1) is based on understanding that spelling involves more than matching symbols to sound patterns; that words do not always sound the way they look. At the beginning of the school year I could not be certain that I had children who had reached this level of word knowledge, as a large group of children, about one-third of the class, produced writing like Sally (Fig. 12.9). These children seemed so conscious that the words they chose must look 'right' that they used only 'safe' words and were severely inhibited by their ideas of correctness. I had to wait some weeks before these writers gained enough confidence in themselves and in me to produce errors! As inhibitions decreased, errors increased. It was obvious that they remembered many more words from their widening reading experience than children at lower

---

FIGURE 12.6 (opposite)

Tom 6y.1m.

'Once upon a time there was three little pigs the mother pig said you must leave home and build your own home but take care the big bad wolf does not blow your home down yes said the first little pig then they set of on the way they met a man with some straw the first little pig asks please give me some staw yes says the man here is your staw says the man back at the first house of straw the wolf was thinking what to do when he had an (idea) I will say little pig little pig let me come in and he did 2 little pigs go on their (way) and take care that the wolf can not see us.'

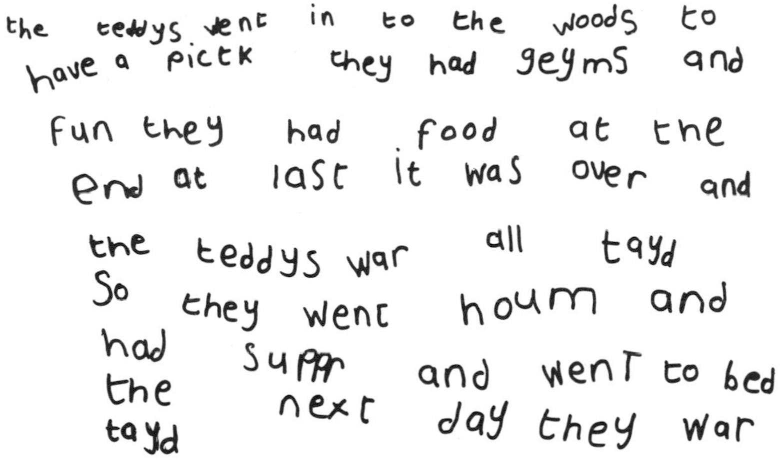

the teddys went in to the woods to
have a pictk they had geyms and
fun they had food at the
end at last it was over and
the teddys war all tayd
So they went houm and
had suppr and wenT to bed
the next day they war
tayd

FIGURE 12.7

Victoria 5y.3m.

TABLE 12.2   *Examples of long vowel errors*

Long vowel 'a'	*Long vowel 'e'*
'teyc' for 'take	'my' for 'me'
'wey' for 'way'	'griyn' for 'green'
'pley' for 'play'	'liyv' for 'leave'
'pleyn' for 'plane'	
'tey' for 'they'	
Long vowel 'i'	*Long vowel 'o'*
'taym' for 'time'	'howm' for 'home
'nayt' for 'night'	'gow' for 'go'
'spays' for 'surprise'	'cowt' for 'coat'
'taykres' for 'tigers'	

levels. These 'sight' words contributed to the large proportion of correct spellings in their work. Their errors made use of the knowledge that extra letters or vowel markers are sometimes used and also that certain letters can be used to represent more than one sound or no sound at all. In the second example of Sally's work (Fig. 12.10) which was four pages long and produced three months after the 'safe' Bob and Ben story, these developments can be observed. Errors such as 'aronde' for 'around', 'carels' for 'cereals', 'knoking' for 'knocking', 'deceid' for 'decided', show her changing perception of what spelling involves.

The final example of children's writing is an extract from David's 'Monkey story' written towards the end of the year (Fig. 12.11). By this time he was well on the way to being a conventional speller. He had the capacity to remember long, complex words which were important to him, 'tyrannosaurus', 'dinosaurs', 'bright', 'enormous', for example. Yet under the stress of composing he still made some errors which demonstrate only phonic analysis. David would correct many of these errors himself on re-reading for a second draft and engage in discussion about some of the complexities of English spelling. But, perhaps most important, he no longer thought that I should write things for him to copy!

None of the children displayed word knowledge at the fourth or fifth stages indicated in Table 12.1. This was hardly surprising, as Henderson (1985) suggests that the doubling principle would be commonly acquired at an age equivalent to that of upper junior or lower secondary children, while derivational constancies require an ability for abstract reasoning more suited to secondary-aged pupils.

On reflection

It is apparent from the examples of work discussed that the children's copy writing had concealed more than it revealed. Many levels of understanding

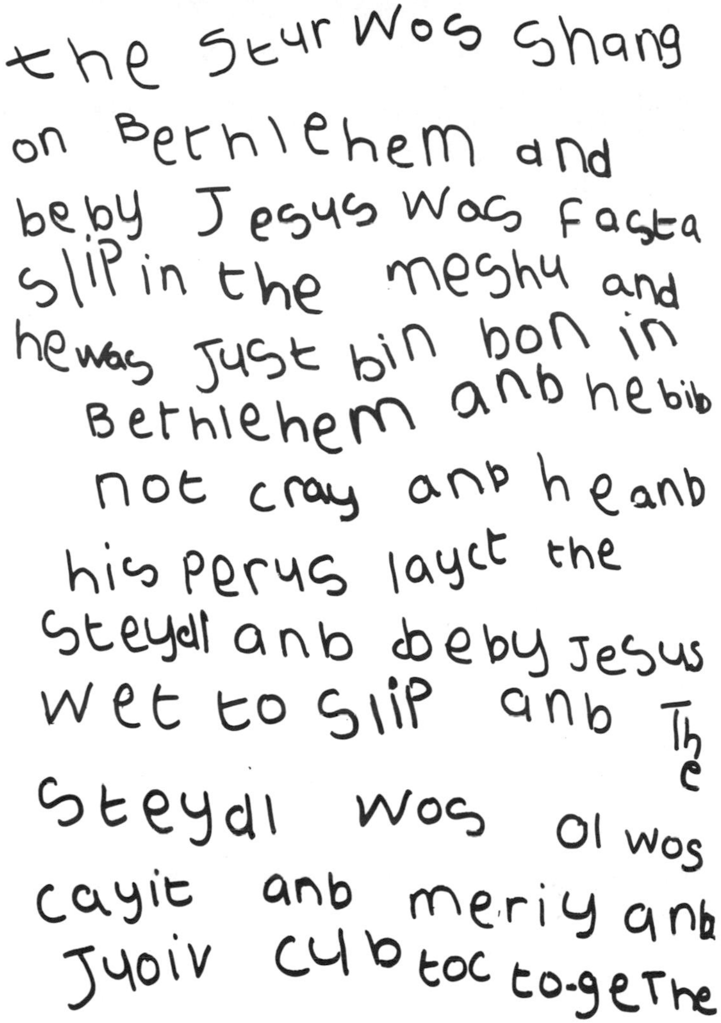

the stur wos shang
on Bethlehem and
beby Jesus was fast a
slip in the meshu and
he was Just bin bon in
Bethlehem anb he bib
not cray anb h e anb
his perus layct the
steydl anb beby Jesus
wet to slip anb The
steydl wos ol wos
cayit anb meriy anb
Juoiv cub toc to-geThe

FIGURE 12.8

Paul   5y.5m.

the stur wos shang on Bethelehem and beby Jesus was fast a slip in
the meshu and he was Just bin bon in Bethleham anb he bib not cray
anb he anb his perus layct the steydl anb beby Jesus wet to slip anb
The steydl wos ol wos cayit and meriy anb Juoiv cub toc to-geThe

'the star was shining
on Bethlehem and
baby Jesus was fast a
sleep in the manger and
he was just been born in
Bethlehem and he did
not cry and he and

his parents liked the
stable and baby Jesus
went to sleep and The
stable was all was
quiet and mary and
Joseph could talk together.'

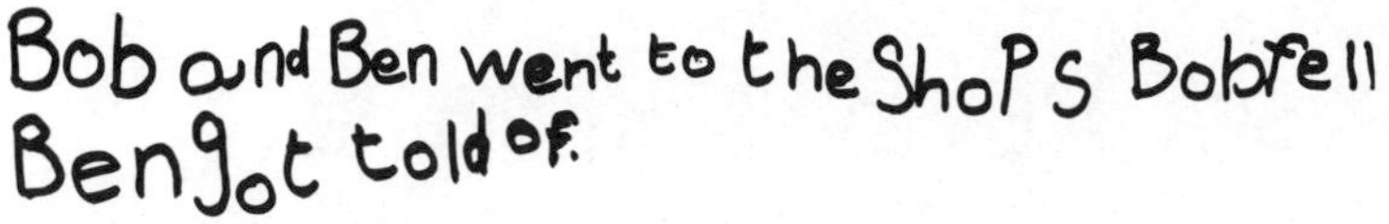

Bob and Ben went to the Shops Bob fell Ben got told of.

FIGURE 12.9

Sally   5y.6m.
> 'Bob and Ben went to the shops Bob fell Ben got told off.'

Sally   5y.9m. (Extract from 4-page story)
> One day Mr. Silly (who was a wolf) went to the shops. he fritend evryone out of the supermarket then he looked aronde and he saw some brecfast carels he ate the carel and the packet. then he saw some cat food he eat the cat food and the tin but it hurt his tonge then he got a trolly and he went aronde knoking all sorts of thing into the trolly. there were biscits and crips and anything you can imagen in a supemarket then he deceid to go home he went home and he saw a invtashen to the faire he cwikly he put on his best clothes and he left.his rele name is Wilfred.

FIGURE 12.10

and skill were displayed when children were allowed to write freely. This wide variety might have been confusing had it not been for the framework provided by knowledge of invented spelling and the security of knowing that other children also used this 'strange language'. Henderson's (1985) work in particular provided valuable guidelines for observing both the level of word knowledge and the progress of the children.

Perhaps one difficulty should be noted here. When children are at the earliest stages of writing development and produce small quantities of text, it is usually easy to see at a glance their level of understanding. As confidence grows in their own ability as writers, the quantity of writing and the intrusion of remembered words can sometimes make analysis difficult for the busy classroom teacher. It is often through discussion that the child's thinking becomes clearer. Justin's worried looks and comments, reported earlier, revealed as much as his strings of letters. A reported conversation between Tom and his mother, while reading at home, was enlightening.

T.   Is that watch?
M.   Yes, that's how you spell watch.
T.   That's not how *I* spell watch!
M.   But, Tom, that's how watch is spelled.
T.   Well it's not how *I* spell it!

David 6y.5m.

A monkey story
by David

Once upon a time there was a monkey. and he had to bright shining eays. One day the monkey who had to bright shining eays went to the zoo and he went to visit the campsignathius and the tyranosaurus rex.

You miat think why I have put dinosaurs names aill tell you why it was a museum so he was only Looking at skeletons but Just then when he was Looking at the compsignatheus he cort his Left eay on one its teeth and it came of. the 1 eayed monkey ran home screming and shoting Led buy a Policeman

When he got home his mum asked wot he had done with his letf eay its a Long Stoury Siad the 1 eayed munkey. the next day he went to the woods to get some bananas for him slef and some mice for old mr weezle and some worms for old mrs blakbird and they both siad the same thing wot had he done with his Left eay

now the 1 eayed monkey did not like this but Just at that moment sumboddey pickit him up and throw him in an old dark dusty storychest so he thought of a plan his plan was to get the keys that were in the storychest and open the storychest so the next day he Did his plan he got the keys from the storychest and at Last he was free he clambered out and waddled down an old passage way at the End of the passage way there was a enormous arch way and unDer the arch way there were a gigantic garden Just Like mr. mcgregars garden in the Tale of Peter rabbit first the 1 eayed monky ate some cabbergers and some Frech Beans then the 1 eayed monkey went out of the gate and was out in the wind world once agian

The End

FIGURE 12.11

As Read (1986) points out, creative spellers at the 'letter name stage' see nothing wrong with contrasting standard spelling with their own. Tom was simply not ready to be influenced by convention. How different from Christopher, whose writing appeared to be at the same stage as Tom's. He asked, 'How do you spell "said"? I always want to write s-e-d.' 'Would that not be all right?' I asked. 'No,' he said, 'it should have something else.' In fact, he was unable to decide what else it should have, but he was showing clearly the beginnings of the move to the next level of understanding.

The guided observation and discussion also enabled me to make informed decisions about the kind of intervention needed for children at each level of understanding. Those at the earliest stages could be encouraged to apply their knowledge of letter sounds, and to try and capture at least some of the sounds in words. But, most of all, they were helped to understand that writing is a means of communicating a message and is intended to be *read* by a reader. Other children, at a more advanced level, were asked to reflect on their ever widening reading experience and to try and recall what words looked like in addition to how they sounded. The most advanced writers were engaged in discussions about the complexities and sometimes apparently illogical aspects of English spelling, although the immaturity of the children obviously limited the depth of these discussions.

My experience of applying the notion of distinct conceptual levels to these children's work caused me to reconsider both the names of the stages and where the boundaries between stages might be drawn. The term 'pre-literate' had caused unease from the beginning. It is possibly acceptable for a child who produces 'scribble', but could it be applied to children who were reading simple texts and demonstrating their awareness of letter shapes and sound/symbol relationships, as well as their understanding of a variety of purposes for literacy? The use of this label seems to deny the growing evidence that children's understanding of literacy begins and continues to develop during their earliest pre-school years (Hall, 1987). In addition, as the knowledge of letter names is not universal, the use of this knowledge should perhaps not be regarded as a criterion for naming a distinct conceptual stage.

While recognising the extensive research behind the stages described by Henderson (1985), I preferred to consider shifts in understanding which were taking place at three points:
first, where children begin to use only letters as opposed to other symbols for writing;
second, where they demonstrate awareness that sound/symbol relationships are important; and
third, where they show that more than sound is involved in spelling.
These major shifts are indicated in Table 12.1.

My experience with this class did not allow observation of the final two stages. It seems at least possible, however, that these could be considered as a refining of awareness developed at the third level; that is that more than sound is involved in spelling. In appearing to criticise Henderson's stage boundaries, I am reflecting only on short experience of their application and on their usefulness to me with a particular group of children. Notwithstanding these comments, the research on children's use of invented spelling provided invaluable guidelines and makes it possible to adopt a reasonably informed and emphatically positive attitude towards the early stages of development in children's writing.

References

BISSEX, G. (1980) *Gyns at Wrk: A Child Learns to Write and Read* (Cambridge, Ma.: Harvard University Press).

GOODMAN, K. S. (1982) In Gollasch, F. (Ed.), *Language and Literacy: the Collected Works of Kenneth S. Goodman, Vol. 1 and 2* (Boston: Routledge and Kegan Paul).

GRAVES, D. (1983) *Writing: Teachers and Children at Work* (New Hampshire: Heinemann).

HALL, N. (1987) *The Emergence of Literacy* (London: Hodder and Stoughton).

HENDERSON, E. H. (1985) *Teaching Spelling* (Boston: Houghton Mifflin).

HENDERSON, E. H. and BEERS, J. W. (Eds.) (1980) *Developmental and Cognitive Aspects of Learning to Spell: A Reflection of Word Knowledge* (Newark, DE.: International Reading Association).

READ, C. (1971) 'Pre-school children's knowledge of English phonology', *Harvard Educational Review*, 41, 1–34.

READ, C. (1986) *Children's Creative Spelling* (London: Routledge and Kegan Paul).

SOWERS, S. (1982) Six questions teachers ask about invented spelling. In Newkirk, T. and Atwell, N. (Eds.), *Understanding Writing: Ways of Observing Learning and Teaching* (Chelmsford MA.: Northwest Regional Exchange Inc.).

WALSHE, R. D. (1981) *Every Child Can Write* (Rozelle: NSW Primary Teaching Association).

Chapter 13

The Development of Coherence in Children's Writing

Bridie Raban

The investigation reported here seeks reasons for the frequent use of 'and' in young children's writing. Comparisons between their speech and writing are reported and further data from opportunities to write at length and from books written for children learning to read are also considered. Children at an early age were found to differentiate between speech and writing and evidence is found which questions the value of the traditional language experience approach to the early stages of writing.

Introduction

As teachers of young children who have just started school, we notice time and again their continual use of 'and' in their writing. For instance,

> I went down the field and I saw an old house and Tracy lived in it
>
> (Judy 5y. 9m.)

> Here is my house and Richard is by the house and the sun is shinning.
>
> (David 5y. 8m.)

> Here is my Daddy's car and it is red and it has stopped by traffic lights
>
> (Andrew 5y. 10 m.)

These are common examples of the writing of five-year-old children and one of the reasons put forward for this behaviour is that these young children write as they speak. It is assumed they have yet to develop a sensitivity towards any distinctions between spoken and written language. They have yet to realise the need for a writer to be more explicit about the connections between different items of information.

Connectives in spoken language

There is an assumption that as children get older 'and' would be used less to express the various meanings for which more specific connectives exist, rather 'and' should be increasingly reserved for simple coordination. However, in their study of the spoken narratives produced by four and nine year olds, Peterson and McCabe (1987) found that 'and' was used the same by both groups of children. 'And' as simple coordination constituted no more than 20 per cent of the relationships, while 33 per cent were simple temporal ordering. The older children were using 'and' no differently from younger children, they were simply using it more. Peterson and McCabe concluded that the role of 'and' in speech seems to be an all-purpose connective, with speakers leaving meaning relations implicit. From their observations, 'and' was most frequently used by speakers to hold their turn in a conversation.

However, Scott and Rush (1986), in their study of adverbial connectives, did find developmental effects with frequency totals rather than relative frequency. They analysed the data of Fawcett and Perkins (1980) of children aged six, eight, ten, and twelve years whose speech was recorded in naturalistic settings. Scott and Rush found that discourse cohesion using adverbial conjuncts was a slowly developing feature of children's speech, being very rare in six year olds and progressing towards, but not approaching, adult levels by twelve years of age. Reporting further data (Scott, 1984) they showed that conjunct use was dependent on the context of the speech, with children using more conjuncts in peer interactions than in interview settings. Also they reported greater use of conjuncts where there was a demand for explicitness. However, in their study of children retelling a story which included 'however', 'though', 'but', 'so', 'for instance', and 'instead', the children's retellings at ages seven, nine and thirteen years of age used 'and', 'but' and 'so' most frequently, with these words accounting for 93 per cent of all the connectives they used. This behaviour is possibly reflecting their earlier finding that children use less variety of connectives in their interactions with adults.

Spoken and written language relationships

However, is facility in oral language a prerequisite for competence in written language? Brown and Yule (1983) have pointed out that logical connectives are more critical in written language and give examples of 'firstly', 'in conclusion' and 'more importantly than' as rarely found in spoken language, but highly significant to the coherence of written text which is generally longer than units of speech and robbed of intonational and situational cues.

Many theorists have stressed the similarity between spoken and written language (Harris, 1977; Lunzer and Gardner, 1979), while others have pointed out their differences (Rubin, 1978; Stubbs, 1980). With respect to young children, however, Perera (1986) has suggested that differentiation between children's speech and writing can best be described as working in two ways. On the one hand, as they grow older, they use grammatical constructions in their writing that are more advanced than those they use in their speech (O'Donnell *et al.*, 1967) and, on the other hand, they use in their speech an increasing proportion of specifically oral constructions.

In her analysis of speech samples collected in naturalistic settings from 48 children aged eight, ten and twelve years of age (Fawcett and Perkins, 1980), Perera (1986) identified eight different specifically oral constructions in these data. Most frequently used was 'well' in initial position, used as a kind of stage setter, through to 'sort of/kind of' and tag statements used least frequently which speakers appear to use for emphasis of one kind or another.

Most striking of all the findings from Perera's analysis was that there was a dramatic increase in the use of these oral constructions from eight to twelve years, an increase of 86 per cent. In total, she found 283 instances of these constructions in the speech of 45 of the children. However, in the writing of these 48 children, Perera reported only two examples of these oral constructions, and both of these were found in the same sentence. This finding is matched by her analysis of 90 pieces of writing from nine-year-old children which she has also analysed from the Bristol Language Development project (Kroll *et al.*, 1980) in which she found only three examples of these oral constructions.

One of the reasons why some constructions occur only in speech and others occur only in writing is because the activity of writing can be given more time than speech, and the writer can take more time to plan than a speaker who may lose their turn if they take too long over what they have to say. Writers can stop and think, in the knowledge that what they have written so far will not be forgotten. Re-reading is a valuable strategy in this respect and while young children need to acquire this ability, some of them do so at an early age.

For instance, Wendy at six years of age, reported in an earlier study (Wells and Raban, 1979), was observed to take her writing 'on the run'. Whenever she stopped to talk to her friends – something which occurred after almost every word – she forgot where she was in composing her story and each time this happened she went back to the beginning of her writing and read aloud until she reached the point where she had broken off, and in this way she managed to sustain the flow and coherence of her writing.

> In the aeroplane the lady said that the aeroplane was going to crash and the lady said don't worry because it wont matter because it will hurt a lot
>
> (Wendy 6y. 3m.)

> The little girl stopped She said all right But you must promise two things First of all you mustnt catch anyone its not allowed
>
> (Wendy 6y. 9m.)

However, some children do appear to write additively, never re-reading their trace and thereby producing written pieces which are largely disjointed.

> I made a obstacle
> I played with my sisters tennis ball
> I made a hole in my trousers
>
> (David 6y. 7m.)

Perera (1984) notes that one of the devices used by children to sustain a text is that of repetition, which is rarely used in their speech. For instance,

On Sunday I went out in the garden
Daddy cut the grass
I helped Daddy dig the weeds
Daddy went into the house
to have a cup of tea
Then we went back into the garden

(David 6y. 7m.)

Perera (1986) further compared the writing and speech of the same children from the Fawcett and Perkins study (1980) at eight, ten and twelve years. She found that the children frequently linked their spoken utterances with 'and' and 'then' with a small number of other time adverbials: 'when', 'first', 'first of all', 'at/in the end'. However, their written accounts included many more. In particular, the ten and twelve year olds used a wide range of these structuring devices to achieve coherence in their texts.

In order to amplify this finding with respect to younger children, the speech data from the six year olds (Fawcett and Perkins, 1980) reported by Scott and Rush (1986) is compared here with the adverbial conjuncts and time adverbials identified in the writing of twenty children at six years of age previously studied by Raban (1984). 179 pieces of writing were collected in school from these children between their sixth and seventh birthdays, pieces frequently written in response to a request by their teacher to write their 'news' or 'a story'.

The results shown in Table 13.1 reveal the marked difference in the use of these constructions in the speech and writing of children as young as six years of age. This difference is evident even when these children can be assumed to have only recently begun writing without needing to dictate to their teacher. However, prior to this age, these same twenty children (Raban, 1984) at five years of age showed a greater range of connectives of these kinds in their speech than in their writing (see Table 13.2).

One reason why these children do not appear to use connectives in their writing may well be because of the writing regime observed in their classes (Raban, 1984). This regime was dominated by the activity of children dictating captions to their teacher and these were frequently single statements. Indeed, Scott and Rush have previously pointed out that children use fewer connectives in interviews with adults and this may well be an example of that limitation. However, this analysis of speech and writing shows that children, even by the age of six years, have begun to differentiate between oral and written language and Perera maintains that one way in which they can learn this is from opportunities to write at length.

TABLE 13.1   *Connectives in children's speech and writing at age 6 years*

Connectives	6 year olds' speech (Fawcett and Perkins, 1980)	6 year olds' writing (Raban, 1984) 179 pieces of writing
and	334	249
but	58	10
then	27	58
so	22	10
or	11	—
though	10	—
now	8	1
anyway	4	—
instead	1	—
when	—	17
because	—	6
first of all	—	4
In writing only		
one day		38
once upon a time		15
today		6
on Saturday		4
on Sunday		2
after/now/next/while sometimes/there was once last night/all night at Christmas/every morning in the afternoon/yesterday on Christmas day/on Friday one sunny day/on Wednesday on Saturday and Sunday		1

Writing at length

Unfortunately, observations of children at different stages of schooling have not shown evidence of children's opportunities to write at length. For instance, HMI (DES, 1982) in their survey of first schools (5–9 year olds) noted a lack of range and variety in the children's writing. In many schools there was an excessive and purposeless use of workcard material. These exercises merely occupied the children who tended to copy without either reading or writing other than handwriting. HMI remarked that the extensive use of copy writing and work cards resulted in children having too little time for any extended writing. These observations were similar to those of five year olds reported by Jackson (1983).

TABLE 13.2 *Connectives in children's speech and writing at age 5 years*

Connectives	5 year olds' speech (Wells, 1985) 4,325 utterances from 334 speech samples	5 year olds' writing (Raban, 1984) 297 pieces of writing
and	74	114
because	41	5
when	18	6
but	20	—
if	20	—
so	8	1
as	1	—
after	1	6
before	—	1
as long as	1	—

It is also interesting to note the findings of the National Writing Project in Sheffield (Harris *et al.*, 1987). The teachers in this project each collected all the writing of three children aged 10–11 years during one week in those schools which fed into three comprehensive schools. In this investigation they discovered that these forty or so pupils exhibited a range of 10–82 per cent of their writing which was of a continuous nature. This finding indicates a wide variation among teachers of children of the same age in the opportunities they provide for writing at length.

Further observations of older children in Scottish secondary schools (Spencer, 1983) indicated that 50 per cent of children's writing in these classes was copied or dictated; single sentences or 'fill-in blanks' comprised 25 per cent, and the remaining 25 per cent was found to be continuous writing in pupils' own words although more than half of this was no more than a few lines and observed mainly in English lessons. Writing for these children was most frequently used to share information for revision, to reinforce memorisation and to allow the teacher to assess knowledge and understanding. When asked, the teachers in this survey did not wish to have their pupils writing at length as this would mean more marking for them.

In further research reported by Thorogood (in prep.), similar writing from two classes of 7–8 year olds illustrated the kinds of differences which can be observed when different classroom regimes for writing are compared. In one class the writing curriculum was teacher directed and the teacher also acted as sole audience for the children's writing. In contrast, the writing curriculum of the other classroom was underpinned by real purposes and a variety of audiences including other children, parents and visitors to the school. The children in this second class were encouraged to edit and redraft their writing. They were encouraged to write together and frequently took their own time to complete their writing.

Six pieces of writing from each child in both classes were analysed for their use of time adverbials (Perera, 1986). Three pieces were collected at the beginning of the school year and three pieces towards the end of the school year. Each group of three pieces included a story, a set of instructions, and a description. Children form both classes showed an increase in their use of time and frequency adverbials from the beginning to the end of the school year. However, those children who were encouraged to write at length, stimulated by real purposes and a variety of audiences, were found to produce more instances of these time and frequency adverbials and a greater number of different items of this kind.

Comparison of the same children's writing at home and at school has been found by Peters (1985) to demonstrate a greater syntactic range in their writing which is purposeful, writing most frequently found at home. This kind of writing which is urgent and demands action provides the context not only for improvement in handwriting and spelling, but also for extending the child's desire to make the whole coherent.

These developments in children's writing arise because of the need to make the message understandable to a reader and this requires the opportunity to write at length and to engage a response partner, either the teacher in conferencing or another pupil sharing in turn. Further examples of 'incoherent' texts which lack any relationship between the items of information are shown below and reveal an apparent disregard for an audience:

> This is a house for my family
> there are four trees in the garden
> the sun is shinning in the sky
>
> (Sandra (5y. 4m.)

> I had a new carpet
> I went to my aunty
> I played with my cousin
> then I went home
>
> (Kathleen 6y. 5m.)

Writing which is disjointed in this way is frequently repetitious and lacks the variety which is clear in speech through the use of paralinguistic features. Speakers can stress important aspects of their message in a number of ways denied the writer. Links between parts of the message need to be made clear by the writer. A writer, unlike a speaker, has to produce a sustained coherent discourse without feedback from a conversational partner. This means that sentences need to link smoothly with the preceding text.

Influence of reading

Frequently, teachers notice that older children's writing reflects their reading, not only in structure but also in style. Indeed, Farmer (1985) has illustrated how this tendency can be used to extend and support children's writing development. It is quite possible, therefore, that young children's writing is similarly influenced although, as Perera (1984) argues, the texts they are required to read may be responsible for their stilted writing. Wade's analysis of young children's reading diet (1982) illustrates the incoherence of many reading scheme books and in order to follow up this anxiety a further analysis was carried out of recently published books for children learning to read. Incoherent texts may well be a feature of past reading schemes as Wade points out, but they may not be an anticipated feature of more recent publications, particularly after all the criticism which has been levelled against reading schemes and the like (Moon, 1986).

Three collections of books for children aged five to seven years were analysed for their use of connectives as an index of coherence in the texts which young children may be required to read for themselves. These included *Reading Tree*: Stages 1–7 (Hunt, 1986/7), *Open Door*: Stages 1–4 (Lawrence, 1986/7) and *Reading World*: Levels 1–3 (Body, 1987).

When the total number of connectives were considered and an index of the number of connectives for each book was calculated, both *Open Door* and *Reading World* books analysed here indicated a greater density of these linguistic devices, with *Reading World*, in particular, using these devices from the beginning of the programme. More books were analysed from the *Reading Tree* programme but considerably fewer connectives were found and those that were did not appear before Stage 5. An inspection of the manual which accompanies this programme provides clues to this discrepancy. The manual provides for extended versions of the stories in the books for reading aloud by the teacher and in one of these extended stories in Stage 2, thirty-three examples of twelve different connectives were found although none of these were included in the book for children to read for themselves. The children's books in this programme were written from tape recordings of children telling the story from the pictures, but as Scott and Rush discovered, young children are unlikely to use a variety of connectives when talking to an adult although they would use them in peer interactions.

TABLE13.3 *Connectives in books for children learning to read*

	Reading Tree	Open Door	Reading World
ages 5–7	Stages 1–7	Stages 1–4	Levels 1–3
No. of books analysed	44	32	34
No. of diff. connectives	8	20	34
Connectives in books	Stages 5, 6, 7	Stages 2, 3, 4	Levels 1, 2, 3
Total no. of connectives	112	584	625
Connectives per book	2.55	18.25	18.38

Conclusion

From the variety of analyses presented here, two general guidelines emerge for the development of coherence in young children's writing. First, time needs to be taken in busy classrooms for children to write at length for real purposes and a wide variety of audiences, particularly from the very first stages. In particular, the practice which requires children to dictate their writing to their teacher needs to be reconsidered. Second, as Perera suggests, it may be necessary to pay due regard to linguistic density with respect to connectives of the written language which we require our children to read for themselves. However, the analysis presented here excludes non-fiction books which are available for young children, books which include a different genre more likely to be dependent upon a wide variety of connectives to make their meaning clear.

References

BODY, W. (1987) *Reading World* (London: Longman).

BROWN, G. and G. YULE (1983) *Discourse Analysis* (Cambridge: Cambridge University Press).

DES (1982) *Education 5–9: an illustrative survey of 80 first schools in England* (London: HMSO).

FARMER, I. (1985) 'Organising writing together' in B. Raban (Ed) *Practical Ways to Teach Writing* (London: Ward Lock).

FAWCETT, R. and PERKINS, M. (1980) *Child Language Transcripts 6–12* Vols 1–4 (Pontypridd: Polytechnic of Wales).

HARRIS, J., S. HORNER and TUNNARD, L. (1987) *All in a Week's Work: Sheffield NWP* (Londons Schools Curriculum Development Council).

HARRIS, M. M. (1977) 'Oral and written syntax attainment of second graders' *Research in the Teaching of English* 11, pp. 117–132.

HUNT, R. (1986/87) *Reading Tree* (Oxford: Oxford University Press).

JACKSON, W. (1983) *The Foundations of Writing Project* (Moray House, Edinburgh).

KROLL, B., KROLL, O. and WELLS, G. (1980) 'Researching children's writing development: the "Children Learning to Write" Project', *Language for Learning* 2, pp. 53–81.

LAWRENCE, E. (1986/87) *Open Door* (London: Nelson).

LUNZER, E. and GARDNER, K. (1979) *The Effective Use of Reading* (London: Heinemann).

MOON, C. (1986) 'Spot and Pat: Living in the best company when you read' in B. Root (Ed) *Resources for Reading* (Basingstoke: Macmillan).

O'DONNELL, R. C., GRIFFIN, W. J. and NORRIS, R. C. (1967) *Syntax of Kindergarten and Elementary School Children: a Transformational Analysis* (Illinois: NCTE).

PERERA, K. (1984) *Children's Writing and Reading: Analysing Classroom Language* (Oxford: Basil Blackwell).

PERERA, K. (1986) 'Grammatical differentiation between speech and writing in children aged 8 to 12' in A. Wilkinson (Ed) *The Writing of Writing* (Milton Keynes: Open University Press).

PETERS, M. (1985) 'Purposeful Writing' in B. Raban (Ed) *Practical Ways to Teach Writing* (London: Ward Lock).

PETERSON, C. and McCABE, A. (1987) 'The connective "and": do older children use it less as they learn other connectives?' *Journal of Child Language* 14, pp. 375–81.

RABAN, B. (1984) 'Observing children learning to read and write', unpublished Ph.D. (University of Reading, School of Education).

RUBIN, A. D. (1978) 'A theoretical taxonomy of the differences between oral and written language' in R. J. Spiro, B. C. Bruce and W. F. Brewer (Eds) *Theoretical Issues in Reading Comprehension* (Hillsdale, N. J.: Lawrence Erlbaum Associates).

SCOTT, C. M. (1984) 'Adverbial connectivity in conversations of children 6 to 12', *Journal of Child Language* 11, pp. 704–708.

SCOTT, C. M. and RUSH, D. (1986) 'Teaching adverbial connectivity: implications from current research', *Child Language Teaching and Therapy* 1, pp. 264–80.

SPENCER, E. (1983) *Writing Matters Across the Curriculum*. Hodder & Stoughton.

STUBBS, M. (1980) *Language and Literacy: The Sociolinguistics of Reading and Writing* (London: Routledge and Kegan Paul).

THOROGOOD, L. (in preparation) M. Phil. thesis (University of Reading, School of Education).

WADE, B. (1982) 'Reading rickets and the use of story', *English in Education* 16, pp. 28–37.

WELLS, G. and RABAN, B. (1979) 'The relevance of applied linguistics for teachers of reading' in R. Shafer(Ed) *Applied Linguistics and Reading* (Delaware, IRA).

Chapter 14

The Child's Sense of Theme as a Response to Literature

Susan Lehr

Researchers have explored the child's ability to generate meaning while reading (Baumann, 1981; Christie and Schumacher, 1975; Otto and Barrett, 1968). Others have explored how well children identify main ideas in expository passages (for example, Brown et al., 1977). However, little research has been done on the child's sense of theme using narrative literature. Children's initial book encounters typically include picture books. Thus, a child's sense of theme may spring from his or her earliest encounters with narrative. This study explored the child's sense of theme with narrative literature.

Defining theme

The term *theme* has been defined by Lukens (1982) as 'the idea that holds the story together, such as a comment about either society, human nature, or the human condition. It is the main idea or central meaning of a piece of writing' (p. 101). Huck *et al.* (1987) writes that 'theme provides a dimension to the story that goes beyond the action of the plot' (p. 19). Thus, a theme is an abstraction and can link stories and ideas in general terms without including specific elements of plot. For example, the story of the three bears may be talked about at several levels of theme such as the perils of disobedience or the thoughtless disregard for the property of others. Without referring directly to the plot of this specific story one can step back and talk about the story in broader terms.

Narrative and expository texts

Since the ability to identify the hierarchy of information received during reading is critical to comprehension (Meyer, 1977; Tierney *et al.*, 1978–79; Trabasso and Nicholas, 1977), it becomes important to explore the young child's construction of meaning. When listening to an adult read a story, how does a child perceive the meaning of the story, and how is this meaning generated? Piaget (1926) posited that children below the age of seven to eight are not able to abstract relevant thematic information, or retell logically sequenced information. Applebee (1978) found that in telling their own stories, children two to five years old did not typically generate a thematic centre or clear focus. However, Korman (1945, cited in Yendovitskayz, 1971) studied the narrative recall of four to six-year-old children in the Soviet Union and found that the material was related in a logical sequence and that certain episodes containing lower-level information were deleted in the retellings, particularly those which were not pertinent to the theme of the story. To extend this work, Christie and Schumacher (1975) tested kindergarten, second, and fifth-grade children, and corroborated that the kindergarten child is more capable of 'abstracting and producing relevant thematic information than has previously been assumed'.

Main idea research using expository passages has accumulated evidence suggesting that young children can recognise main ideas, but lack the ability to generate main idea statements (Baumann, 1981; Dunn *et al.*, 1979; Otto and Barrett, 1968; Taylor, 1980; Tierney *et al.*, 1978–79). However, expository texts are structurally quite different from narrative texts (Meyer, 1977), and are also less frequently encountered by young children (Baker and Stein, 1981; Baumann, 1981). Children with experience listening to and reading stories would tend to have a tacit knowledge of narrative forms; therefore, their ability to form narrative categories and generate organisational structures for the recall of themes might develop at an early age (Flood, 1977; Mandler and Johnson, 1977; Stein and Glenn, 1978; Whaley, 1981).

Studies of children's ability to generate meaning from narrative passages have concluded that elementary-age children do have the ability to interpret themes in narrative (Brown *et al.*, 1977; Christie and Schumacher, 1975; Danner, 1976; Meyer, 1977; Waters, 1978). However, in these narrative studies, researchers did not clearly distinguish between identifying theme and generating statements of theme. Children were not specifically asked to generate themes, and results were based on analyses of children's retellings of stories. In the passages used in these studies, story elements were often manipulated or deleted; some of the passages also included intrusive elements that students were forced to ignore. Some of the passages were too short to develop a meaningful context or were of low interest. And, in some cases, simplified texts were used for all ages tested.

Illustrated books

In the narrative studies cited, prepared passages were presented instead of real books with pictures. It could be argued that these were unnatural book-sharing experiences for the children tested, and that, as a result, the researchers were unable to elicit natural responses. Huck points out that the picture book 'conveys its message through two media, the art of illustrating and the art of writing. In a well-designed book in which the total format reflects the meaning of the story, both the illustrations and text must bear the burden of narration' (1987, p. 197). Thus, as Cochran-Smith argues, 'it seems problematic to separate text and pictures, rather than to treat them as integral parts of the beginning reading/comprehension' (1984, p. 11). Because of this interdependency, texts from picture books may 'suffer a loss of meaning and significance when separated and displayed' (Marantz, 1977, p. 148). Therefore, it can be argued that using materials with children that omit illustrations alters the child's ability to build meaning and discuss ideas related to the book.

Purpose of the study

The major purpose of this study was to characterise the nature of the child's sense of theme in narratives as it develops across three age levels, and to determine the role of literature in that development.

Subjects

Subjects were chosen from twenty classrooms of children in kindergarten, second, and fourth grade, in the same school, in a middle-class suburb of a large metropolitan Midwestern city in the United States. The children were given a literature inventory (Revised Huck Literature Inventory, Lehr, 1987) to determine their exposure to literature. High and low-exposure groups were then chosen from the ten highest and ten lowest-scoring students in each grade, for a total of 60 subjects.

Books used for the study

Books for this study were chosen from the wide variety of children's books available. Books chosen reflected a concern for quality of text and illustrations and also were appropriate to the children's cognitive development as outlined in *Children's Literature in the Elementary School* (Huck, 1979). Three books in each of two genres – realistic fiction and folktales – were chosen for each grade level.

Books were chosen, such that, for each grade and each genre, two of the books clearly shared a common theme, whereas the third did not. Adults in a children's literature study group rated the books thematically.

Procedures

Children attended two reading sessions on different days, and on each day I read three books aloud to them in a room separate from their main classroom. Children were then given ten to fifteen minutes to draw pictures about the themes of the books, and meanwhile were interviewed individually, apart from the other children.

First (Task 1), the child was asked to identify two books with similar themes. Next (Task 2), the child was asked a series of interview questions, adapted from guide questions to aid in story retelling developed by Goodman and Burke (1972). The questions provide a variety of perspectives and encourage the child to consider the books from the author's perspective and from former book experiences, and to make personal evaluations about the stories. The following are the questions used:

1. Match two titles. Why did you choose these two books? What are they both about?
2. Can you tell me what the whole story was about, in a few words or in short form?
3. Are these stories similar to any other stories you have read? How?
4. What were the authors trying to teach you when they wrote these stories?
5. What are the most important ideas in these stories?
6. Pick a story. Why did it end like it did?
7. Is there anything you would have changed?
8. Did you like the story? Why or why not?
9. Would you have changed the ending?

During the interview, the books were in visual range and within easy reach of the child. The child could handle the books if he or she chose to do so. All interviews were conducted in the familiar environment of the school, and the child sat close to me on a couch or rug.

Scoring

Interview transcripts were analysed for whether children were able to generate a thematic statement which would reflect the overarching concept of meaning for books heard. Theme statements were rated for congruency with text as well as for level of abstraction. For example, a concise restatement of the plot might be considered a concrete theme statement compared to a theme statement that generalised information from the story. Because no scale existed which measured the abstraction level of theme statements, I adapted Otto and Barrett's (1968) scale for evaluating statements of main idea. However, Otto and Barrett gave students lower ratings for responses that did not link general and specific *elements* than for more general statements. Thus, in response to a passage about various places birds build their nests, a child was ranked lower for saying the main idea was 'where birds like to build nests', than for saying 'Birds build nests in different places' (Otto and Barrett, 1968). The former was considered too general, whereas the latter was considered a correct blending of general and specific information. But according to Lukens (1982) and Huck *et al.* (1987), the concept of theme in narrative is more abstract than that of the main idea of an exposition, that is more directly tied to specific information. Moreover, according to Applebee (1978) a more abstract response denotes a higher cognitive level of the child's development of story understanding. Therefore, it was necessary to add a seventh and highest level to the Otto and Barrett scale, for answers that were generalised statements of theme.

Findings

Identification of theme

All children interviewed, except for one child in the second grade who did not understand the concept of theme, attempted to match two books that the child perceived as being thematically matched selections. Table 14.1 shows the percentage of children's choices for thematically matched books.

Children at all grade levels were more likely to identify the titles adults had selected as thematically matched with realistic books than with folktales. Older children made the same selections as adults more often than kindergarten children; however, there was no difference between the choices of the second and fourth-grade children.

Generation of theme

For Task 2, all analyses were based on transcripts of the 120 interview responses (one for each of two genres, for 60 subjects). The thematic

TABLE 14.1   *Children's choices for thematically matched books*

Realistic fiction	
Titch/The Carrot Seed	16
Titch/New Blue Shoes	2
The Carrot Seed/New Blue Shoes	2
Let's Be Enemies/The Hating Book	20
Stevie/Thy Friend, Obadiah	20
Folktales	
The Three Little Pigs/The Three Billy Goats Gruff	7
The Three Little Pigs/The Gingerbread Boy	12
The Three Billy Goats Gruff/The Gingerbread Boy	1
Tattercoats/Snowwhite	12
Tattercoats/The Swineherd	8
Dawn/A Japanese Fairytale	12
The Stonecutter/Dawn	4
A Japanese Fairytale/The Stonecutter	4

statements of children were all given a score on the Thematic Scale. Kindergarten scores showed a positive correlation of .76 for realistic fiction and .69 for folktales between RHLI (Revised Huck Literature Inventory) and Thematic Scale scores. Average kindergarten scores on the Thematic Scale were 3.1 for realistic fiction and 3.55 for folktales. At the second-grade level the low-exposure group had more scores clustered at the concrete level of stating theme for realistic fiction – which corresponds to a four on the Thematic Scale – than did the kindergarten low-exposure group. The second-grade scores showed a positive correlation of .82 for realistic fiction and .5 for folktales between RHLI and Thematic Scale scores. Average second-grade scores on the Thematic Scale were 4.3 for realistic fiction and 3.1 for folktales. Continuing the trend of the second-grade children, seventeen of the twenty fourth-grade children were able to verbalise themes for realistic fiction. Fourth-grade scores showed a positive correlation of .5 for realistic fiction and .61 for folktales between RHLI and Thematic Scale scores. Average fourth-grade scores on the Thematic Scale were 4.8 for realistic fiction and 3.9 for folktales. Three boys from a classroom in which a lot of literature was used by the teacher did not score high on the RHLI and were able to generate theme statements which were ranked quite high on the Thematic Scale.

Within grades the differences between groups were even more pronounced. In all three grades there was an upward parallel growth pattern in ability to generate theme, in relation to score on the RHLI for both genres. The mean difference between high and low-exposure groups for scores on the Thematic Scale within grades varied from 1.95 to 4.7 for kindergarten, 2.5 to 4.95 for second grade and 3.25 to 5.4 for fourth grade.

Children in all three grades scoring low on the Thematic Scale tended to offer answers that were too general or that contained misinformation that did not mesh with the story. Children's thematic responses, however, ranged from concrete to abstract generalisations for both genres. The context shaped the natural flow of the conversation as the child's own answers built on themselves during the course of the interview.

Responses for realistic fiction

Some children attempted unsuccessfully to link two books with a theme statement. For example, 'cause both of them have blue', was an attempt on the part of a five-year-old child to link *Titch* and *New Blue Shoes* thematically.

Some children were able to identify thematic elements for both stories, but were unable to verbalise themes. For example, one child linked *Titch* and *The Carrot Seed* by stating that 'they both had things that were growing'. This information is important in developing a theme for both books; however, as it stands, the statement is too general and does not establish a theme.

Other statements included absolutes which did not mesh with information in the story like this second-grader's response to *The Hating Book*: 'Even if you don't think you like the person it always ends up that you like the person'. Answers which included absolute statements were most frequently given by children in the low-exposure groups in all three grades, but occurred most frequently with folktales.

Many children offered statements that were concretely tied to the plot, and were actually main ideas, corresponding to a four on the Thematic Scale. When asked why *Titch* ended as it did, one kindergarten child responded perceptively: 'He needed to have something that was bigger. He wanted it to grow.'

The younger children's statements were distinctly different from adult responses, whereas older children, particularly in the fourth grade, offered statements that were more closely aligned to adult perspectives with differences that were more subtle. One kindergarten child talked about *Titch* from the vantage of sharing whatever you're doing and justified her position within the book with a direct reference to the illustrations and the text. This occurred most frequently at the kindergarten level and suggested the child can take on the perspective of another, although it may differ from the view of the adult.

Eight of the kindergarten children in the high-exposure group, fourteen of the second-grade children, ten of whom were in the high-exposure group, and seventeen of the fourth-grade children, ten of whom were in the high-exposure group, scored at or above the level of four on the Thematic Scale for realistic fiction. Of those responses six second-grade children and eight fourth-grade children scored at the two top levels on the Thematic Scale which are abstract responses. For example, at a generalised level in the fourth grade is Nat's (age, 10y. 5m.) thematic response linking *Stevie* and *Thy Friend, Obadiah*: 'Be nice to your friends while you still have them'. This response steps back from the literal plots of both stories and links them successfully with an overarching idea that holds both stories together. His perspective differed from the adult subject's by degree.

Responses for folktales

With folktales children in all three grades injected more misinformation about the text into their comments. Statements that were not congruent with the text primarily originated in the low-exposure groups for all three grades. 'They're basically, they're both in foreign countries', was offered by one fourth-grade girl for *Dawn* and *The Stonecutter*, and when probed further she added that 'they both had boats'.

Some of the children indicated a basic understanding of a character's internal dilemma and struggle, but responded with absolute values that were not appropriate in relation to the larger context of the story. 'Don't go across bridges', was offered by one kindergarten child in response to *The Three Billy Goats Gruff*. The child's perspective is that of avoiding danger without thought of the danger of starvation.

A common response for *The Three Little Pigs* or *The Gingerbread Boy* was 'they both got eaten up'. Mary (age, 5y. 6m.) added that the story ended like it did because 'you can't blow down brick houses'. Answers of young children were less concerned with becoming independent than they were with being safe. 'Build your house strong.' The books teach you 'Not to trust strangers that you don't know'. The fate of the two foolish little pigs and the foolish gingerbread boy was mentioned by eleven children, but not by one adult. With *folktales* kindergarten children did not offer statements that matched adult statements of theme. Rather, they had formed their own perspectives of the stories and had constructed meaning systems based on their background knowledge about how the world functions.

Many statements were literally tied to the plots, such as this second-grade response to *Tattercoats*: 'two people being mean to another person'. Second-grade children primarily gave concrete statements of theme for *Tattercoats* and *Snowwhite* which referred to both characters as having someone that hated them, as being the prettiest and as getting married to a prince. These were summary types of statements which contained no abstractive levels of theme.

At a high level of abstraction Cary (age, 8y. 0m.) stated that in *The Swineherd*, 'You don't get everything and that's how life goes'. His statement can stand alone as a theme for Zwerger's tale. 'You can sacrifice things to make people happy', was offered by Dave (age, 10y. 1m.) in response to *A Japanese Fairytale* and *Dawn*. His statement reflects a clear understanding of the overarching concepts explored in the books. Dave's skilful linking of the two folktales steps back from the plots and identifies common ideas in language similar to adult statements for the same books.

Text congruency

The children's thematic statements seemed to fall into three categories:

(a) *adult-congruent*, in which the child's answer matched the adult choice of thematically matched texts;
(b) *text-congruent*, in which the children's answers were plausible based on the book itself, but did not match the adult choices; and
(c) *not text-congruent*, in which children generated theme statements which did not match information given in the book itself.

Kindergarten children gave text-congruent responses more often than second and fourth-grade children and the nature of the responses changed as the child got older. The differences between fourth-grade responses and adult responses were more subtle.

Characteristics of the child's sense of theme

Ability to summarise

In linking the two selections for *realistic fiction* Mary (age, 5y. 6m.) concretely identified the theme of *Titch*, after talking about the plot of the

story: 'They both (child refers to two books in front of her) have a plant
that grows. . . They (points to older brother and sister in *Titch*) get all the
biggest things. He (points to Titch) ends up with the biggest.' When asked
why the story ended as it did she responded, 'He needed to have something
that was bigger. He wanted it to grow.'

She summarised the story, identified the literal thematic elements of the
story, was aware of character motivation and made a concrete statement
of theme. Her response is generally aligned with adult responses.

Eight of the ten kindergarten children in the high-exposure group were
successfully able to summarise at least one of the stories heard for the
realistic fiction selections, which resulted in a theme statement.

Awareness of character motivations

Children in all three grades talked at length about characters and their
internal motivations. One kindergarten child enlarged upon the theme of
sharing in *Titch*:

> They're going real fast up the hill. And here they won't let him try
> to fly the kites. Here they couldn't let him try their instruments.
> Here Titch he had to hold the nails and they had to the hard jobs.
> That's not fair. . .Right here they won't let him put any dirt in or
> hold it. They only let him handed the seed. . .it grew bigger until it
> was bigger than them. . .at the ending the plant grew out and it got
> those two.

This answer indicates an awareness of internal reactions of characters and
a sensitivity for Titch's plight as the youngest child. His world view included
a system of concrete rewards and punishments and provided a satisfying
ending.

Ability to analyse and make generalisations

Cary's statements for *The Swineherd* reflect an ability to analyse and make
a generalisation about the story. Cary (age, 8y. 0m.) stated,

> The princess learns a lesson. . .She was someone that wanted just
> about everything and that's how she learned her lesson. . .You don't
> get everything and that's how life goes.

Fourth-grade responses for *Dawn* and *A Japanese Fairytale* further
illustrate the language which the nine or ten-year-old child brings to an
understanding of literature. 'You can sacrifice something for something
else,' (Chris, age 9y. 2m.). 'You can sacrifice things to make people happy',
(Dave, age 10y. 1m.). The language used and the concepts revealed in
these statements matched adult statements for the same books, and were
at generalised levels for stating theme.

Physical use of texts

Children used the books as references during the interview and opened them, pointed at illustrations, browsed while thinking about an answer, and at times, even hugged the book while explaining an answer. This literal use of the book decreased with age. Seventeen kindergarten children opened the book as they talked. Second-grade children pointed to and held the book. In contrast, fourth-grade children rarely opened or touched the books, but would occasionally nod in the direction of the book under discussion. This indicated a literal movement from the concrete toward the abstract across age levels in using the physical text as a reference.

Manipulating endings

Kindergarten children typically did not want to change endings or actions of characters in realistic fiction. At the second-grade level children suggested a more active role for characters in changing what they didn't like in the stories. Themes for *The Hating Book* and *Let's Be Enemies* ranged from 'She wanted to find out why her friend was mad at her. . .She was misunderstood', to 'Make friends and don't let an argument separate you'. Fourth-grade children were also able to manipulate story elements. The older children talked about changing characters and their actions, as well as altering endings with both genres. For example, in *Thy Friend, Obadiah* children wanted to delete Obadiah's act of cruelty toward the seagull. In *A Japanese Fairytale* children wanted the hero to regain his good looks, because he had sacrificed them willingly.

Story expectations

Some children altered story events to match their own individual story schema and background knowledge. Zwerger's retelling of *The Swineherd* does not end typically. Yet three children used the predictable 'they lived happily ever after' response to the story when verbalising themes. This suggests the child's strong sense of story and expectations for story parts to behave in a predictable manner which did not mesh with a princess sitting alone out in the rain at the end of a fairytale. The child's ending was much more satisfying and predictable.

Conclusions

Identification of theme

Kindergarten children were able to identify thematically matched books 80 per cent of the time for realistic fiction and 35 per cent of the time for folktales, thus indicating that thematic identification is a fairly early developmental strategy. As an identification task only, children in second and fourth grades matched adult choices more often than kindergarten, particularly with folktales, suggesting that world view or perspective becomes more closely aligned with that of adults as the child matures. This suggests that acculturation occurs at a fairly young age.

Generation of theme

Children verbalised themes for books heard in relation to exposure to children's literature. Children having a low exposure to children's books, as tested by the Revised Huck Literature Inventory (Lehr, 1987), most frequently responded at levels too general to be considered thematic responses. In contrast, children familiar with a broad range of children's literature and genres typically responded to interview questions with thematic statements that were at or above concrete levels on the Thematic Scale used to rate responses.

Second-grade children paralleled kindergarten response patterns at a slightly higher thematic level. That is, the second-grade low-exposure group generated a range of thematic responses that included answers at the concrete level of stating theme and the high-exposure group included more abstract thematic responses to books heard, than did the high kindergarten group. This indicated a developmental trend for group levels within and across grades.

Fourth-grade children continued the developmental parallel growth pattern of thematic response across grade and group levels, but included more variety within the low group in response to realistic fiction. This indicated a developmental awareness of themes for realistic fiction and a facility with generating a statement in that genre. At this grade level the high-exposure group generated more abstract thematic statements than any other group. In all three grades there was an upward parallel growth pattern in ability to generate theme, in relation to score on the RHLI.

Characteristics of child's sense of theme

Children in kindergarten were able to summarise stories heard when asked to tell what the story was about in a few words or a short form or when probed about the story from a general perspective. This ability to summarise the story enabled the child to talk about theme at a concrete level of meaning and seemed to assist the child with ensuing theme questions that asked for important ideas or evaluative statements. In contrast, Applebee (1978) found that children of this age were unable to summarise stories, but had a tendency to retell entire stories. The structure and content of the interview might account for this difference. During interviews I specifically asked the child to retell the story in a few words or a short form.

Children at this age level were also aware of internal motivations or reactions of characters. Seventy per cent of the kindergarten interviewed for realistic fiction mentioned the internal thought processes which motivated character actions in the stories. This ability assisted the child in determining themes of books heard. Knowing how or why the characters responded as they did in particular episodes was often included in thematic responses. Mandler and Johnson (1977) found that children omit internal reactions of characters during spontaneous recall. The variety of perspectives which the interview questions included may have acted as a catalyst in this respect. This supports the idea that children do take on the perspectives of others (Donaldson, 1978; Paley, 1981).

Second and fourth-grade children, particularly those in the high-exposure groups, were able to respond to stories with thematic statements which were at analysis and generalisation response levels in Applebee's Developmental Formulation of Response Categories (1978). This finding was interesting because Applebee asserts that children in the concrete operational stages of development are typically unable to analyse and generalise thematic statements about stories. Older children in this study were able to generate thematic statements which matched adult responses. The quality of the language used was most complex with the fourth-grade high-exposure group. Children were given access to books as points of reference during the interview and were also given time to draw a picture about what the books were about. This presumably focused the children on the thematic content of the stories and gave them an opportunity to consider themes for the books.

Implications

The use of physical texts from children's literature as a research tool elicited a high quality of response from children in kindergarten, second and fourth-grade classrooms in the present study. The interview format which encouraged children to consider the story from several different perspectives was also helpful in eliciting a wide range of responses from children in all three grades. Future studies might include real books with illustrations and might encourage formats which are natural contexts in which children explore their perceptions of books. Since this study was conducted with individual children future studies might include interactive contexts in which children discuss books.

Since exposure to children's literature had a strong correlation to the child's level of thematic awareness, teachers might be encouraged to provide students with a rich literature background in a variety of genres. Giving children opportunities to listen to books and to read books in the classroom can increase the child's background knowledge about the world and increase a child's ability to generate theme.

This study specifically found that giving children the opportunity to talk about their ideas regarding the book can help them verbalise themes and explore character motivation and elements of plot. Since so many perceptions of the children were different from adult perspectives, the notion of right and wrong regarding discussions of books is less useful than the notion of sharing ideas. Future studies might explore interactive contexts in which books are shared and discussed and the child's perspective is valued.

References

APPLEBEE, A. (1978) *The Child's Concept of Story: Ages Two to Seventeen* (Chicago, IL: University of Chicago Press).

BAKER, L. and STEIN, N. (1981) 'The development of prose comprehension skills' in C. Santa and B. Hayes (Eds.) *Children's Prose Composition* (Newark, Delaware: International Reading Association).

BAUMANN, J. (1981) 'Children's ability to comprehend main ideas after reading expository prose', paper presented at 31st Annual Meeting of National Reading Conference, Dallas, TE, December.

BROWN, A., SMILEY, S., DAY, J., TOWNSEND, M. and LAWTON, S. (1977) 'Intrusion of a thematic idea in children's comprehension and retention of stories', Technical Report No. 13, Center for the Study of Reading, University of IL, February.

CHRISTIE, D. and SCHUMACHER, G. (1975) 'Developmental trends in the abstraction and recall of relevant versus irrelevant thematic information from connected verbal materials', *Child Development*, 46, pp. 589–602.

COCHRAN-SMITH, M. (1984) *The Making of a Reader* (Norwood, NJ: Ablex).

DANNER, F. (1976) 'Children's understanding of intersentence organization in the recall of short descriptive passages', *Journal of Education Psychology*, 681, pp. 174–83.

DONALDSON, M. (1978) *Children's Minds* (London: Collins).

DUNN, B., MATTHEWS, S. and BIEGER, G. (1979) 'Individual differences in the recall of lower level textual information' (Technical Report No. 150, Center for the Study of Reading, University of IL: ERIC No. ED 181 448).

FLOOD, J. (1977) 'Parental styles in reading episodes with young children', *Reading Teacher*, pp. 864–867, May.

GOODMAN, Y. and BURKE, C. (1972) 'Additional guide questions to aid story retelling', revised for *Reading Miscue Inventory Manual: Procedure for Diagnosis and Evaluation* (Basingstoke: Macmillan).

HUCK, C. (1960) *Huck Inventory of Literary Background* (Boston: Houghton Mifflin).

HUCK, C. (1979) *Children's Literature in the Elementary School* (3rd ed.) (New York: Holt, Rinehart and Winston).

HUCK, C., HEPLER, S. and HICKMAN, J. (1987) *Children's Literature in the Elementary School* (4th ed.) (New York: Holt, Rinehart and Winston).

LEHR, S. (1987) 'Revised Huck Literature Inventory' in White, M. (Ed.), *Instructor's Manual for Children's Literature in the Elementary School* (4th ed.) (New York: Holt, Rinehart and Winston).

LUKENS, R. (1982) *A Critical Handbook of Children's Literature* (Glenview, Illinois: Scott, Foresman and Company).

MANDLER, J. and JOHNSON, N. (1977) 'Remembrance of things parsed: Story structure and recall', *Cognitive Psychology*, 9, pp. 111–151.

MARANTZ, K. (1977) 'The picture book as art object: a call for balanced reviewing', *Wilson Library Bulletin*, pp. 148–151, October.

MEYER, B. (1977) 'The structure of prose: effects on learning and memory and implications for educational practice', in R. Anderson, R. Spiro and Montague (Eds.) *Schooling and the Acquisition of Knowledge* (Hillsdale, NJ: Erlbaum).

OTTO, W. and BARRETT, T. (1968) 'Two studies of children's ability to formulate and state a literal main idea in reading', Report from the Reading Project, Wisconsin Research and Dev. Center for Cognitive Learning, June.

PALEY, V. (1981) *Wally's Stories* (Cambridge, Mass.: Harvard University Press).

PIAGET, J. (1960) *The Language and Thought of the Child* (London: Routledge and Kegan Paul). (Originally published 1926.)

STEIN, N. and GLENN, C. (1978) 'An analysis of story comprehension in elementary school children' in R. Freedle (Ed.) *Discourse Processing* (Norwood: NJ: Ablex).

TAYLOR, B. (1980) 'Children's memory for expository text after reading', *Reading Research Quarterly*, 15, pp. 399–411.

TIERNEY, R., BRIDGE, D. and CERA, M. (1978–79) 'The discourse processing operations of children', *Reading Research Quarterly*, 14, pp. 539–73.

TRABASSO, T. and NICHOLAS, D. (1977) 'Memory and inferences in the comprehension of narratives', Paper presented at conference on Structure and Process Models in the Study of Dimensionality of Children's Judgements, Kassel, Germany, June.

WATERS, H. (1978) 'Superordinate-subordinate structure in semantic memory, *Journal of Verbal Learning and Verbal Behavior*, 17, pp. 587–97.

WHALEY, J. (1981) 'Reader expectations for story structures', *Reading Research Quarterly*, 1, pp. 90–114.

YENDOVITSKAYZ, T. (1971) 'Development of memory', in A. Saparozhets and D. Elkonin (Eds.) *The Psychology of Preschool Children* (Cambridge, Mass.: MIT Press). (Originally published 1964).

Chapter 15

Assessing Inquiry Reading

Ronald Fyfe and Evelyn Mitchell

Children's problems in handling reading and writing as tools of inquiry were investigated using small-scale inquiry activities based on two-dimensional matrixes. Pupils used small collections of books to find information to complete blank cells in the matrixes. Good inquirers were opportunistic and willing to take risks, usually well-founded, when carrying out inquiry tasks. This was shown in the planning, searching, recording and editing phases. Strategies which adults regard as desirable and effective in inquiry work – asking open questions, using indexes, browsing in a controlled manner, composing rather than copying, inserting examples and so on – may be high-risk strategies for children to use. These strategies depend on prior knowledge of subject matter, of books and of expository writing, prior knowledge which children do not possess to the degree that adults do. That poorer inquirers use less effective strategies is, therefore, understandable in the circumstances, but these strategies are unlikely to lead to satisfactory progress in the long run.

When children work on topics, themes and other forms of inquiry work they are expected to learn many things. One of these is how to use reading and writing as tools of inquiry. However, it is not easy for teachers to monitor the progress that individual pupils are making in the use of these tools. Inquiry work is complex and much of what goes on may be cooperative in nature. It is difficult to be sure just how much any one child has contributed to the work of a group. It is also difficult to identify how much of the material presented has been culled through reading and to what extent the pupils' written work has been copied or paraphrased from texts rather than composed by the children themselves.

One solution to these problems would be to try to break down inquiry work into discrete subskills and test these separately. However, it is unlikely that this kind of approach would produce a true picture of what children actually do in real situations. Neville and Pugh (1977), for example, found that pupils who *could* make use of indexes when asked to do so none the less ignored them when actually engaged in inquiry work. In our work on the assessment of the reading and writing elements in inquiry work we tried to find an approach which would:

1. allow assessment to be carried out in a context where pupils were finding out about a topic currently being studied by the class as a whole;

2. involve pupils in something approaching a 'complete' inquiry in the sense that they would have to deal with the different elements and tasks usually found in an inquiry;

3. allow teachers to observe more easily how pupils handled these different tasks and elements so that diagnosis of the pupil's difficulties could begin.

Our overall approach will become clearer when we describe the assessment activities themselves.

The assessment device: the matrix

The assessment activities were small-scale inquiries based on two-dimensional matrixes prepared for different topics, printed on card and subsequently laminated. Accompanying each matrix was a small collection of information books typical of those found in school libraries. One of the matrixes we prepared is reproduced in Fig. 15.1. It was used with P7 children who expressed an interest in 'Birds' as a topic for investigation. Each column of the matrix is devoted to one species of bird: each row is prefaced by a question to be answered about each of these species. The pupils were asked to undertake the following tasks.

1. *Search*. Pupils used the collection of books to find information which would complete the blank cells in the matrix.

2. *Record*. Pupils noted down relevant information on adhesive slips and attached these to the appropriate cells in the matrix.

3. *Edit*. Once pupils had completed a matrix, they were asked to use the information gathered in each column to produce a paragraph of running prose that could be understood by a child one year younger than themselves.

4. *Plan*. Pupils were asked to expand the matrix on which they were working by adding an extra column (sub-topic) and row (question) or they were asked to prepare a completely new matrix on a related topic.

Using the matrix in this way separates these four tasks reasonably clearly while ensuring that the pupils are still working in the context of a reasonably complete inquiry. This is particularly the case if the matrix is based on a sub-area of a more general topic on which the class is already working.

To make detailed observation and diagnosis easier, the activities were designed so that teachers can vary the support given to pupils or groups of pupils. The underlying idea is that teachers can gain useful information about pupils' difficulties by investigating the kinds and degrees of support they need in order to succeed in a task which they cannot as yet carry out independently (Vygotsky, 1978). In the 'Birds' matrix, for example, support is given by providing column and row headings for pupils. This gives them a plan to work to. Again, incorporating completed cells in the matrix offers support by showing pupils the kind of information they have to look for. Teachers can reduce that support by omitting some or all of the completed

	Robin	Oystercatcher	Swallow	Kingfisher
What are the colours of the parts of the bird?		It has a glossy black head, upper breast and back. The underparts, and a stripe on the wing and across the base of the tail are white. It has a long orange-red bill. Its legs are pink. 		
What kind of food does it eat?				It feeds on small fish like sticklebacks.
Where does it build its nest?			Usually their nests are inside buildings. They are made on beams or joists or stuck onto a wall.	
What is its nest made of?	Its nest is made of grass, moss, wool and hair.			
What sort of movements does it make when it flies?		Its flight is fast and straight. Its wingbeats are rather shallow.	Swallows usually fly quite near the ground and they perform daring acrobatics to avoid things that are in their way. They often swoop low over water, darting about as the chase insects. Sometimes they just skim the surface of water and scoop up a little water to drink.	

FIGURE 15.1 *Prepared Matrix*

cells (so making recording more difficult) or by asking pupils to supply some or all of the column and row headings (so increasing planning demands). By observing the effect of these different kinds of support teachers can begin to work out where pupils' weaknesses lie. In inquiry work children are encouraged to take responsibility for their own learning. This makes it particularly suitable for the application of the support approach to assessment.

Books themselves vary in the amount of support they give to the reader. Unfamiliar vocabulary, conceptual difficulty and grammatical complexity in the texts used are all likely to make an inquiry task more difficult. Perhaps less obvious is the fact that a search task becomes more difficult when books offer the required information at a level either more specific or more general than the question demands. For example, suppose a group of pupils is trying to find out what adult puffins do when their chicks are ready to fly. Here are three texts which would supply the answer.

> The (puffin) chick is tended by both parents, but before it can fly or swim is deserted and has to find its own way to sea.
>
> (Leigh-Pemberton, 1967)

> At fledging-time the young sea-bird discovers that its parents are growing indifferent to its food-begging advances, and will ultimately repulse them, or will abandon the chick completely (tubenoses, gannets and puffins).
>
> (Fisher and Lockley, 1954)

> By the end of July Puffin, now six weeks old, had grown into a fat contented little fledgling. But this safe and sheltered time came to an end. The tired parent birds returned to the sea, to drift away and moult their feathers and change to winter colouring. Puffin waited in the nest a week or more, then ventured out – not in the strange disturbing daylight, but at night. He saw the moonlit water and scrambled towards it through the rough grass (for he had not yet learned to fly), hopped over the edge of the cliff, dropped down two hundred feet, and spent his first night in the open splashing about in the shallows.
>
> (King, 1984)

The first text gives the relevant information directly though in quite difficult language. Indeed the sentence could be copied down as an answer to the question. From the second extract (again difficult) children might be able to *deduce* the answer but the author is writing at a level more general than the one at which the question is set, that is he is writing about sea birds rather than puffins. The third passage is more appealing and easier to understand. However, children using this passage would have to *generalise* from what happened to the puffin in the story in order to produce a statement about puffins in general. This is always a risky procedure. Even adults may be unsure of the extent to which they can legitimately generalise from the experiences of the puffin in the story. Are all puffins deserted by their parents? Do all puffins leave the nest for the first time at night? Rising above the level of ordinary particulars is a crucially important thinking skill and a hallmark of scientific thinking (Medawar, 1985). It mirrors in the handling of print what children must also do when learning more directly from their immediate environment. Teaching children how to move across different levels of generalisation should be treated as a major goal of inquiry work and one which can be developed through reading and writing. However, such thinking is difficult. The first step in assessing inquiry work will usually be to ensure that children can handle texts in which target information appears at a level which directly answers the questions set.

This, then, was the approach we used in investigating how pupils tackled the reading and writing elements in inquiry work. It is one which teachers can adapt for use with their own materials. In the next section we summarise what we found out using this approach and point out some of the things that teachers might look out for when observing how their own pupils perform.

What to look for when observing inquiry work

Our findings led us to formulate the following hypothesis: those who make better or more efficient use of reading and writing in inquiry work are flexible in their overall approach and are prepared to take well-founded risks. On the other hand, poorer performers are inflexible, even rigid in their approach, and are unwilling to take risks. We use pupils' work in planning, searching, recording and editing to illustrate the kind of evidence which led us to this hypothesis.

(a) Planning

The most elementary form of planning in inquiry work is the preparation of a list of key questions to be answered. How good are children at producing such questions?

Before embarking on our work with the matrix tasks we interviewed a large number of children and asked them to suggest topics that they would like to investigate. We then asked them to choose one of these topics and tell us the kind of things they would want to find out about it. In this kind of situation a simple and safe tactic is to ask questions to which the answers are already known or, failing that, to ask very specific questions the answers to which are likely to be easily recognised even if not so easily found. These were, in fact, the kinds of questions pupils tended to ask. For example, one P4 pupil suggested that 'Football' would be an interesting topic and thought that he would need to find out:

> Not to tackle behind their legs
> You are not allowed to hack

The goalkeeper is not allowed out of his box
handling the ball.

(It was not always easy to detect that pupils were asking questions to which they knew the answers. One child, talking about 'Music' as a topic, suggested that she would like to find out the names of the notes. After a pause she added, 'Like crotchet, minim and quaver'.) Very specific questions were easily spotted: 'When did the last dinosaur die? What was the smallest dinosaur? What was the fiercest dinosaur?' Neither kind of question is likely to open up a topic for investigation. One thing that might be developed through inquiry work, then, is the ability to formulate questions which genuinely inquire. How can we check whether pupils have acquired this ability and, just as important, whether they are willing to use it?

Our solution was to ask pupils to extend the matrix they were working on by adding a new column heading and row question. Pupils were extremely unlikely to know the answers to this question – several answers had to be found, one for each cell in the row. Furthermore, the questions had to be sufficiently general to apply across all the columns. The pupils we worked with found this task quite difficult, but the matrix seemed to make them aware of what was required. In this sense it supported their thinking. (They were also helped by the fact that they had just completed the original matrix.) As a result most of them were able to offer suitable headings and questions. For example, pupils working on a 'Wild Flowers' matrix offered as additional questions, 'Where are the common places to find them?', 'Name any flower in the same family' and 'How tall will it grow?'

Pupils found preparing a matrix on a new but related topic much more difficult. Once again, however, the matrix seemed to help to clarify their thinking. One pupil quickly produced 'Dog, Cat, Budgie and Fish' as column headings for a matrix on 'Pets' but found setting row questions more difficult. However, he was able to see, unaided, that the first question he prepared – 'What colour is this pet?' – could not be applied to the animals as he had listed them. He said, 'But you would need to have a certain kind of dog, a certain kind of cat and a certain kind of . . .'. He had recognised that a general question about colour could only be asked about specific instances within each category of pet. He then changed his column headings to 'Terrier, Siamese, Parrot and Goldfish'. We suspect that the structure of the matrix may encourage children to think in terms of generic questions. Because such questions can be asked about all the subtopics they are very likely to be fruitful ones to explore in an inquiry. Children who in planning habitually ask specific questions or questions to which they already know the answers may reveal that they can do better when given the support provided by a simple matrix. The basis for a worthwhile investigation may be created by what is really a quite simple device.

(b) Searching

Successful searchers began by 'screening' the set of books in order to identify the ones most likely to provide the information they wanted. Sometimes they rejected books after a quick glance at the titles and cover illustrations. They would often, however, look at the contents sections or indexes in those volumes which survived that first quick inspection. Eventually, they selected a book for closer inspection. When screening books pupils must use prior knowledge of the topic to sift out volumes which are unlikely to give the information required. Sometimes, of course, the children's screening decisions were 'wrong'. (Not infrequently this was because titles and cover illustrations did not accurately reflect the contents of the books. For example, the fullest account of the kingfisher to be found in our collection of books was in a book about 'Garden Birds'. Many pupils understandably rejected this volume during screening because they did not regard the kingfisher as a garden bird.)

Less successful searchers followed an inflexible, but potentially safer, tactic: they picked up a book, seemingly at random, and proceeded to go through it methodically. That book dealt with, they chose another. No screening took place. Occasionally we asked poorer searchers who were 'stuck' to sort the books into 'likely' and 'unlikely' groups. Pupils who were able to do this usually found the target information quite quickly. However, when they encountered similar difficulties during a later search these pupils did not spontaneously attempt another screening. Poor searchers may need to be encouraged to screen books but any training must emphasise why screening is useful and be based initially on topics with which the pupil is already reasonably familiar. Indeed, any assessment of pupils' competence in inquiry reading should compare how pupils search topics they know well with their performance on less familiar ones.

Good searchers also differed from poorer searchers in the way that they studied individual books. Poor searchers page-turned; that is they systematically turned over one page at a time and studied each page as they came to it. Indeed, some pupils proceeded page by page through a text until they reached the index. Only then did they use it to look up individual pages! Good searchers, on the other hand, 'browsed'. They moved back and forth through the book, using the index, subheadings, pictures and other cues within the text to guide their searches. They were very quick – sometimes too quick – to decide that a page or a book was going to be unhelpful. (By contrast, poor searchers were reluctant to abandon a book or a page which had helped them to complete a previous cell.) Browsing is, we feel, a significant advance on page turning. The browser, unlike the page turner, is in control of the text and is not constrained by the sequence in which authors happen to present their information.

Using indexes and contents sections is the first and most elementary step readers can take to wrest control of their search away from the author. However, neither good nor poor readers made as much use of indexes as we expected. This may be because information books for children do not always have indexes and, where indexes are provided, they are often of poor quality. Experienced searchers recognise shortcomings in indexes and generate alternative keywords under which the topic they are working on may be listed. Pupils who are not immediately successful are more likely to conclude that indexes are simply not useful. The consequences of failing to use an index or using an index carelessly are seldom apparent to such pupils. They are seldom made aware of what they have passed over when they prematurely discard a book.

Poor searchers adopted a systematic, laborious and essentially inflexible approach to searching, an approach which almost guarantees success if pursued consistently to the bitter end. Few, however, had the time or the resolve to achieve success. Good searchers were much more flexible, but ran the risk of passing over target information and neglecting sources which at first glance seemed unpromising. Their approach was more enjoyable and more active. They had to think all the time about what they were doing.

(c) Recording

Once they had found the information they were looking for pupils recorded it temporarily on the adhesive slips provided. The safe tactic in recording is to copy information verbatim. Perhaps because our questions were relatively specific in their demands what pupils copied was selective and relevant. None of the pupils we worked with produced 'chunk copying' where any relevant material is lost in the large amount of irrelevant material which surrounds it. Some pupils were more adventurous and composed rather than copied their entries. Here is a passage from Ardley (1976) which many pupils used as a source of information about the colouring of kingfishers.

Kingfisher *Alcedo atthis*
A glimpse of a kingfisher is one of the most spectacular sights of the bird world. An iridescent blue-green above and a rich chestnut beneath, the kingfisher is probably everyone's candidate for the most beautiful British bird.

Here are cell entries produced by two pupils working from this source. The first pupil copied from the text. The second composed his entry after reading this extract and studying an illustration found in another book.

An iridescent blue green above and a rich chestnut beneath.
(Selective and relevant copying)

The kingfisher has a ritch chestnut underneath and a Green head and wings also a blue back and neck with a bit of white.
(Composing)

Pupils who compose entries are much more likely to introduce errors or misinterpretations into their texts. The more work a pupil puts into an entry the more likely he or she is to fail to meet three constraints that are imposed by the task: namely, the cell entry must be relevant to the question, accurate in substance and written in an acceptable form. Consequently, while working to produce one's 'own' text may be considered more desirable by the teacher, the rewards for doing so may be few and pupils may even feel that they are being 'punished' if they are asked to rewrite and correct their work. One advantage of the matrix approach is that it firmly separates recording from editing: both those who copy and those who compose are expected to revise (compose) and rewrite as a final step.

Good recording can be encouraged in the initial stages by setting relatively specific targets. This tends to eliminate unthinking 'chunk' copying. Once pupils have become proficient in searching for such targets, they can be asked to look for less precisely specified information and to use multiple sources and sources other than text (for example, pictures or real-life objects). This encourages composition rather than copying though, when texts alone are used as sources, composing may take place during editing rather than recording.

Two further differences between good and poor inquirers are worth noting. First, poorer inquirers were anxious to complete or 'close down' cells as quickly as possible and often did so prematurely. Once they had found some information to enter in a cell they were unlikely to notice, far less look for, additional information. Recording ended their search. On the other hand the better inquirers were willing to add to their entries and sometimes deliberately set out to find additional material. For them, recording merely punctuated their search. Second, poorer inquirers filled in the cells in the order in which they appeared in the matrix, usually column by column but often row by row. Better inquirers were much more opportunistic. Though they began by focusing on one column they were prepared to move from column to column as information came to light. They would not bypass information on the grounds that it was not relevant to the cell they were currently working on. They seemed to maintain a grasp of the whole matrix task while they were working.

(d) Editing

Pupils were asked to use the material they had gathered to produce a text suitable for pupils one year younger than themselves. Although they worked hard very few could be described as good editors. Most were content simply to proof-read. This was again a safe tactic: few new errors were introduced and some errors were eliminated. A few bolder spirits went beyond this. They re-ordered sentences, attempted simplifications, inserted 'helpful' examples and added information. This was a riskier strategy because it sometimes led them to introduce new errors. One pupil, for example, decided to amplify what she had actually found out about oystercatchers' nests. Her original cell entry

> They build nests on the shore but sometimes they build them inland on the heather.

became, in her paragraph about oystercatchers,

The oystercatchers build their nests on the shore but sometimes they build them inland on the heather according to the weather.

The final 'improving' phrase was added without any attempt to check whether it was accurate or not. (Note, however, the helpful way in which 'They' in the original has been changed to 'The oystercatchers'.) The most impressive editor we came across was unconcerned about low-level editing of spelling and grammar. He was much more interested in trying to explain ideas. In the following extract he is writing about aeroplanes. The section beginning 'just like you need' was added to help younger readers.

Also to help control the plain sort of flaps on the wings tilt the plain by one going up and the other going down the plain needs to tilt when it turns because it is going very fast, just like you need to when you ride a bike other wise you'd fall off or even not turn and skid.

The addition is very effective, but he has not reduced the number of errors in the text. More lower-level editing is required.

Conclusions

Strategies which adults see as efficient and effective in inquiry work are risky ones for pupils to use. When conducting a search adults will almost always have significant prior knowledge not only of the topic being investigated but also of how authors conventionally arrange and present information in books. This knowledge enables them to screen books and browse through them efficiently and effectively. Pupils often lack both of these kinds of knowledge.

There is, however, another source of difficulty. Adults use indexes effectively not only because they know how to handle them but also because indexes in adult books are of a reasonable quality. Children's information books seldom have good indexes and pupils' frustrating experiences with them may explain why neither good nor poor searchers made as much use of indexes as adults might expect. Again, browsing is effective when a text is well structured and when chapter headings, subheadings, illustrations and more subtle cues in the text are present to help readers to make use of that structure for their own purposes. Children's books often lack structure and are idiosyncratic in their choice of content. Given these limitations in the books they have to use, the poor inquirer's choice of approach may be quite rational. Teachers face a 'bootstrapping' problem: in the long run inquiry work will give pupils an increasing knowledge of subject matter and of texts which will then enable them to carry out inquiry work efficiently! If we want to help pupils to do this we need to support them not only by introducing them to good habits but also by ensuring that, as far as possible, the books we offer them can be used to demonstrate that these habits are indeed effective.

References

ARDLEY, N. (1976) *Birds of Coasts, Lakes and Rivers* (New Maldon: Almark Publishing Company).

FISHER, J. and LOCKLEY, R. M. (1954) *Sea-Birds* (London: Collins).

KING, D. (1984) *Puffin* (London: Jonathan Cape).

LEIGH-PEMBERTON, J. (1967) *Sea and Estuary Birds* (Loughborough: Ladybird Books).

NEVILLE, M. H. and PUGH, A. K. (1977) 'Ability to use a book: further studies of middle school children', *Reading* 11, 3, pp. 13–22.

MEDAWAR, P. (1985) *Limits of Science* (Oxford: Oxford University Press).

VYGOTSKY, L. (1978) *Mind in Society* (Cambridge, Mass.: Harvard University Press).

This paper is based on the findings of a research project funded by the Scottish Education Department (Research Project JHK/7/16). The authors are grateful to the Department for its support. The views expressed here are, however, their own.

Chapter 16

Nursery Children's Views About Reading and Writing

Nigel Hall

It has always been difficult to find out about how children think about reading and writing. Most direct questions of the kind 'What is reading?' yield distinctly unhelpful answers. In an effort to consider the problem in a different way a group of nursery-aged children were asked about animals being able to read and write. The children demonstrated very clear views about the possibility and those views were consistent with the kind of experience that young children have of reading and writing.

> You'll never be a good writer, my lad. You have not a steady hand, but never mind. They can teach a pig to write, but they cannot teach it to think, and you can think.
>
> (John Sykes, *Slawit in the sixties*, p. 23)

> *Mrs Pugh*: Some persons were brought up in pigsties.
> *Mr Pugh*: Pigs don't read at table, dear. Pigs can't read, my dear.
> *Mrs Pugh*: I know one who can.
>
> (Dylan Thomas, *Under Milk Wood*, 1954)

Introduction

How do young children view the activities of reading and writing? Do they see them as reasonable activities and what is it that they think those activities are? During the last thirty years there have been many attempts to answer those questions. Mostly the investigations have used interviews (sometimes with other instruments) and have asked central questions such as 'What is reading?' (Weintraub and Denny, 1965; Johns and Johns, 1971; Johns, 1974; Johns and Ellis, 1976; Tovey, 1976; Canney and Winograd, 1979; Mayfield, 1983; and Robinson *et al.*, 1983).

There are, however, problems with asking young children such a direct question. The question is highly abstract. Choosing a response to questions such as 'what is reading?' or 'what is reading for?' is not an easy task for an adult, let alone a young child faced with a strange questioner in an environment often different from the classroom the child is used to.

In the studies noted above the interviews tended to be highly structured and demanded single answers (and it is clear from the way the studies were reported that the investigators had a very clear idea of what an appropriate response was). For example Johns and Ellis (1976) asked only three straight questions, the answers to which were transcribed and classified. It does not appear from their description that the children were given any chance of open-ended discussion. The same appears to be true for all the other studies noted above. Thus the young child had to make a first-time response to specific questions of a highly abstract nature.

Such studies generally came to depressing conclusions about the understanding by children of the nature of reading. Johns and Ellis (1976) claimed that 57 per cent of the children they interviewed either failed to respond or gave vague or circular responses: Robinson *et al.* (1983) claimed 42 per cent of such responses, Tovey (1976) 29 per cent of such responses, and Weintraub and Denny (1966) 27 per cent of such responses.

However, recognition that structured interviews had some limitations led Johns (1986) to hesitate about drawing too many conclusions about young children's understanding of reading. In general others (and Johns in previous studies) were not so reticent and had been happy to describe the vast majority of children as having 'little or no understanding of the reading process' (Johns and Ellis, 1976, p. 127). This kind of conclusion agrees with those of the slightly more open-ended interviews of Reid (1966) and Downing (1969). However, such conclusions leave open the question of what it is that children actually do believe and do know.

In an attempt to pursue young children's notions about literacy a more devious approach was adopted. The approach derived from discussion with a group of children in response to a story about a child who went to the zoo to help the animals learn to read and write. The child was somewhat unsuccessful, having a number of failing adventures and eventually being sent home in disgrace. This attempted comic tale led to the children debating whether, in fact, animals could learn to read or write. The children taking part in this discussion clearly had differing views and the expressions of those views seemed to suggest different understandings of what reading and writing were. The story was read to, and discussed with, other groups of children and again there appeared, through the responses, to be different conceptions of reading and writing being used.

It was decided to investigate this further by inverviewing a number of children from different age groups about the possibility of animals being able to read or write.

This study reports the first phase of the investigation; interviews with nursery children about the topic. The interviews all took place in a writing centre in a nursery school and were carried out during a three-month period when the author was working in the centre with the children. Each child was interviewed at a time when it was working on its own in the writing corner and the interview was begun as a continuation of a casual conversation that had been going on between the author and the child. The children were not told they were being interviewed; the interviewer simply shifted the topic by saying 'can I ask you some questions about reading and writing'. The interviews were recorded using a Walkman positioned in a pocket and a minute lapel microphone. None of the children appeared to notice the microphone.

The questions fell into four general categories.

Can animals learn to read?
Can animals be taught to read?
Can animals write?
Can animals be taught to write?

Within the constraints of the categories the responses of the children were explored by asking further questions and engaging in discussion.

Can animals read and can they be taught to read?

An initial assumption had been that there was a possibility that the nursery children might suggest that animals could read and write. The stories that children of this age hear are replete with animal characters who act like human beings. A whole parade of well-loved animals, from Peter Rabbit to the Church Mice manage to talk and engage in all types of human behaviour. Old Mother Hubbard's dog certainly had literate inclinations:

> She went to the cobblers,
> To buy him some shoes
> But when she came back,
> He was reading the news.

However, the children's initial response to the question was always 'no'. The 'no' was frequently accompanied by a laugh or chuckle. Their reasons were fairly consistent. They were either:

> They 'aint go no hands.

> They 'avn't got arms.

or

> They can't talk.

> Because they can't hear properly.

> Because they can't talk, they can just noise.

Another child offered what appeared at first sight to be a different response, 'No because they've got to be grown up'. However, when this response was pursued and she was asked whether a dog or a cat could read she said, 'No, because he would bark it and you don't bark to read' and 'It would Miaow it'. Thus her original response still fell into 'they cannot talk' category. One three and a half year old, when asked whether a dog could learn to read, answered 'No, because he's small and can't open his mouth'. One child was asked,

Q: Is reading something we do inside our heads or is it something we do with out mouths?

A: With your mouth.

Both major types of response were explored. The response 'Because they can't talk' was followed up by identifying an animal that can, in some senses, talk – a parrot. Some of the children were resolute:

'No because he can't – no animals can read.'

While others were prepared now to make concessions:

Q: What about a parrot – could a parrot learn to read?

A: Yes.

Q: Why could a parrot learn to read?

A: Cos he can talk.

The children who had replied by stating that animals could not read because they did not have hands were asked, 'Why did they need hands?' The answers were straightforward:

Or they wouldn't be able to hold the book.

British children are certainly not the only ones to respond like this. Rachel, the daughter of Scollon and Scollon (1981) claimed that her baby brother would be able to read when his hands grew but, 'The dog, though, would never be able to read because he had no hands' (p. 62).

Children who responded like this were offered the example of an animal with hands – a monkey. Some answers suggested the influence of home:

Q: Do you think that because a monkey's got hands it could learn to read?

A: Yes.

Q: How would it do it?

A: It would have to wash its hands.

Q: Wash its hands – why?

A: Cos it's been in the mud!

One child volunteered that a monkey could read because:

A: They've got 'ands.

Q: And what do they do with their hands then?

A: Scratch!

And one child would not accept that monkeys had hands – they had paws. When the children were asked whether the interviewer could read something without holding it the answer was an emphatic 'no':

Q: Could I learn to read if I didn't have any hands?

A: No

Q: Suppose I put my hands behind my back?

A: No.

Q: Why should I need hands?
A: Because you won't be able to hold the book.

Q: Suppose I look at that and say 'Do you think animals can read?', am I reading it?
A: No
Q: What am I doing?
A: You're just looking like that – you're just looking at it.

In general, though, children remained unconvinced by the example of a parrot and a monkey and stuck to their response that animals could not read, primarily because of the inability to talk, although one child invoked personal experience, 'I've got a dog and it can't read'.

Their responses to the question 'Could we teach an animal to read?' were, on the whole, consistent with their previous responses.

> You cant explain the reading 'cos he doesn't know what the words are.

But a couple of children were prepared to consider it:

Q: How would we teach a parrot to read?
A: Get a book.
Q: And what would it do?
A: Sort of read it – he would.

Or:

Q: How could we teach it though?
A: If we said 'pretty Polly' – it might do it – mightn't it?

Only one child gave a clear response which related to some internal aspect of reading:

Q: What about those fish over there – do you think we could teach them to read?
A: No
Q: Why not?
A: They don't think – animals.

Can animals write and can they be taught to write?

The children when asked the first question responded, on the whole, with:

> No – because he 'asn't got any hands.

> Because he's got no fingers.

> No they ain't got no hands.

When asked a particular question about whether a dog could write, all the children except one denied it:

I wouldn't know how a dog could hold a pencil.

Because he's only a dog and you can't explain.

No cos he asn't got any hands.

Cos he's a puppy.

Because they don't know what they're doing.

One child was prepared to speculate:

He could have the pen in his mouth – he might.

Which was followed by:

It might know how to write 'cat' or 'dog'.

But the children as a group, were more prepared this time to speculate that a monkey might be able to write.

Q: What sort of things do you think a monkey could write?
A: 'Hayley is my friend.'
Q: How would the monkey know what to write?
A: Well – if it – the monkey – gets a piece of paper he could write it.

The reasoning behind several of the answers was interesting, for example:

Q: How would a monkey know what to put down on the paper?
A: He could write 'monkey'
Q: How would he know how to write 'monkey'?
A: Do a 'm' first
Q: But how would the monkey know that it began with a 'm'?
A: Because he was a monkey!

Summary of nursery children's views

From the interviews it would seem that the nursery child's notion of reading and writing is of them as very physical manifestations – reading is holding something printed and saying the words, and writing is apparently exclusively the ability physically to grasp a pen or pencil and make certain kinds of movements.

The existence of these beliefs should not be surprising. Much of our knowledge is rooted in experience and it is the experience of young children that people speak when they read, and that they hold what they read. Silent reading is eliminated as a type of reading; my three-year-old niece when asked what her mother was doing replied, 'Nothing, she's just looking at the paper'. Young children's experience is of having books read to them, of asking 'What does that say?' and having the reply spoken aloud, and of being told, 'Hold the book properly or I won't be able to read it'.

There were a few examples that hinted at some internal criteria, in particular the girl who said, 'They don't think – animals'. Another child offered, 'You can't explain the reading' and 'Because he's only a dog and you can't explain him', but it is unclear in this example whether the verb 'explain' is simply being used as a form of 'tell'.

Several children felt that animals which had hands might be able to write their name. It would seem that, typically, the children were claiming that ownership and knowledge of the name is an essential part of being the animal.

It would be difficult to see the children's statements as evidence of confusion. It is certainly the case that their views, by adult and conventional standards, are incomplete or even wrong. However, their beliefs are rooted in their experience and are hardly invalid in terms of that experience. The children do not exhibit signs of confusion and are not bothered in the slightest by any inconsistencies in their accounts. On the whole they use their criteria quite consistently.

What these children have said may not explain why Tovey (1976) found children who said reading was 'breathing' or 'spelling' (p. 587), but they might help explain why he found young children who said that reading was 'talking'.

It appears in the end that young children, are not the remotest bit convinced that animals can read or write. They clearly accept traditional rhymes in the spirit in which they were intended. Old Mother Hubbard's dog is just a good joke:

> This wonderful dog was
> Dame Hubbard's delight,
> He could sing, he could dance,
> He could, read, he could write.
> *Mother Goose's Nursery Rhymes*, 1924

References

CANNEY. G. and WINOGRAD, P. (1979) 'Schemata for reading and reading comprehension performance' (Technical report No. 120, Urbana, Illinois: Center for the study of reading).

DOWNING, J. (1969) 'How children think about reading', *The Reading Teacher*, 23(3), pp. 217–30.

JOHNS, J. (1974) 'Concepts of reading among good and poor readers', *Education*, 95, pp. 58–60.

JOHNS. J. (1986) 'Student's perceptions of reading: thirty years of enquiry', pp. 31–40 in Yaden, D. and Templeton, S. (Eds.) *Metalinguistic awareness and beginning reading* (New Hampshire: Heinemann).

JOHNS, J. and ELLIS. D. (1976) 'Reading: children tell it like it is', *Reading World*, 16, pp. 115–28.

JOHNS. J. and JOHNS, A. (1971) 'How do children in the elementary school view the reading process?', *The Michigan Reading Journal* 5, pp. 44–53.

MAYFIELD. M. (1983) 'Code system instruction and kindergarten children's perceptions of the nature and purpose of reading', *Journal of Education Research*, 76(3), pp. 161–68.

REID, J. (1966) 'Learning to think about reading', *Education Research*, 9, 56–62.

ROBINSON, A., LAZARUS, A. and COSTELLO, G. (1983) 'Beginning reader's concepts of reading: an international survey', *Reading-Canada-Lecture*, 2(1), pp. 12–17.

SCOLLON, R. and SCOLLON, S. (1981) *Narrative, literacy and face in interethnic communication* (New Jersey: Ablex).

TOVEY, D. (1976) 'Children's perceptions of reading', *The Reading Teacher*, 29, pp. 536–40.

WEINTRAUB, S. and DENNY, T. (1965) 'What do beginning first-graders say about reading?', *Childhood Education*, 41, pp. 326–27.

Chapter 17

English Language in Scottish Schools: Reading Ability Assessed and Compared to Performance in Other Modes

Mary Neville

In 1984 the English language competence in both oracy and literacy of almost 5,300 Scottish schoolchildren was tested in a national survey. The representative sample was made up of approximately equal-sized groups of lower and upper primary, and lower secondary, pupils. So that valid comparisons could be made between school stages, almost all tests, or a 'core' of their subtests (including the reading tests), were the same for all the ages tested. The overall testing design ensured that children were tested in a minimum of two language modes.

Five tests of reading were used, including the Edinburgh Reading Test *which had been employed in earlier primary surveys. For two other reading comprehension tests (cloze and recall), comparable listening tests were also developed; both these types of test used narrative and expository stimulus passages. Two further tests assessed reading study and reference skills; an attitude to reading questionnaire was also administered to sub-samples of the primary and secondary pupils.*

The results gave comparisons with the earlier surveys and of reading performance at the three stages. Results in other modes showed the need to view reading in a language context rather than as a literacy skill to be taught per se *without consideration of either the pupils' ability to comprehend written language aurally or their level of functioning when using more informal forms of oral language.*

Introduction

In May and June of 1984, at the end of the school year, a nationally representative sample of schoolchildren was, for the first time in Scotland, tested for competence in the English language. This testing programme, funded by the Scottish Education Department, was of both oracy and literacy. The children tested were at three school stages: Primary 4 (aged eight to nine), Primary 7 (aged eleven to twelve) and Secondary 2 (aged thirteen to fourteen). These school stages were chosen because, by Primary 4 (P4), basic literacy should have been achieved; Primary 7 (P7) is the final primary school year; after Secondary 2 (S2) more specialised examination curricula are introduced in the secondary schools.

Our project 'team' comprised two, plus a full-time secretary, and we were given just fifteen months to develop, produce and distribute our tests to the schools by the testing date. We thus had to be very economical of effort and this forced us to produce a tightly structured testing design as well as encouraging us to maximise the use of our testing material. In some earlier testing of reading in the Lothian Region of Scotland, Helen Mulholland (1984), using her own cloze tests, had found that they gave a good spread of scores over an age range as wide as nine to fifteen. (This result was subsequently confirmed by another national Scottish cloze testing exercise (Mulholland, 1986b).) We therefore decided to use the 'Mulholland' cloze tests for all the ages of our sample and, wherever possible, with other tests which we developed ourselves for writing, speaking, listening and also reading we used the same test materials for all ages. Some skills-based tests such as spelling and punctuation, or dictionary and reference skills tests, had 'core' subtests common to all stages, but with an easier first subtest for the youngest children and a harder final test for the two older stages. Thus, performance on at least parts of all but one test could be directly compared for the three stages without the confounding factor of different test content affecting the results.

We also used the same materials for tests in different modes. We had the same cloze tests of reading and of listening and Helen Mulholland carried out exactly the same detailed, in-depth analyses on all the cloze test responses. As well, we used the same task for writing and for speaking and some speaking responses provided the stimulus transcripts for listening tasks. In addition, we devised an integrated test (Neville, 1986) which, by means of one stimulus passage, tested reading, listening, writing and speaking; each child performed one receptive and one productive language task in this test which was also basically the same for all three stages. Because we also wished to compare the performance of the *same* children when they read or listened to (and wrote or spoke about) narrative and expository text, the cloze tests, as well as the integrated test, had narrative and expository (informative) subtests.

Detailed information on all aspects of the testing programme is given in the report to the Scottish Education Department (Neville, 1985) but the characteristics of the sample and testing design can be summarized as follows: total sample size, P4: 1,692; P7: 1,800; S2: 1,774. The schools taking part in the testing programme were a proportional sample, weighted with regard to school roll size and stratified according to educational authority regions. Numbers of schools returning test papers were: P4, 112; P7, 113; S2, 97. The mean sample size in individual schools was, for each stage: 15.1 (P4), 15.9 (P7) and 18.3 (S2), the smaller school-group sizes in the primary schools reflecting the falling rolls in many Scottish primary schools. Within each school, testing was carried out by teachers in subgroups of the school sample in such a way that each child was tested in about half the tests of two language modes. These could be: reading and listening;

reading and writing; listening and writing; speaking and the integrated test (that is, reading/writing, reading/speaking *or* listening/writing, listening/speaking).

Thus, we obtained results which enabled us to make cross-mode comparisons and also to compare performance at different stages. As well, mode-by-stage interaction could also be examined and, for some tests, comparisons of results for narrative and expository material could be made.

This national survey-cum-monitoring testing programme was planned and designed so that it was also really an educational experiment but with very large and nationally representative samples at three school stages – an enviable situation since most researchers normally count themselves fortunate if they can achieve the 'large' sample size of thirty desirable for statistical treatment of experimental results.

Testing reading

The tests

THE EDINBURGH READING TESTS

We had five tests of reading and one of them, the *Edinburgh Reading Test* (ERT) had been used in two earlier P4 and P7 surveys in Scotland. Thus, from the results from this test, we hoped to gain some comparisons of 'standards' in our two primary stages. The ERT is a standardised test of reading comprehension with several subtests testing more specific aspects of comprehension such as vocabulary knowledge, skimming, and comprehension of main ideas. Although there are different 'stages' of this test, the test content, and even the types of subtests, are different for each stage. Thus, although raw scores can be compared within stages for the test results from different test years, comparisons between stages can only be made using the standardised Reading Quotients (RQs).

THE INTEGRATED RECALL TEST

The reading (and listening) sections of the integrated test measured comprehension by means of recall. After reading (or listening to) the stimulus passage, children spontaneously wrote down (or recorded on tape) what they had just read (or heard). Immediately after this writing or speaking, probe comprehension questions on the main points of the passage were asked so that if the children had, for any reason, omitted to record a part of the passage which they comprehended, they could still gain marks by their answers to the probe questions. The final comprehension marks were thus made up of main ideas and details given in the writing or speaking *plus* any extra main points given in answers to the probe questions. For the reading test, a reading rate score of words per minute (wpm) was also obtained by briefly stopping the children half-way through the time allotted for the reading and asking them to mark the word they were reading at that moment. There were two forms of this test, a narrative, and informative (expository); the narrative was a folk tale from the Western Isles and the piece of information was about keeping rats and mice as pets. The readability level of the folk tale was about 8.5 years and, of the information, about 9.5 years. All stages received exactly the same passages but P7 and S2 had a further extra section of information from the 'Rats and Mice' text so that their final scores had to be standardised to make them comparable to the P4 scores. Almost all children took both forms of the test.

CLOZE TESTS AND RESPONSE ANALYSES

The cloze reading tests were in two forms, 1 and 2, and each form comprised a narrative and an informative subtest. Some of our subjects, at each stage, took one form of the test as a reading test and the other form as a listening test and, in that way, we could relate the reading and listening performance of *individuals* on comparable tests; as well, of course, we could compare the reading and listening cloze performance of different *groups* of children on exactly the same forms of the test. Helen Mulholland (1984, 1986a) had used a computer programme to analyse cloze reading responses according to thirteen categories which she had found to be very valuable in diagnosing areas of difficulty in reading comprehension; she also carried out the same type of analyses on all the responses (approximately 64,000) from both the reading and listening cloze tests administered in our survey to all three stages.

READING STUDY SKILLS

Although the tests of comprehension of information could be contrasted with comprehension of narrative, we needed to have a more specific test of reading study skills. We therefore used the chapter about keeping rats and mice as pets from which the recall passages had been taken and made it into a booklet with the text subheadings, the table of contents and the index from the original book. All school stages worked from this 'real book' as they performed four study skills subtests: skimming and scanning (A); reference skills (B) – P4 answered only the first half of these questions; finding the topic sentence in a paragraph (C); distinguishing fact from opinion (D).

DICTIONARY USE TEST

Ron Fyfe and Evelyn Mitchell (1986) had carried out in Aberdeen some interesting work into children's use of dictionaries and we developed a dictionary use test incorporating some of their ideas. We used actual pages from dictionaries to make up booklets for the children to use, but we used different dictionaries for the P4 and for the P7/S2 stages. Thus results from these two tests could not be directly compared although we later realised that we could have used the same dictionary booklets for all stages (perhaps with bigger print for the youngest children) and varied the difficulty of the subtests as we did for the other writing skills tests. In the P4 test there were three subtests: finding the correct meaning (A), finding the correct sub-entry meaning (B), choosing the correct meaning from two or more listed (C). P7/S2 had a further type of subtest (D) where the meaning of the target word was affected by its grammatical function.

ATTITUDE TO READING

It must be clear that, wherever possible, we used work already carried out or in progress in Scotland and so, for testing attitude to reading, we used the questionnaire devised by Jim Ewing and Margaret Johnstone (1981). My research assistant, Sheila Kydd (1986) further developed their ideas to produce attitude to writing, listening and speaking questionnaires; all the attitude tests were administered to local sub-samples of our total survey sample. These questionnaires, as well as the questions for structured interviews which Sheila Kydd also conducted with about half the 'attitude' samples, were the same for all stages.

Reading test results

The interpretation of the results are those of the author and do not necessarily reflect the views of the Scottish Education Department.

The results are given in numerical detail with appropriate statistical treatment in the full report (Neville, 1985) and their implications for teachers are fully explained in Neville (1987). Here only the most important findings will be presented and discussed.

THE EDINBURGH READING TEST

For the *Edinburgh Reading Test*, the results for all stages in 1984 were almost the same as for the standardisation data, that is means ($\overline{X}$s) of about 100 and standard deviations (SDs) of about 15. The exception was a very high SD (18.4) for P4 in 1984 although in the earlier surveys of 1981 and 1978 the SDs had been 15.5 and 15.8 respectively. The subtest raw scores for P4 in 1984 showed that there were proportionately more zeros on all subtests, except one, and also proportionately more very high scores than in the earlier and much larger samples. However, the mean age of the 1984 P4 sample was somewhat lower than the earlier groups and thus the test and the norms were probably not well suited to the 1984 P4 sample. Nevertheless, the increase in the proportions of scores at the extremes of the scale was very marked and this was a pattern which was repeated for P4 on our other tests – and sometimes also for S2. However, for the ERT, the results for S2 were little different from the standardisation data while for P7, too, there seemed to be little change over the three surveys.

THE INTEGRATED RECALL TEST

The means for the main ideas in the integrated recall test are given in Table 17.1. They show that the narrative form of the test was much easier for every stage than the informative. Fig. 17.1 also shows that many more main ideas were given spontaneously for the narrative, particularly for P7 and S2, than for the informative form of the test where, for any stage, about as many main ideas were given in response to questions as were freely written down or recorded on tape. The children seemed to need the help of the probe questions to cue their recall of facts.

Stage	Main Ideas (Means)		Probe (Means)	
	Narrative*	Informative**	Narrative*	Informative**
P4	4.4	2.3	2.8	2.8
P7	7.8	3.6	2.6	4.3
S2	8.3	4.5	2.5	4.6

* *13 main ideas*
** *13 main ideas for P4; 20 main ideas for P7/S2 standardised to a 13 main-idea score.*

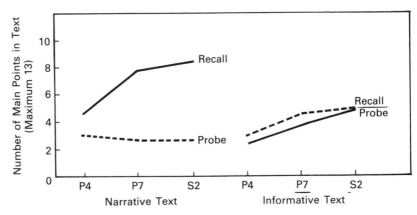

FIGURE 17.1 *Means of main ideas and probe points for integrated recall test plotted for narrative and informative texts*

The mean reading rates (wpm) were, for the narrative: P4, 153; P7, 205; S2, 217. For the informative passage the means were lower: P4, 107; P7, 172; S2, 163; but the SDs for both types of text were very large, ranging from 40 to 75. In fact, although the difficulty level of the passages should not have caused any problems for either the P7 or the S2 children, there were great variations in rate; over half the S2 children, for instance, read the piece of information no faster than, or even much slower than, the rate of speech (that is around 115 wpm).

CLOZE TESTS AMD RESPONSE ANALYSES

The cloze test means plotted in Fig. 17.2, also show the low informative subtest means compared to the narrative although the readability levels of all passages used in these tests ranged between eight and ten years whereas the chronological ages of our subjects ranged between eight and fourteen

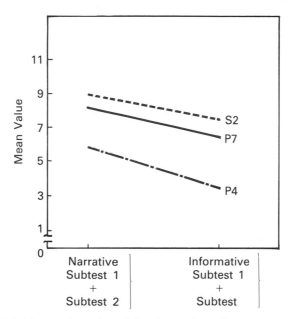

FIGURE 17.2 *Mean values plotted for the reading cloze test (Forms 1 and 2)*

plus years. However, many of the older children did find the narrative passages quite easy, so that the $\overline{X}$ for S2 was 8.9 (max. possible mark 13); the $\overline{X}$ for the informative subtests was 7.5. When all the cloze responses were categorised and the patterns of responses analysed, a picture emerged of the best readers, *at any age*, having a good appreciation of the whole test paragraph as a 'coherent unit', particularly when it was a narrative. The younger children and the poorer readers, at all ages, seemed to deal with text in a much more fragmentary way, making errors that had no connection with the whole passage although they were also more successful with narratives than with expository text. The poorer readers seemed to deal with small sections of the text almost as though they were independent of the rest of the paragraph, perhaps because these readers were not yet fully familiar with the type of language structures employed in the written text.

STUDY SKILLS AND DICTIONARY USE TESTS

The mean values for the study skills subtests (P7/S2 subtest B scores standardised to a 10-point scale) are shown in Fig. 17.3. This figure, as well as Figs. 17.1 and 17.2, shows that, even allowing for the different age difference between P4 and P7 compared to P7 and S2, there was a greater difference in performance between the two primary stages than between P7 and S2. The figure also shows that skimming and scanning and finding

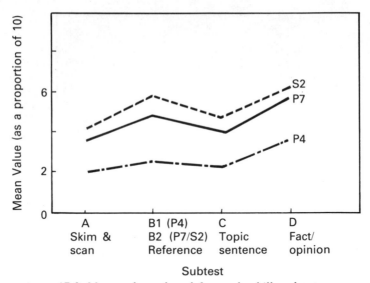

FIGURE 17.3 *Mean values plotted for study skills subtest scores*

the topic sentences were harder subtests *at any age* than the other two subtests. That is if children found the subtests hard (or easy) at P4, they found them about as hard (or easy), relatively, at later ages. The study skills text, again, should have been 'easy' for the older pupils so that, if the pupils had been taught these study skills as they progressed through school (and how to apply them to their reading), the pattern of subskill scores really should not only have improved but, by the higher stages, also have 'flattened out'.

The dictionary use test results for P7 and S2 showed quite a good grasp of the skills tested by the three easiest subtests although many points were lost because the children were very slow at locating information. Subtest D, where grammatical function had to be understood before the correct definition could be identified, was very difficult for both P7 and S2 children. For P4, there was a good spread of marks on all three subtests.

READING DIFFERENCES BETWEEN BOYS AND GIRLS

The performance of boys and girls at each stage on all the tests was compared. For the ERT results there were no sex differences but, for the cloze test, P4 and P7 girls had higher mean scores than boys; for the recall test the girls were better than the boys at P4 and then only for the narrative passage. However, for the dictionary use tests girls at all stages were better than the boys; for the study skills test the same effect was found although, at the S2 stage, the difference between the means of the boys and the girls was not statistically significant. That is, we found an early difference for reading in favour of girls which tended to disappear. But the opposite situation was found for the attitude to reading questionnaire. Attitude was related to performance on the reading tests at all stages but this relationship was more pronounced by the two older stages. The boys' attitudes were more negative than the girls' at all ages but only became significant by P7 and more highly significant by S2. That is the boys' early lack of reading success, relative to the girls, seemed to have a lasting and increasingly negative effect on their attitude to reading even though the differences in ability appeared to be disappearing.

Reading and the other language modes

Reading is concerned with the written form of the English language and this has a style and form rather different from spoken language. In writing, the message must be conveyed wholly by the marks on the page because no paralinguistic aids to meaning are available. Even when conversation is written down, its form must be carefully structured so that meaning can be obtained from written clues alone. Writers have time to think up particularly apposite and perhaps idiosyncratic vocabulary as well as to organise and arrange these words; many a phrase and clause can be elegantly inserted to construct a compound or complex sentence. This produces a language form rather dissimilar to the conversations we conduct with our friends and families. When we designed some of our listening tests we tried to control some of these oracy/literacy differences by using the same written language forms in both oral and written modes and, in the listening tests, by using recordings rather than the face-to-face communication act. Although this produces a somewhat artificial oracy situation it is one which is common enough when pupils listen to a teacher reading, to some types of 'talk' and to certain tape recordings or radio programmes. Our listening cloze and recall tests were controlled in this way in language type and administration although, as already noted, we did have a listening test where the stimuli were recordings of conversational language and also tests of speaking where the children used quite informal and even colloquial language forms with a child partner.

When we compared the results of the cloze and recall reading and listening tests we found similar results. This surprised us since we had expected that the P4 children would, for example, do better at listening than at reading whereas the older children, accustomed to studying information in books would do better at reading expository texts than listening to them. Although these effects were found to some extent for the cloze informative subtests, they were present neither for the cloze narrative nor for any of the recall tests. The quality of the writing and speaking responses in the recall test were also not affected by whether children had read or heard the stimulus passage. What was more, the patterns of cloze responses were almost the same for listening and reading *at all stages* although there was a tendency for rather more careful and more locally constrained language processing in reading than in listening. This is perhaps not surprising given that the readers actually had the test text before them while the listeners had to rely on their memory of what they had heard before they filled a cloze 'gap'. Nevertheless, as Helen Mulholland concluded:

> Overall, it is the similarity, rather than the differences between the two modes that is apparent. It appears that subjects were responding to the message rather than the mode in which it was presented.
>
> (Mulholland in Neville, 1985, p. 208)

The differences between the scores of boys and girls in the recall and cloze listening tests are also of interest. Now it is the boys who are superior to the girls at cloze listening in S2 and, at P4, in listening to the piece of information to be recalled. It is also interesting to note that, in the writing tests, the girls excelled at the *language and style* component of the writing score but not necessarily in the *content* component. When the topic was quite factual or transactional, the content of the boys' writing was often superior to that of the girls'. In speaking, however, few sex differences were found.

Intertest relationships showed that all the tests employing written language forms, in both the oracy and literacy modes, were quite highly related and especially so at P4. *Per contra*, the relationships between content in writing as well as the listening test employing spoken language forms, and the other tests, were generally lower and especially so at S2.

Conclusions

We all glibly say that reading and the other language modes are interdependent, but we rarely spell out the relationships. Our tests seemed to show that reading and writing and the tests of listening employing *written language* forms are so interdependent that, if a text is not understood when it is read, it is generally not more likely to be understood when it is heard. Instances where children's aural comprehension of a written text is much better than their reading comprehension clearly should alert teachers to reading, rather than language, disabilities. But, more often, performance is poor in both oral and written forms of the language of literacy so that reading teaching needs to be supported by listening to 'the language of books' whether this is presented by tape, by reading or telling stories, and even by conversational language which uses grammatically correct and fairly complex language.

It seemed to us that too many children were making only rather slow progress in reading (and writing) in the lower secondary stages and yet their performance on other language tests showed that they had a command of *spoken* language and good ideas for their language work; they simply had not adequately developed the skills of literacy. One of the reasons for this is possibly indicated by the sex differences in literacy that we found. Perhaps, for socio-psychological reasons, girls early begin to read and enjoy 'stories' and so practise reading narratives more than the boys, at the same time also acquiring more knowledge of such writing skills as spelling and punctuation and of the form and style of written language. Although the boys catch up with the girls, at least in reading performance, their attitude towards reading and writing becomes steadily more negative in the older stages.

Perhaps some children, who may be boys, need more chances, from an early stage, to read and write about factual and circumscribed topics which may appeal more to them than reading long narratives and producing 'creative writing' epics. Such a varied reading diet (and more controlled and restricted writing experiences), supported by oracy practice of written language forms, might enable more children to reach a level of literacy at least commensurate with their oral language abilities.

References

EWING, J. and JOHNSTONE, M. (1981) *Attitudes to Reading* (Dundee: Dundee College of Education).

FYFE, R. and MITCHELL, E. (1986) *Reading Strategies and Their Assessment* (Windsor: NFER Nelson).

KYDD, S.C. (1986) 'Attitudes to Language: relationships between attitude and age, sex and language performance', unpublished M.Ed. thesis (Dundee: The University of Dundee).

MULHOLLAND, H. (1984) 'The Interaction with Text of Failing and Normal Readers', unpublished Ph.D. thesis Milton Keynes: The Open University.

MULHOLLAND, H. (1986a) 'Cloze procedure in the diagnostic assessment of reading', in D. Vincent, A.K. Pugh and G. Brooks (Eds) *Assessing Reading* (Basingstoke: Macmillan Education) pp. 81–97.

MULHOLLAND, H. (1986b) 'Cloze Tests of Reading Using Subject Area Texts', Report to the Scottish Education Department, Edinburgh.

NEVILLE, M. (1985) with MULHOLLAND, H. and KYDD, S.C. 'English Language in Scottish Schools: a monitoring project', Report to the Scottish Education Department, Edinburgh.

NEVILLE, M. (1986) 'The Scottish national assessment of reading', in D. Vincent, A.K. Pugh and G. Brooks (Eds) *Assessing Reading* (London: Macmillan Education) pp. 11–28.

NEVILLE, M. (1987) *Assessing and Teaching Language: literacy and oracy in schools* (Basingstoke: Macmillan Education).

Chapter 18

WWB at Sheffield City Polytechnic

Asher Cashdan, Linda Fessler, Patrik Holt, Kathryn Kohl, Vanessa Pittard and Noel Williams

We first heard of Writer's Workbench (WWB) in 1983 when Asher Cashdan met Charles Smith of Colorado State University who was experimenting together with Kate Kiefer with Writer's Workbench with their composition students (Macdonald et al. 1982). Infected with Charles Smith's enthusiasm for the software and its potential for helping students, Asher Cashdan was delighted to discover that two of his colleagues at Sheffield had already decided to move into this field. In a preliminary paper to the 1984 UKRA conference, we discussed WWB and explained our intention to mount a pilot project to evaluate it with British students (Cashdan and Williams, 1984). It was not, however, until the autumn of 1985 that we were able to start our pilot project, having by then secured financial help from both the British Manpower Services Commission and IBM (UK). On completion of the pilot evaluation in spring 1986 we were convinced that this type of writing help had a definite future. We were able to persuade both of our sponsors to give us funding for a more substantial study and this commenced in the spring of 1986 and will be completed by spring 1988. The current project has three major aims:

1. *To establish a working writing laboratory with long-term prospects.*
2. *To mount, customise and further develop WWB.*
3. *To develop our own new software in this field, provisionally entitled Ruskin.*

WWB – what and why

WWB is a suite of programs originally compiled to help technical personnel of the Bell/AT&T Corporation. It still constitutes the most comprehensive software available to help students – and others – to evaluate and improve their written style. IBM's Critique (originally developed under the title 'Epistle') has larger aims and looks like being a very exciting package, but it is not yet available. Meanwhile, the original version 2.0 of WWB which we used in our pilot study has been replaced by version 3.0 and there is also a specially tailored Collegiate version specifically for use in colleges. Although version 3.0 is the most advanced, with some new programs, all the versions are highly similar and carry out much the same functions. There are over thirty programs, some single function and others multiple, which work independently of each other. They range from a spelling checker through readability indices to a number of word lists and some grammatical analyses of style. There is a fairly accurate parser, which enables a number of useful analyses (for example proportions of passives or of different types of sentence openers). WWB has the general advantages of any form of computer-assisted learning. It is student driven, 100 per cent accurate within its own terms, provides quick feedback, carries out elaborate computations quickly and frees tutors to provide more individual and in-depth help to students. Trials at Colorado State showed the system to be highly acceptable to most students, to be efficient and cost effective. Nevertheless, it has a number of limitations which we shall be discussing later in the paper.

The pilot investigation

As we have explained, we carried out a feasibility study with WWB at Sheffield over a six-month period from October 1985 to Easter 1986. The study aimed to investigate both the usefulness and acceptability of WWB in helping students and executives to write more accurate, better structured and more effective reports. Its wider aim was to test market interest in the whole idea of learning to write using computer assistance, not necessarily tied to WWB alone.

Informal trials were carried out with volunteer academics and some undergraduate writers. Following this, a major systematic evaluation of the software was carried out with sixty undergraduates. A short study of literary consistency was also undertaken. Finally, a selection of executives both within and outside Sheffield City Polytechnic constituted a further test group.

Of the five assessment phases we shall describe only one in detail. (The whole project report is available in Cashdan, Holt and Williams, 1986.)

The main student report writing study

The main objectives of the student investigation were:

1. to examine whether feedback from WWB would improve the written style of undergraduates being taught report writing,
2. to examine user acceptance of WWB and its documentation.

We studied two groups, each of thirty first-year undergraduates, taking degrees in Applied Statistics and Systems Modelling. The two degrees have a common first year programme and all students are required to follow a course on human communication.

This course usually involves two written assignments, one being carried out in the autumn term and the other in the spring term. Prior to the first assignment, students are given lectures and handouts on report writing and after the first assignment each student receives individual help.

WWB feedback was inserted into this assessment schedule to examine whether students improved on specifically defined criteria and students also completed questionnaires on the perceived effectiveness of WWB.

The sixty students were initially pseudo-randomly allocated to two groups. Both groups would receive the normal instruction and feedback on their written work. Additionally, one group would receive feedback from WWB after their first assignment. The group not receiving WWB feedback after the first assignment did so after their second assignment.

Each assignment required students to write a 2,000 word report using a specified format. The task in both assignments involved extracting, summarising and effectively presenting information which was provided in a poorly presented and confused state.

Feedback given to students

All sixty students received extensive two to three page feedback on their reports emphasising presentation and structure, but features such as spelling, grammar, length of sentences and paragraphs were also commented on. The thirty students in the extended feedback group were also given Writer's Workbench feedback using thirteen selected programs:

1. Style (a multiple program)
2. Findbe (use of the verb 'to be')
3. Organisation
4. Spelling
5. Punctuation
6. Double words
7. Word choice
8. Split infinitives
9. Abstract words
10. Acronyms
11. Sexist (language)
12. Syllable count (lists of longer words used)
13. Topic (incidence of major words)

The 'Style' program included among its analyses three readability indices, the incidence of simple and compound sentences, types of sentence openers used and the incidence of passives.

In addition to the feedback, students were also provided with an explanatory handbook specifically written to help them understand the WWB output. This was developed from a booklet designed for the same purpose by Smith and Kiefer at Colorado.

After receiving the WWB feedback, all participants were asked to complete a questionnaire which asked about the usefulness, relevance and presentation of both the feedback document and the handbook.

A number of language variables were statistically analysed, including marks awarded, readability scores, length of reports, spelling errors, word length, content words, use of 'to be', use of passive verbs and type of sentence used. The main hypothesis tested was that students receiving WWB feedback would show greater improvement or change as compared to students who received only 'normal' feedback.

In fact, this predicted difference only appeared in the analysis of word choice (number of clumsy phrases). However, this result was not clear cut as it shows that students receiving WWB feedback use clumsy phrases equally frequently in the first and second assignments while the students receiving ordinary feedback became significantly worse in the second assignment! If this is to be interpreted as showing improvement due to WWB then it must be assumed that WWB prevented the students from getting worse! It seems more natural to assume that the effect was spurious.

There *were* a number of significant changes between the first and second assignments:

1. Marks improved overall (57.6–60.4 per cent).
2. Readability level went up (11.6 years–12.3 years).
3. Word length, content word length, and the length of reports overall, all increased.
4. Both sentence length and the number of spelling errors increased slightly.
5. The use of 'to be' increased.
6. The use of compound sentences and auxiliary verbs both diminished.

User reactions

Listed below are the WWB categories used by us ranked in order of perceived usefulness from the most to the least useful. (The scores are on a scale of 1–7, 1 representing least useful and 7 most useful.)

Category	Score	Category	Score
Word choice	5.0	Abstract words	3.7
Spelling	4.9	Syllable count	3.3
Style	4.8	Acronyms	3.0
Topic	4.4	Double words	2.8
Punctuation	4.3	Split infinitives	2.7
Findbe	4.1	Sexist	2.6
Organisation	4.1		

WWB feedback

Students felt that the WWB feedback was fairly useful, clear and relevant. The majority thought that the length of the feedback document was right, although a substantial minority felt it was too long. Similarly, most thought the level of complexity about right, but some felt it was too high.

The handbook

Respondents felt the handbook to be clear and comprehensive, and also very useful and relevant to understanding the feedback. When asked about length, detail and complexity, the majority answered that these were satisfactory.

Excluding categories

When students were given an opportunity to indicate if they thought any categories would be better removed, the following main results emerged:

	N		N
Sexist	11	Double words	7
Findbe	10	Syllable count	6
Split infinitives	9	Acronyms	5
N = number of respondents			

Conclusion

Overall, the feedback from WWB was not extensively used by students to improve their written style, apart from word choice which was also seen as the most useful category of feedback. The question of why the students paid such limited attention to the stylistic feedback merits some attention and possible answers may lie in the nature of our assessments and the method by which the WWB feedback was administered. Our main criteria for awarding high marks stress format and layout rather than written style. In retrospect, the study expected too much from students in terms of being able to assimilate and transfer learning on the basis of feedback on one assignment only. Making students re-write their assignments using WWB feedback would seem a more satisfactory arrangement. However, it is clear from the responses to the user questionnaire that students perceived WWB to be a useful tool in improving their written communication skills.

WWB and its problems

For the pilot study, we typed in the students' reports for them. In computer jargon, they were batch processed. We did this for two reasons, both of which are highly significant. First, we found that the analysis took a great deal of time, unless one was running WWB on a large mainframe. The programs run under the Unix operating system, which is a 'greedy' one, and it was quite a technical triumph for us to succeed in mounting and running it efficiently on an IBM PC-XT. However, that meant waiting over twenty minutes for a 2,000 word report to be analysed and the computer printout to appear. Second, most British students do not type well. So it would have taken the students a great deal of time and effort to produce their own reports on a machine. Batch processing, in the sense in which we are using the term, would not be a problem for the average executive or academic, if they have a secretary to type in their work, or if they acquire effective keyboard skills. Nevertheless, WWB could hardly be described as interactive. However, we are working on these points, as will be described later.

More significantly, WWB is a post-writing aid only, offering no help in composition or during the act of writing. The output is unfriendly; we soon realised why the Colorado group had designed a manual to use alongside the printout. One could, of course, incorporate more advice and explanation on the printout itself, but this would be cumbersome and repetitive.

In the learning situation, not many students would be able to customise their own analyses, an aspect of WWB that we have not fully exploited, but which certainly has considerable potential. What it means is that one can add words to the spelling dictionary and to the lists of jargon and cliched expressions. In everyday executive use such features would be more helpful.

WWB also requires the commitment to revise which may not suit many people's work patterns. It seems clear to us that none of these criticisms mean that one should give up the whole enterprise, but rather that there are some pitfalls. At present, WWB seems to us highly useful as part of major office/text systems such as IBM's PROFS. Otherwise, smaller, less comprehensive systems such as Rightwriter (1985) might suit the ordinary user rather better. However, as we shall see later, this is a fast changing field.

Help at different points in the writing process

Marcus and Blau (1983) note that professional writers devote 85 per cent of their total writing time to pre-writing, 1 per cent to actual writing of anything like finished copy, and 14 per cent to re-writing. Students, and writers in the workplace, typically spend little or no time pre-writing and re-writing, but rather churn out one version which they may edit perfunctorily during the typing or re-copying stage. However, post-writing packages such as *Writer's Workbench* and *Rightwriter* may, if used conscientiously over time, help students to hone their editing skills and improve the quality of their finished work through re-writing.

However, many people feel that writers who switch to word processors alter their writing behaviour and actually begin to experience writing *as a process.* The mobility of text, the immediacy of the transfer from thought to printed text (on screen or hard copy), the ease of text editing, beginning anew and saving scraps of text may encourage writers to redefine their writing style.

One study, by John Gould (noted in Marcus and Blau, 1983), found that writers who use word processors actually spent 50 per cent *more* time composing than writers who wrote by hand, but less time from start to finish, if typing of final hand-written copy was included. One reason given for the change was that those writing on a word processor enjoyed what they were doing and were in fact unaware that they spent longer composing by word processor. The quality of the work produced by the two modes of writing was not noticeably different; what was significant was the change in behaviour and attitude of the writers using word processors.

Pre-writing software engages writers in various 'getting started' exercises not unlike those which teachers, or indeed writers themselves, may use. These may include brainstorming (whether for writing topics or points related to an already selected topic); 'free writing' (writing as quickly as possible in a stream-of-consciousness fashion in an attempt to 'warm up' to the writing task); and questioning strategies, which serve to focus the writer's thoughts, without inhibiting a broad approach to the subject matter.

William Wresch's *Writer's Helper* (1985) is such a pre-writing package. It includes a text analyser or post-writing package but merits a mention here especially for its pre-writing section, entitled 'Find and analyse a subject'. Writers engage in many activities designed to help them locate and refine a topic. Interesting aspects include a free-writing exercise in which the program judges the user's typing speed and inserts dots if he or she pauses.

Again, 'Crazy Contrasts' asks students to consider their topics in relation to unrelated subjects. Our initial scrutiny of *Writer's Helper* casts doubts on the usefulness of comparing, for example, image clusters in Sylvia Plath's poetry to a ski lift or leftover meatloaf! But Wresch is inviting students to widen their perspective and think creatively, which is praiseworthy.

Other exercises aim to help students to organise their thoughts into categories, 'trees', outlines and, finally, the old American freshman composition stand-by, the five-paragraph theme.

One pre-writing technique which seems particularly interesting is called 'invisible writing', and is featured in a package from UCLA, called *HBJ Writer* (Herrard, 1986). As with free writing, students write as quickly and continuously as possible, but with invisible writing the screen stays blank until they have typed at least 100 words. This may discourage writers from editing prematurely, and in turn open them up to the possibilities of their subject and to the utility of drafting.

Other pre-writing and post-writing software tools are discussed in a useful research report by Hazen *et al.*, 1986.

Conclusion

As part of our IBM funded project we now have a fully equipped Writing Laboratory both for studying the writing process and for everyday student use. We are convinced that computer software can play an important role in teaching students and in helping working professionals. But we need even better software and well presented, 'friendly' advice. Our current work includes improving WWB, particularly on the presentational side, and creating our own software, based on new principles. We hope to report on the progress of these studies at later UKRA Conferences.

References

CASHDAN, A. and WILLIAMS, N. (1984) 'Teaching written style by computer', *Annual Conference of the United Kingdom Reading Association*.

CASHDAN, A., HOLT, P. and WILLIAMS, N. (1986) 'Report to the Manpower Services Commission on a Pilot Investigation into the Assessment of Written Style by Computer' (Manpower Services Commission, Moorfoot, Sheffield).

HARRIS, J. and WILKINSON, J. (1986) *Reading Children's Writing: A Linguistic View* (London: Allen and Unwin).

HAZEN, M., EICHELBERGER, J., KILLION, S. and O'SHIELDS, M.E. (1986) 'Report on the Writer's Workbench and other Writing Tools (University of North Carolina).

HERRARD, R. (1986) *HBJ Writer* (New York: Harcourt Brace Jovanovich).

MACDONALD, M.H., FRASE, L.T., GINGRICH, P.S. and KEENAN, S.A. (1982) In, L.T. Frase (ed) Special Issue: 'The Psychology of Writing', *Educational Psychologist*, 17, pp. 172–9.

MARCUS, S. and BLAU, S. (1983) 'Not seeing is believing: invisible writing with computers', *Educational Technology*, April, pp. 12–15.

RIGHTWRITER (1985) (RightSoft Inc.).

SMITH, C.R. and KIEFER, K.E. (1982) *Manual for Writing with Computer Assistance* (Department of English, Colorado University).

WRESCH, W. (1985) *Writer's Helper* (Conduit: University of Iowa).

The work reported in this paper is supported by the British Manpower Services Commission and by IBM (UK).

Chapter 19

New Directions in the Study of Reading

Margaret M. Clark

Fifteen years ago there was already a growing awareness of the skills brought by a child to the task of learning to read. Evidence from a study of young children who could already read with understanding and enjoyment on entry to school has added further insights, as have the studies of young pre-school children's attempts to understand the print in their environment. The importance of experience of written language in a variety of contexts to children's developing competence in reading and writing is increasingly apparent. It is therefore important that any assessment of children's progress should not prevent such experiences. 'Back to the basics' must not prevent the insights developed over the past fifteen years leading to 'new directions in the study of reading'.

Introduction

Fifteen years ago as President of UKRA I organised the Annual Conference in Hamilton College of Education in 1972. The title of that conference, 'Reading and Related Skills', already reflected a growing awareness of the need to consider in any study of reading, 'the language prerequisites for reading' and the contribution of the homes of many children both pre-school and out of school to the success of their children in literacy learning. In my introductory paper to the proceedings (Clark, 1973) I stressed a number of features whose importance I felt were increasingly being appreciated, some to which I felt too little attention was being paid – and still others which were being neglected. In doing so I cited the then recently published book of Frank Smith, *Understanding Reading* (Smith, 1971). He stressed that two things are noteworthy about the child on entry to school. One of these is the impressive array of skills which the child, as a user of language, brings to the situation of learning to read. The other is how little credit the child is given for these. In a more recent publication entitled *Awakening to Literacy* more recent evidence is presented (Goelman, Oberg and Smith, 1984) and in *New Directions in the Study of Reading* (Clark, 1985).

Young fluent readers

Already by 1972 I was able to cite some preliminary evidence from my study of young children who were reading fluently with understanding and enjoyment on entry to school at five years of age. That study was of thirty-two young children, their strengths, and weaknesses, in spite of which they had learnt to read. Their homes provided dynamic interactions with adults around them in a warm supportive environment. I felt, and still feel, such studies contain many lessons for the understanding of all children and ways of improving the teaching of reading and related skills. The study published in 1976 as *Young Fluent Readers* (Clark, 1976) showed how intimately these children's reading progress was bound up with their language learning, and their active and creative attempts to make sense of their environment. That print was an interesting aspect was apparent, whether in books, on signs, on car numbers – or on television. The parents had not 'taught' these children to read in any didactic sense. Indeed, most were embarrassed by their childen's precocious interest and development which was often viewed with suspicion by those around them, including the children's teachers.

The children's strengths were predominantly understanding and processing of language and were less evident in visual perception tasks unrelated to language and their motor coordination. Some of the children were indeed not even average in motor coordination. A warning about regarding such aspects of development as necessary precursors to acquisition of reading skill was sounded. Predictions of failure based on tests of reading readiness of which motor coordination and visual recognition tasks were a major component could lead, I suggested, to the embarrassing situation of identifying as a potential failure a child who is already a highly successful reader! This might indeed still happen, as I discovered recently.

That study has been fully reported elsewhere (Clark,1976) and more recently aspects of the children's spelling have been further analysed, showing the children's developing awareness of which words they could and couldn't spell and the approximation to the probabilities of English in their attempts (Clark, 1984).

The importance of the parents, often father as well as mother, to the children's success was clear. Among these children were some from non-professional homes and indeed with characteristics which in other studies had been too readily identified with subsequent failures, or where any success had been attributed only to the school. Some of the children were from so-called working-class homes, and indeed homes with few books and/or where the parents themselves had not been successful at school. The common feature was the dynamic interactive nature of the children's involvement with adults. Clearly this was not sufficient explanation for the children's precocious development and some of the explanation lies also in the children's own strengths, precocity of development and ability to concentrate.

The children could read, and did read widely and for enjoyment at five years of age. They read a variety of materials, some of which might have been read to them. They thus had freedom to read or reread favourite stories and other material they sought out themselves, for example non-fiction and other sources of information. Many of these children read silently and did not appear to have gone through a stage of oral reading. Their understanding of print became apparent to the adults only gradually as a result of their responses to the print in their environment. One example was the child who on seeing on a bus a notice which read 'Friday night is danger night' commented to his father:

> It's a good thing it's Saturday!

The relationship of reading development to competence in other aspects of literacy development, including spelling, was observed. Not that they could already spell all the words in English that they required. They already knew what they did know, and did not know, and were sensitive to the likely alternatives for words they did not know. This meant that their errors were often readable because of their approximation to English. These children were also showing their sensitivity to other aspects of written language, for example in retelling their favourite stories in ways that captured the style of the author. By seven years of age their attempts at written language were creative and showed clearly the influence of their wide reading. Their style was far removed from the 'speech written down' of many young children, or even older backward readers.

Developing awareness of print

In the past fifteen years further insights have been developed from case studies of a number of young pre-school children and their developing awareness of print. Also shown has been the richness of the dialogue which surrounded story reading in the home and the children's own attempts at written representations of print. Two interesting examples of such studies are those by Payton of her daughter Cecilia (Payton, 1984) and Butler (1975) of her multiply-handicapped granddaughter Cushla whose pre-school development was greatly enriched by the story-reading sessions she shared with her parents:

> It seems clear that access to a wealth of words and pictures, in a setting of consistent love and support has contributed enormously to her cognitive development in general and her language development in particular . . . But perhaps, most of all, Cushla's books have surrounded her with friends; with people and warmth and colour during the days when her life was lived in almost constant pain and frustration.
>
> (Butler, 1975, p. 102)

Bissex studied her son Paul's earliest attempts at written communication and their increasing approximation to correct written English (Bissex, 1980, 1984).

Before entry to school many children are already framing and testing hypotheses about the world of print around them. They are actively seeking for meaning in an environment which is print filled. They gradually learn that drawing and writing are different. Even in their 'pretend' writing they represent some of the conventions of print, including the linear representations, the need for a finite number of different symbols for words and that numbers and letters have different functions. They are no different from adults in sometimes framing hypotheses and confirming them from too little evidence, or in their reluctance to relinquish a hypothesis on receiving the first contradictory information. Studies such as those by Ferreiro (1982 and 1985) of attempts at representation of written language, its features and its functions, based on careful observation of young children, can give the adults insights into the stage of development of children's understanding. The adults are then able to present situations and offer explanations appropriate to the stage of development.

Learning to read and write

We are inclined to assume that children should enter school ready to read, but not too ready. In Britain we tend to assume that five years of age is the appropriate age for starting school, and reading. Furthermore it is often suggested that teachers of pre-school children should not interfere in what has been seen as the prerogative of the 'real' school. It is ironic therefore that children should not, in many parts of England particularly, be starting school at the beginning of the school year in which they will be five years of age. Thus some children will be only four years of age on entry. When this is the case, in many instances there is very quickly a start to the more formalised teaching of reading and writing, including handwriting; that is with children previously thought to be too immature!

Likewise so often in Britain it is assumed that children should be able to read by seven years of age, otherwise they are likely to suffer from long-term failure. In the light of evidence from countries where children do not even start school until seven years of age it is perhaps pertinent to question whether it is necessary and valuable to embark on the formal processes of learning to read and write so soon, to regard delay as dangerous. Furthermore we should question whether and why failure to learn to read by seven years of age should lead to long-term educational failure. Such may not be inevitable but a consequence of the educational structure of our system and its expectations.

Testing of reading progress

To revert to 1972 and the paper at the conference referred to earlier, note was made of the recommendations of a Government Committee published in that year, namely the Tizard Report (DES, 1972). That report on *Specific Reading Difficulties* recommended screening of all children for reading difficulty at seven years of age, or the end of the infant department. The aim was, however, highly practical as a way of screening to monitor closely any children at risk of more permanent difficulties and to lead to action to help such children. Observation and monitoring of progress by teachers can and should be an important aspect of teaching. Time spent on testing unless it can, and does, lead to more sensitive teaching appropriate to the developmental needs of the children is a waste of resources. Testing 'products' in formal reading and writing tests at seven years of age for the purpose of comparisons of standards between children and schools is dangerous as well as unprofitable. Use of resources in the development of such tests, whether group or individual, in their administration and scoring, is unlikely to produce information which is or even can be used diagnostically. It is sad if, fifteen years after warnings on the use of so called 'standardised' tests on young children, scarce resources which could more profitably be employed in observation and recording children's progress appropriately and in a variety of settings, on a range of tasks related to literacy, are used for such a purpose. It is ironic that adequate resources were not made available to implement the recommendations of the Tizard report, or indeed those of the Bullock Committee, which held its first meeting in 1972 and reported in 1975 (DES, 1975).

Any attempt to assess children's attainments or the competence of teachers from assessments on a national test at seven years of age is misguided. Teacher competence assessed by this crude measure is almost like reverting to 'payment by results', as if the task of teaching all young children was comparably easy or difficult irrespective of their stage of development and home support towards literacy. Such a policy flies in the face of fifteen years of accumulating evidence on the importance of a variety of contexts to make an assessment of the competence of young children. Equally important is the need for a variety of language experiences to the development of literacy. Early standardised assessment is more likely to result in treating children on entry to school as homogeneous in their level of attainment and needs according to age. The focus is likely to be excessively on the 'features' of print, accurate reading of words and sentences, neat formulation of letters and correct spelling of words as first steps to literacy and an anxiety to be *seen to be teaching the basics* to all children as soon as possible.

The features and functions of print

The features of print *are* important if a person is to be functionally literate, able to read for a variety of purposes and to communicate in writing precisely, effectively and creatively. There is already evidence on the relationship between story reading pre-school to children and their later attainment. A study of the complexity of language, richness of vocabulary and sequential nature of the themes and implicit meanings in the best and most popular stories for young children shows just why reading and rereading of such stories does give many children such a 'head start' and creative experience from which to develop literacy. Analysis of children's retelling to others, who do not know the story, of short well-written stories, with fun in the plot and the language, shows just how sensitive young children can become to the patterns of written language. Such experiences help children to grasp the themes and gradually the styles of written language. Some children, even quite young children, can capture such language in their written attempts also when the pressures to spell correctly or write a certain amount are removed. A rich variety of such experiences can also stimulate many children to create their own stories on similar themes. Some older children categorised as reading failures do have difficulties specific to reading and/or writing. Others have problems which are much more far-reaching. Some have not grasped the functions of written language. Others cannot cope with processing with understanding written language even when presented orally. They may fail to identify the theme, to separate the essential from the detail. If children are to become functionally literate, to listen thoughtfully, to read with understanding and enjoyment for a variety of purposes, and to write effectively and creatively, then not only the written but the spoken word has an important part to play. The importance of a variety of 'creative contexts' for the successful development of literacy is becoming increasingly clear.

Conclusions

Children must be shown from the earliest stages the 'functions' of reading and writing. This cannot be left until they have been taught its 'features', otherwise some may never appreciate its functions – and will have a very confused grasp of its features. Let us ensure that any 'new directions in the study of reading' do take account of the increasing evidence that children can be active and creative in their search for meaning – if the situations we provide enable them to engage in such explorations. It is to be hoped that any move towards 'the basics', is not 'back to the basics' if by that we risk ignoring the new insights we can utilise and new directions we can explore in what is an increasingly print-filled environment.

References

BISSEX, G.L. (1980), *Gnys at Wrk: A Child Learns to Read and Write* (Cambridge, Mass: Harvard University Press).

BISSEX, G.L. (1984) 'The Child as Teacher', in H. Goelman, A. Oberg and F. Smith (Eds), *Awakening to Literacy* (London: Heinemann), pp. 87–101.

BUTLER, D. (1975) *Cushla and her Books* (Sevenoaks: Hodder and Stoughton).

CLARK, M.M. (1973) The teaching of reading and related skills in M.M. Clark and A. Milne (Eds) *Reading and Related Skills*, (London: Ward Lock), pp. 3–13.

CLARK, M.M. (1976) *Young Fluent Readers* (London: Heinemann).

CLARK, M.M. (1984) 'Literacy at Home and at School: Insights from a Study of Young Fluent Readers' in H. Goelman, A. Oberg and F. Smith (Eds) *Awakening to Literacy* (London: Heinemann), pp. 122–30.

CLARK, M.M. (Ed) (1985) *New Directions in the Study of Reading* (London: Falmer Press).

DES (1972) *Children with Specific Reading Difficulties* (London: HMSO) (The Tizard Report).

DES (1975) *A Language for Life* (London: HMSO) (The Bullock Report).

FERREIRO. E. and TEBEROSKY. A. (1982) *Literacy Before Schooling* (London: Heinemann) (UK translation 1983).

FERREIRO, E. (1985) 'The relationship between oral and written language: The Children's Viewpoints' in M.M. Clark (Ed) *New Directions in the Study of Reading* (London: Falmer Press) pp. 83–94.

GOELMAN. H., OBERG. A. and SMITH. F. (Eds) (1984) *Awakening to Literacy* (London: Heinemann).

PAYTON, S. (1984) *Developing Awareness of Print*, Educational Review, Offset Publication No. 2. (Available from Faculty of Education, University of Birmingham, England B15 2TT).

SMITH, F. (1971) *Understanding Reading* (New York: Holt, Rinehart and Winston).

Chapter 20

Watching the 'p's and 'q's

Doug Dennis

This paper seeks to identify some classroom implications of reports and research in reading and language since the publication of the 'Bullock' Report. It adopts the view that children will learn most effectively where there is a clear and important (to them) purpose for that learning. It also assumes that children will do their best to make sense of a learning situation in the light of their knowledge and experience. The teacher's role is seen as capitalising on what the child brings to the learning situation and not getting in the way of learning by over-insistence on teaching.

I have interpreted my title in terms of the relationship between research findings and the things we say and do in our teaching of reading. Reading has always been one of the most researched (and most tested) areas of the curriculum and yet there is a recurring cycle of anxiety, in political circles at least, about standards of reading teaching in British schools.

A recent diatribe in the educational press prompted an examination of the history of reading research (Venezky, 1984), and this, in turn, revealed a comment of considerable moment. Venezky, discussing the current interest in Huey's 1908 text, *The Psychology and Pedagogy of Reading*, notes the appropriateness of Kolers' remarks introducing the 1968 reissue: 'remarkably little empirical information has been added to what Huey knew, although some of the phenomena have been measured more precisely' (p. xiv).

In practical terms this raises the questions whether the researchers are spending much of their time reinventing the wheel; and whether the recurring anxieties about reading relate more to the fact that teachers' classroom activities in reading do not reflect the findings of the researchers. The excellent and often recurring ideas to be found in the government's reports on education over the last fifty years bear testimony to the degree of inertia within the system.

It is my intention to focus on British research in this paper because there are, to my mind, significant differences between the UK and both America and Australia which would make one wary of considering an instant application of the findings of research from these sources to British classrooms. Nevertheless it is encouraging to be able to find parallels between all the major points of the US Federal Report: *Becoming a Nation of Readers* (Anderson, 1985) and the findings of research conducted in the UK since the *Bullock Report* (1975).

First, it seems important to be clear what we are talking about when we refer to 'reading', and to whether a child can or cannot 'read'. Bullock (1975, para 6.5) offered an interesting trio of definitions which pointed up very nicely the difference between what most of us say we are teaching, and what most of us still test as evidence of reading progress. If we test only word recognition then we have collected no evidence with regard to either understanding or the reader's response, yet this lack of compatibility between word and deed does not appear to trouble the majority who continue to collect reading ages from word recognition tests. Where an explanation is thought necessary it usually relates either to the demands of the headteacher, or the parents – or perhaps both. I find it unprofessional to agree to continue supplying information about children's progress which may be inappropriate, incomplete or even inaccurate.

Huey (1908) had an appropriate comment:

> Reading as a school exercise has almost always been thought of as reading aloud, in spite of the obvious fact that reading in actual life is to be mainly silent reading. The consequent attention to reading as an exercise in speaking, . . . has been heavily at the expense of reading as the art of thought-getting and thought manipulation.
>
> (p. 359)

which fits excellently with the findings of the Vera Southgate (1981) study and her analysis of the reading lesson in which the teachers work to capacity and the children hardly work at all. Her analysis showed that teachers spent an average of thirty seconds of time solely devoted to one child and comments:

> No effective teaching or help can be given in such a short time, particularly when the teacher is constantly being interrupted by other children asking for help or advice, or is dealing with other kinds of interruption. Nor is merely prompting the child when he fails to read a word an effective teaching technique.
>
> (p. 320)

These comments by Southgate also echo one of the findings of the Morris (1966) survey in Kent, more recently reinforced as an important variable in pupil progress by Bennett (1976), namely 'time on task' as opposed to 'time allocated'. The significance of time devoted to a particular activity seems very likely to increase as central control of the curriculum decreases the options available to schools and individual teachers. Scrutiny of the data relating to lengths of school days reported by HMI reveals some interesting facts, for example in secondary schools the difference between the shortest school day and the longest amounted to almost four terms of extra schooling between the ages of eleven and sixteen; in primary schools if the teachers divide their time entirely into individual instruction (assuming classes of thirty) they have a total of approximately four weeks with each child between the ages of five and eleven. Two things seem to emerge for urgent consideration: the amount of time available and its effect on teaching and learning; and the importance for the child of incidental learning – one definition of subnormality is failure to profit from incidental learning opportunities.

Increasingly the importance of the interaction between reading, writing, talking and listening is being emphasised in studies of children's progress or lack of it, and this seems to be another suitable area to examine. The natural progression of the four aspects of language is listening, speaking, reading, writing and one would normally expect children's performance in listening and speaking to be in advance of their competence at reading and writing. The reading–writing relationship between author and reader is based upon a presumption that they hold a body of language in common – it is this commonality which enables meaning to be given and received. To ensure that this continues to be the case, thus allowing for successful and meaningful reading experiences, it is essential that language development in terms of listening and speaking is systematically maintained at a level in advance of that which may be required by any written text encountered. This is particularly important in the early secondary years when pupils are being introduced to a wide range of specialist subject texts.

At the earlier phase the children cannot bring to bear on a decoding problem strategies beyond a simple sound to symbol matching if the word being studied is one they do not know and won't recognise, nor will they be able to check their performance against previous experience. This is a major problem if our aim is to make children independent readers as soon as possible. In the look and say approach the child either recognises the word or asks the teacher. Children always seek to make sense of a situation and interpret on the basis of the best evidence available to them at the time; sometimes this leads to miscues and amusing misinterpretations which can contain an interesting sidelight on the school system.

For example:

Age 7   'My friend says my dad is a red but he isn't he's a bus driver.'

Age 8   'To have a baby the mother has to lay an egg then the mail cracks it.'

Age 7   'I nearly know how to have babies but we don't do it till next term.'

Age 16   'Red Indian's shoes are called Mackesons.'

Age 16   'Rivers are essential to keep sea level in its right place.'

The work of Wells (1985) and Tizard and Hughes (1984) among others has emphasised the social nature and importance of language to young children. What is also clear is that children learn rather than are taught. What characterises this early learning is its purposefulness; in other words language is used as a means to achieve some non-linguistic end, it is a vehicle for social interaction. The adults observed in these studies, chiefly parents, facilitated but rarely instructed children in their attempts to create and understand meanings. Naturally this leads to an unsystematic, perhaps spasmodic, development since skills and information are acquired as and when the need arises to achieve some other purpose. What is clear is that children's learning is spectacularly successful, and it is not achieved via a series of carefully presented skill hierarchies.

One classroom lesson we can derive from this is that where there is a powerful external reason for acquiring some knowledge (skill or information) children will acquire it to achieve the external purpose. This is a much more powerful motivation than learning on the basis of possible future utility. Some impressive examples of this kind of motivation are given by Lorac and Weiss (1981) and by Bacon and Porter (1987). Other points relating to classroom implications can best be made by a series of contrasts.

At home	*At school*
The child initiates learning and language activities	The teacher initiates activities
The child is an equal partner in decision making	The programme is predetermined
Literacy activities are grounded in the child's own experience	Activities are not grounded in experience and consequently often lack meaning
Constant supportive feedback produces feelings of confidence	The focus is on identification and correction of errors, which produces feelings of inadequacy

Clearly the school cannot hope to emulate the one-to-one relationship which characterises young children's learning at home; however, this does not mean that it is impossible to allow the child to initiate or to participate in decision making. Nor does it allow for the most basic rule of teaching – 'Start where the children are' – to be ignored.

Children, then, bring with them to school a range of knowledge, skill and experience in the areas of listening, talking, reading and writing. The problem lies in the fact that every child's combination of experiences will be unique and different, thus a major task initially is to establish exactly what each child's starting point is. The work of Clark (1976), Reid (1966), Downing (1969, 1979), Clay (1972, 1979) has served to identify differences between young fluent readers and others, and also drawn attention to what gaps there might be in a beginning reader's knowledge about the nature of print and of books. The Cognitive Clarity Theory (Downing, 1979) elaborates the idea that children's learning will be more effective if they know exactly what it is they are trying to do and why. This makes it all the more surprising that so many reading schemes appear to work from the premise that the child brings nothing to the task of learning to read, and so must be taught an initial sight vocabulary. This vocabulary may well be totally divorced from the child's background, and its presentation in the early reading books is certainly divorced from the levels of language competence which children of five have reached. The naming or labelling behaviour required by the early scheme books is far more typical of a child of between fifteen and eighteen months than of a five year old. Thus it is not meaningful and does not permit the child to utilise skill and experience in responding. This can be demonstrated (Fig. 20.1) by reference to the idea that children respond to the gestalt or whole shape of the word initially and not to its component parts.

The fact that (a) is relatively easy to read while (b) is apparently impossible, relates not to the difficulty of the individual words involved but to the meaningfulness of the two selections. Because (a) has continuity and meaning it is possible to behave towards it in an intelligent way bringing experience and reasoning to bear on the decoding problem; (b) lacks these qualities so the child is not in a position to use his previous knowledge to help him. The implication here is clear – if you want children to respond sensibly to tasks, give them sensible tasks to respond to. Of course, if all you want is for children to indicate their mastery of sight words then the significance of the exercise in Fig. 20.1 is lost.

If we accept that children bring with them to the task of learning to read considerable experience of language gained through listening and talking, that is both reception and production of language, evidence from studies of early language development shows that children attempt from an early age to identify and apply rules to their utterances. It seems reasonable, therefore, to assume that children might adopt this approach towards reading. If this is the case they will have:

1. Syntactical rules in the mind for combining words into a basic sentence frame.
2. Transformational rules in the mind for converting the basic frame into its final form.
3. Semantic rules in the mind for interpreting the meaning of the sentences.
4. Phonological rules in the mind for converting the thought into the sounds of language.

(a)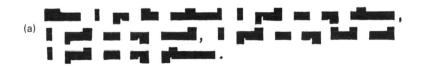

(b)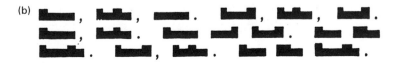

FIGURE 20.1

This will lead them to process text in the light of their existing understandings. A model of this processing might be as in Fig. 20.2. It would, for example, explain the difference in response to (a) and (b) in Fig. 20.1.

The importance of assuming an information processing model rather than a 'whole word recognition' model or a 'phonic word construction' model is further emphasised by the work on cohesion (Halliday and Hasan, 1976;

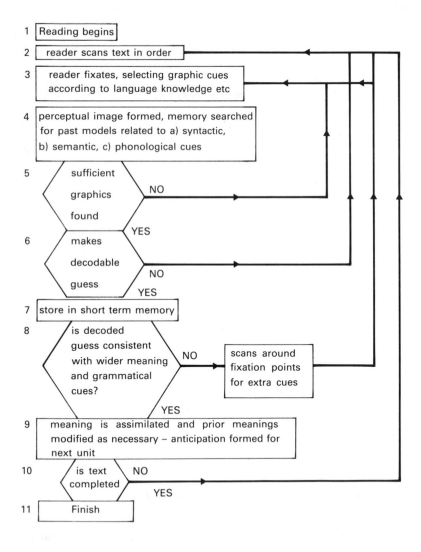

FIGURE 20.2 *Model of processing text*

Chapman, 1983) which has shown the importance for comprehension of selecting units greater than the sentence or even the paragraph. Without this wider canvas the importance and meaning of references and connectives cannot be properly grasped. This is a crucial awareness for children at the secondary stage as each subject in the curriculum has its own characteristic set of connectives together with its favoured sentence structures and styles of reference. The young reader needs to come to terms with these in order to understand the discipline of the various subjects and thus be able to think and write like a geographer or historian or scientist by selecting and presenting ideas and evidence appropriately.

This implies a greater depth of comprehension than is normally necessary to succeed in school comprehension exercises. The work of Lunzer and Gardner (1979, 1984) and Davies and Greene (1984) has shown the importance of encouraging reflection upon what has been read – particularly through small group discussion to allow the possibility of alternative interpretations, and of requiring the child to re-present information in some alternative form to demonstrate comprehension. The Directed Activities Related to Text (DARTS) described by Lunzer and Gardner, Davies and Greene (1984) represent a very substantial advance on the more typical textbook exercise (Fig. 20.3) which produces information about knowledge of sentence structure rather than knowledge of word meanings.

Read the following sentence carefully, then answer the questions.

One grod he drakened this brod and did not shak that the knronit cha in the glend nird griking.

What did he do?
When did it happen?
What did he draken?
Where was the knronit?
What was the knronit?
What did he not shak?
Who was griking?

Even the stricture to 'answer in a sentence' does not require any higher level of 'understanding' to respond.

FIGURE 20.3 *Typical textbook exercise*

Conclusion

If we are to concentrate on reading 'as the art of thought-getting and thought manipulation' (Huey, 1908 p. 359) then we must ensure that the activities we undertake with our young readers will actually lead to achievement of the aims we have set for them by allowing them to learn.

NOTE   Text of Fig. 20.1:
(a) When I go to school I put on my shoes, I put on my coat, I put on my hat and I put on my gloves.
(b) Come, John, come. Look, John, look. Come, John. Come and look. See the boats. Look, John. See the boats.

References

ANDERSON, R.C. (Chmn) (1985) *Becoming a Nation of Readers* (Washington, D.C.: The National Institute of Education).

BACON R. and PORTER, A. (1987) 'Parents of the Future' in Smith P. *Parents and Teachers Together* (London: Macmillan).

BENNETT, N. (1976) *Teaching Styles and Pupil Progress* (London: Open Books).

BULLOCK, SIR. A. (Chmn) (1975) *A Language for Life* (London: HMSO).

CHAPMAN, L.J. (1983) *Reading Development Cohesion* (London: Heinemann).

CLARK, M. (1976) *Young Fluent Readers: What Can They Teach Us?* (London: Heinemann).

CLAY, M. (1972) *Sand* (London: Heinemann).

CLAY, M. (1979a) *Stones* (London: Heinemann).

CLAY, M. (1979b) *The Early Detection of Reading Difficulties* (London: Heinemann).

DAVIES, F. and GREENE, T. (1984) *Reading for Learning in the Sciences* (Edinburgh: Oliver and Boyd).

DOWNING, J. (1969) 'How Children think about Reading', *The Reading Teacher*, 23, iii, pp. 217–30.

DOWNING, J. (1979) *Reading and Reasoning* (Edinburgh: Chambers).

HALLIDAY, M.A.K. and HASAN, R. (1976) *Cohesion in English* (London: Longman).

HUEY, E.B. (1908/1968) *The Psychology and Pedagogy of Reading* (Cambridge, Mass: MIT Press).

LORAC, C. and WEISS, M. (1981) *Communication and Social Skills* (Exeter: Wheaton).

LUNZER, E. and GARDNER, K. (1979) *The Effective Use of Reading* (London: Heinemann).

LUNZER, E. and GARDNER, K. (1984) *Learning from the Written Word* (Edinburgh: Oliver and Boyd).

MORRIS, J. (1966) *Standards and Progress in Reading* (Slough: NFER).

REID, J. (1966) 'Learning to think about Reading', *Educational research*, 9, pp. 56–62.

SOUTHGATE, V., ARNOLD H. and JOHNSON, S. (1981) *Extending Beginning Reading* (London: Heinemann).

TIZARD, B. and HUGHES, M. (1984) *Young Children Learning: Talking and Thinking at Home and School* (London: Fontana).

VENEZKY, R.L. (1984) 'The History of Reading Research' in P. David Pearson (Ed) *Handbook of Reading Research* (New York: Longman).

WELLS, G. (1985) *Language, Learning and Education* (Windsor: NFER-Nelson).

Chapter 21

Beyond the a b c

Keith Gardner

Forty years ago, Schonell set out the a b c of reading instruction that was destined to dominate classroom practice in the 1950s. Twenty years later the Bullock Report Survey showed that little had changed. After the passage of nearly another two decades the position is still much the same. If reading standards were satisfactory and educational knowledge had stood still there would be no need for concern. But standards are not satisfactory and knowledge has not stood still. What then should be the a b c of reading instruction for the 1990s?

There comes a time in every Conference when the participants begin to wilt under the barrage of words that has assailed their ears. To provide time for recuperation the Conference Organiser builds into the programme an adult version of the infant school 'story time'. This is a session for relaxation and enjoyment with, perhaps, the potential for some educational enlightenment just in case someone asks a few awkward questions about wasting time.

It is an ideal moment to wheel on one of those senior citizens of reading who can meander gently back into history, produce a few amusing anecdotes, and, if pushed, even draw the odd conclusion or two.

It is forty years ago that I was seconded to Birmingham University to study for a Diploma in Psychology. There I was introduced to the a b c of teaching reading according to Schonell. The method was simplicity itself. Start by teaching children a basic sight vocabulary of some fifty words, using repetition as your main weapon. Repetition in the graded reader, repetition in flash card drills, repetition in wall displays. Then, with this bank of words safely memorised, the pupils could be introduced to the key to unlocking the sound of unfamiliar words – phonics.

When I worked with the Bullock Committee in the 1970s I was surprised to learn that teachers still worked to the Schonell approach. They did use different books, and there were extra frills added such as language experience, but the fundamental method was still

    (i) Start with the basic sight vocabulary.
    (ii) Use phonics as the main weapon in attacking new words. Nor
       have things changed very much in the 1980s.

None of this would matter if the standard of reading in school and beyond school caused no concern. If there was general satisfaction with the state of literacy there would be no need to question the long rule of look and say and phonics in the classroom.

But the state of literacy in the nation has caused concern, and is still causing concern. Many schools have to make elaborate arrangements to deal with reading problems. For many years subject areas like Science and Geography have retreated from the use of text because too many pupils were unable to use written language as a means of learning. There have been constant grumbles from industry and commerce, and the need for help for adult illiterates is widely recognised.

Perhaps there would be little need for comment if knowledge had stood still and the theoretical underpinning of old and trusted methods had remained intact. But the fact is, knowledge has been widened and there have been developments in both linguistics and learning theory that should have had some impact on classroom practice.

Certainly, efforts have been made through an expanding network of short courses, one-year diplomas, and elements in some in-service degrees to communicate with classroom practitioners and disseminate new knowledge. Discussion has raged within educational establishments and some thoughtful and thought-provoking essays and dissertations have been written. But teaching methods have remained stubbornly entrenched.

At the same time reading progress among our pupils has also stayed close to an old and familiar pattern. Only a minority of children from the Campari and soda belts exhibit serious problems with reading. It is in the areas of Brew X1 or similar ales, where remedial classes multiply and reading problems abound.

This proven and long-standing link between social status and reading achievement should be a source of great concern. It has survived a reduction in the size of classes, dramatic changes in teacher education, and a revolution in book production. It remains the greatest single indictment of the way literacy is approached in our schools.

In my most cynical moments I believe that our successful pupils succeed in spite of the inadequacies of their teaching. They are able, by virtue of intellectual, linguistic and emotional advantage to paper over cracks in their instruction, to generalise from imperfect models, and to practise their growing skill in an environment rich with opportunity. On the other hand, our less successful pupils seem to receive little intellectual stimulation, are often condemned to work with inferior language models, and are faced with damaging strains and stresses.

Where, then, has methodology gone wrong?

It would be presumptuous of me to pretend I have a complete answer to that question. After all, in my years in the classroom I produced as many backward readers as most. But I can outline how some of my beliefs have changed over the years and the effect this has had on how I teach reading. Whether this has any significance or not, others must judge.

First, forty years ago I believed that repetition was a powerful means of compelling children to learn. In common with most other young teachers of the time the daily drill of hearing a page from Janet and John and reinforcing the ditherers with flash cards was the classroom manifestation of this belief.

Doubts were created by the personal observation that one exposure to 'elephant' was sufficient to trigger a successful response for ever, but 'was' and 'saw' were still mixed up after 50,000 exposures in a variety of settings. It was obvious that word recognition rested on a wider base than just mere repetition.

I have long since discarded the simple behaviourist learning theories I once believed could lead me to a perfect teaching method. Today, I have a sneaking suspicion that different children learn in different ways; I suspect that attitude and interest are powerful determinants of what we choose to learn; I have a growing conviction that our own perception of what we consider important to learn is probably the greatest single factor in personal achievement. So purposeful activity would figure largely in my present-day regime.

Second, I used to believe that learning to read had to be a solitary exercise, and each solitary performance had to be perfect. In short, I heard individual pupils read aloud and corrected every error.

Doubts about this began when I realised that it might be OK for those youngsters who could read, but it must have been sheer hell for those who couldn't. I gave the able an opportunity to show off, but the less able had a painful reminder of how inadequate they were.

Then I looked at other aspects of my practice. Good readers were reading more text than poor readers. Those who needed practice most were getting least. What I was asking pupils to read had little content or purpose. Above all, it suddenly dawned on me that I was concentrating all my effort on stupid, over-simplified texts, when the real reading lay within the covers of the story books which were reserved for private reading.

Today, I believe children should read what good authors produce. They need to experience models of good written language and sense something of the unlimited universe that an understanding of written language opens up.

Again, I once believed that the individual word was the key to reading and once a pupil could recode written words into spoken words then they were readers. Of course, the royal road to recoding was by blending the sounds of separate letters in a written word. At least, this was supposed to work for 'regular' words. 'Irregular' words had to be learned by sight.

My pupils soon taught me the folly of these notions. There were those who could parrot their way through Book 3, but had forgotten how to parrot Book 2; there were a good number of excellent parrots who had no idea at all about the content of their reader. It became very clear that recoding did not lead to comprehension, and just to complete the collapse of my morale, I met my first 'non-reader' who appeared to understand a great deal of what he couldn't read. As for 'building words from their sounds . . .'! Every day I listened to pupils who got the sounds wrong and the word right, and I also listened to pupils who got the sounds right and the words wrong. You didn't have to be a genius to realise that the pupils had found ways of recognising words that had not been mentioned by Schonell.

I could go on, but the message is clear. There was no necessity to go on a refresher course to find out that my classroom procedures were suspect. The pupils were shouting it out every day.

There is much more to tell, but perhaps I have said enough to communicate the essence of what I have been forced to discard. I must emphasise, though, that I have discarded little in response to intellectual argument or a desire to follow a new and passing fad. My dissatisfactions stemmed from how children behaved and the overwhelming evidence they provided that my understandings and my teaching were faulty.

But what has taken the place of my old beliefs?

Today I know that print is not divided into 'sight' words and 'phonic' words. Rather, when we scan a page of writing we process the total display using a variety of intake cues. Some parts of the display we process very quickly – so quickly, in fact, it is almost instantaneous. This is the nearest we get to the 'sight vocabulary' I once cherished. But it is not just the vocabulary that we process. Rather, it is complete chunks of meaning.

I know that in processing print our prediction of meaning plays an important role; I know that familiarity with linguistic sequences and linguistic structure helps us along; and I also know that when we need to pause and check a specific word we draw on a knowledge from within word features to confirm or deny a preliminary prediction.

Believing this means a complete change in my classroom procedures. For instance, the only way young children can meet the forms and structures of written language is by hearing them. Hence, reading to children becomes fundamental, and the choice of what we read, fiction and non-fiction, is as critical as our choice of what books we offer children. Drawing attention to the features of written language is far more important than teaching phonic rules which do not work.

Because this immersion in written language is so critical to reading success I now believe a partnership between home and school is essential. My generation once told parents to leave the teaching of reading to the professionals. Unfortunately, for many children, they did. Reading cannot be taught in school. The classroom can only put flesh on the existing bone structure. If circumstances force the school into isolation then the results are likely to be disappointing.

Then, because I now know that the most efficient learning is often what we learn for ourselves, and because I now know that interest, purpose, and motivation are major factors in successful learning, I can no longer treat reading as a solitary, painful slog through word lists masquerading as books. Much of my classroom practice would be built around group activities with discussion and mutual support combining to maximise the understanding of texts that had something to communicate. Let children learn to read by learning purposefully from real texts.

Some of you in my audience will recognise echoes of 'The Reading for Learning' project in my last statement. As this project was concerned with secondary schools I must emphasise that the principles of the activities developed for post-primary pupils apply with equal force to both infant and junior pupils.

But even as I articulate the new approaches I have developed in my own teaching down the years I realise that these are not the true a b c of my methodology. For beyond the a b c of action lie the fundamentals, without which, in one sense, the acquisition of reading is impossible; in another sense, the acquisition of reading has no point, and lacking purpose will wither as soon as the demands of school are left behind.

I believe these fundamentals are:

(i)   The willingness of the pupil to learn. Without this all is lost, and a major part of school time is best spent fostering a vision of learning that, in these hard times, if they are hard times, must have a practical relevance, but must also go beyond immediate needs.

(ii)   A realisation that written communication relies on a common knowledge which must be assumed to exist between writer and reader. Without this common knowledge there can be no comprehension no matter how many 'comprehension skills' are taught. Therefore, growth in reading follows growth in knowledge . . . it is only the proficient reader who can add substantially to knowledge by reading.

(iii)   A teaching approach that recognises that the function of teaching is to give shape and form to the thinking of pupils. Then, it follows that we, as teachers, first engineer experience, then we provide time for pupils to discuss among themselves and sort out their own thinking, then we teach . . .

It seems that I have talked myself into a position where I am saying that successful readers teach themselves to read . . . teachers exercise their skills when they can make pupils aware of what they already know, and can utilise their knowledge to further their own learning.

This is what lies beyond the a b c . . .

Chapter 22

Reading, Communication and Context

Roger Beard

This paper will argue that British reading studies need to go 'beyond the a b c' to take a realistic account of the communicative context of written language and it will take a deliberately cautious look at some of the possibly exaggerated claims in recent debates about the use of 'real books' in early reading development and the associated 'apprenticeship approach'. The paper will explore several dimensions of this context, including the sense of authorship in young children's early reading experiences, the sense of readership in children's writing and the importance of considering 'the text in context' in literacy development in homes and schools.

Anyone who has taken a close look at British reading studies in recent times will have been struck by the rich store of knowledge to which teachers now have access. Teachers entering the profession are heirs to a far more comprehensive range of publications and related practices than was the case when I began teaching in a primary school some twenty years ago. At that time, like many of my contemporaries, I had little awareness of the nature of the process of reading which had become part of me earlier than I can remember. Perhaps I had more awareness of the ways in which reading can be applied for different purposes, although I lacked a language for referring to what seemed to be involved. I was very conscious of the rewards which literature can bring and excited by finding that children's literature was going through something of a second 'golden age'. To help meet the needs of children in my class who were experiencing difficulties in learning to read, I attended a six-evening course in Oxford run by the late John Downing who, I found, reassured me on my commitment to providing a sense of purpose and pleasure in literacy, as well as a commitment to diagnosing where children's difficulties lay and whether they could be considered 'dyslexic' or not.

Professional progress in reading

Since then, there has been a great deal of water under the bridge and a great many words on the page about reading. We now have something resembling a properly *professional* awareness of what the reading process seems to involve and several influential studies of how literacy *emerges* in children (see, for instance, Hall, 1987). As a consequence, reading assessment has become better informed and proportioned. We have the benefit of a number of studies which have given us some *terms of reference* for the efficient and effective use of written resources. The *dyslexia* debate drags on, still founded on exclusive definitions (Ellis, 1984) and a constellation of possible symptoms (Money, 1962), although Bryant and Bradley (1985) have recently provided some evidence to counter the deficit model which has often been assumed, suggesting instead that much can be gained from a study of the *continuum* related to children's *phonological processing*.

Finally, the vision of a second golden age of *children's literature* has been shattered by the assertion of a new social realism. This has replaced the rather smug and cosy world in the recurrent theme of the celebrated fantasies of the late 1950s and 1960s: 'the rediscovery of the past', found for instance throughout the books of William Mayne, Philippa Pearce, Joan Aiken, Alan Garner and, later, Penelope Lively. According to Carpenter (1985), there had been a similar theme in the first golden age, at the turn of the century, focused on 'secret gardens' (the river bank, the Never Never Land, the rural retreats of Westmoreland, the slopes of a railway cutting, the Wonderland). But, as Leeson (1985) reminds us, realism broke through this 'bourgeoise hegemony' in 1977 when *The Turbulent Term of Tike Tyler* won both the Carnegie Award from 'the establishment' and the 'Other Award' of the 'new left' in children's literature, the *Children's Book Bulletin*. Yet, through all this, there has been a growing recognition of at least a glittering era in young children's picture books which have been seen as an under-rated resource in early reading development (Bennett, 1982), although questions remain about administration, structure and sequence.

Communications on reading

At the same time, the news from classrooms does not necessarily reflect the fulfilment of the promise of this burgeoning of professional activity and publication. Just a few snapshots can act as sharp reminders of the continuing need for substantial in-service investments to be made on reading studies. The HMI survey of first schools reports that, 'In almost all schools the youngest children were introduced too quickly to published reading schemes and phonic practice, with the result that some were confused and made little progress' (DES, 1982 p. 5). Bennett's (1984) study of sixteen 'better than average' teachers reports that, on language work in general, 'In most cases there was a lack of sequence structure and development' (Bennett, 1984, p. 128).

Almost all the eighty schools in the first school survey lacked guidelines on the extension and development of reading (DES, 1982 p. 5) and only about half of the sixty-five schools in the eight to twelve middle school survey had such guidelines (DES, 1985 p. 7). The commentary on the published reports by HMI on individual schools, *Education Observed 2*, concludes 'Once they are reading fluently, children could with profit be challenged more than they are in order to extend their reading skills, and most need to encounter a wider range of information books and good fiction than they do' (DES, 1984 p. 1).

Reading as communication

But it would be misguided to respond to these indications from observational research by a commitment only to dissemination, awareness-raising and action. For it can be argued that reading research, publications and teaching have been rather narrow in focus and have not taken full account of reading as part of an *act of written communication*. Even the recent 'avant-garde' movement to promote the use of 'real books' in early reading development has not really adopted the purest perspectives on the communicative context in which written language is generated and validated. Those involved in this movement have certainly encouraged us to look more closely at the psychological and organisational appeal of texts, especially those in the narrative mode, but they have tended not to look beyond stories and the sympathetic adult who introduces them to children.

I have found it helpful to go 'beyond the a b c' of the text to the communication which it represents and the *context* in which the communication is set. The integral nature of the various components is traditionally represented as a triangle. Drawing out some of the conceptual links between the various components can illuminate some of the crucial dimensions involved in using written language (Fig. 22.1).

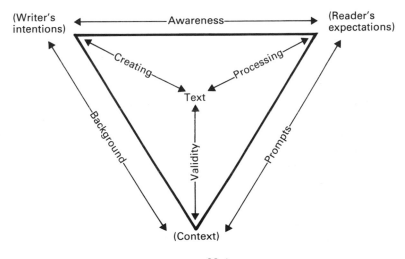

FIGURE 22.1

A fundamental insight from this framework is the reminder that written language is created by someone within some communicative setting. It also serves as a sharp reminder to those who draw unsubstantiated parallels between learning to talk and learning to read. For it is plain to see that talkers and readers are at different apexes of the triangle and that they are engaged in different, though perhaps complementary, tasks and draw differentially upon the contextual support of shared reality.

It may be helpful to pull out some of the principal implications from this basic framework, although some of the related ideas run more thematically through a recent book (Beard, 1987b). There seem to me to be major implications for our work in fostering children's sense of authorship, their awareness of readership and the promotion of the curriculum context in which early literacy develops.

Communicating authorship

The triangle illuminates the integral relationship of writer and reader. The text may well effect the communication more permanently, completely and elaborately than talk may be able to do. And this takes us to the heart of the *purpose* of written language. Research such as that of Hazel Francis (1982) warns us that reading stories to children or using some published teaching approaches, such as that embraced by *Breakthrough to Literacy* (Mackay *et al.*, 1979), may do relatively little for some children. Her research revealed how some children seemed to confuse the invention of their own stories with fabrication. Furthermore, they seemed to see much sentence construction, even in so-called language–experience approaches, as meaning-less because it is neither a proper story nor intended as an everyday act of communication.

approach' to early reading development seems to rely rather heavily on the use of *Breakthrough to Literacy*, curiously described as a 'stimulus for writing' (Waterland, 1985, p. 16). More recently, it has been claimed by the same author that *Breakthrough* 'enables the child to see how speech relates to print, how words convey personal meaning and, of course, gives the child that important sight vocabulary, but within the context of the child's own personal, meaningful "homemade" books' (Waterland, 1987, p. 5). It seems paradoxical that these words come from an author who has been associated with widespread criticisms of materials specifically published for teaching early literacy. Moreover, they do not deal satisfactorily with the question mark which has hung over *Breakthrough* from its inception, that it may not facilitate the growth in the use of 'connected prose' (Reid, 1974). More recently, Kress (1982) has explored some of the main differences between speech and writing and suggested that an early emphasis on 'sentence-making' may be misplaced. His investigations suggest that, because of the chain-like structure of clauses in speech, children may be more predisposed to produce '*textual*' rather than syntactical units, in which two or three 'sentences' are run together and punctuated as if they are one.

This new emphasis on *text* creation rather than sentence making can take us back again to the *why* of text production. It is a little strange that the notion of apprenticeship has not been explored with regards to *writing*, in which it may well have a more clear-cut and less ambiguous application. Reading aloud with a child does, after all, fall some way short of indicating the silent generation of meaning which constitutes the 'real' nature of reading for most of us (poetry readings being perhaps a notable exception). What is more, authentic writing may well be more explicitly tied to *context* and thus be more educationally significant than the kind of serendipity which can be a feature of the contexts in which books are encountered.

This more directive role by the teacher as a kind of 'initiator' has many parallels in the teaching of music, the coaching of games and indeed underpins one of the most established of the major theories of education (Peters, 1964). Moreover, it helps to counter the fears that the extreme child-centred ideologies associated with the approaches to writing espoused by Graves (1983) will lead to little more than undifferentiated 'knowledge-telling' outcomes within a fairly limited range of genres (personal narratives, stereotyped war stories, unconvincing fantasies). The informed and decisive teacher can ensure that children are helped become more flexible and accomplished writers by ensuring that they are encouraged to tackle non-narrative and more discursive modes of writing. For writers need *discourse knowledge* as well as *content knowledge* and they seem more likely to become alert to this aspect of the *'how'* of writing if the teacher draws attention to the structural features of recipes, instructions, advertisements, arguments, reports, requests and commentaries and *reads them aloud to children* (Bereiter and Scardamalia, 1987).

Furthermore, writing such texts in front of the children engenders both credibility and recognition of a kind which may help us get behind the taken-for-grantedness of writing, to recognise its problematic nature and to examine more critically its potential in children's reading development.

Communicating readership

If we look at the dynamics of written communication, we can also recognise the implications for children becoming aware that they are part of a readership. Here, again, the teacher can lead the way by regularly writing for the children and helping them to write for each other. The reciprocal awareness can enrich the processing of texts which others have created within a shared context.

This perspective raises big questions about the use of published books, too. Anyone who has worked closely with a professional author will confirm the spell-binding influence which their presence can have on children. Yet authors seem under-used in reinforcing the sense of readership, although some magazines such as *Puffin Post* and *Books for Keeps* carry regular features on them. The presentation of even the most celebrated books in children's literature seem to underplay the role which John Burningham or Quentin Blake or Pat Hutchins played in their creation.

At the same time, if the sense of readership were explored further, there could be some anomalies thrown up. Roald Dahl, for instance, is writing for readers who he sees as being 'only half civilised, laughing at things which make adults squirm' (Dahl, 1985). His startling frankness may belie the notion of the author as innocent entertainer which seems to be sometimes assumed. Maurice Sendak once spent a good part of the *Book Programme* on BBC 2 talking to Robert Robinson about the thinking which went into the hidden themes of *Where the Wild Things Are*. Eric Carle was trying to do more than tell a story in *The Very Hungry Caterpillar*. In fact, John Rowe Townsend has sensed that there is now a new didacticism at work in some children's literature which compares with that of the nineteenth century. Today many children's books seem to be being used to distil desired attitudes to race, sex and class (cited in Hadley, 1980).

In fact, the variable intentions of authors towards their readership could, *in principle*, point up an underrated strength of some reading schemes. Their recurring sense of shared context, their consistent style and their incremental, serial-like nature might provide a reliable sense of tacit support to young readers which might be missing if they moved uncertainly from author to author without being able to establish a silent rapport with the face beneath the page and the pen behind the words.

A closer look at the sense of readership can take us on to some of the idiosyncrasies behind the conditions in which writers choose to write (Beard, 1987a) and how the author interacts with the available content in the light of perceived audience needs. This leads beyond words and sentences to the *modes of discourse* (Kinneavy *et al.*, 1976). Two years ago, I set out a framework which can help us look at the resulting links between reading and writing (Beard, 1986) (Fig. 22.2).

Interestingly, we can see these modes at work in the recent debate about the texts for use in early reading development. Several contributors to the debate have called for narrative to be the predominant basis of early reading experience. But these writers have had to use modes *other than* narrative to argue their case. They employ *descriptions* of the weaknesses of reading scheme materials, they set up *classifications* ('real books') and they work towards *evaluations* of the quality of early literacy experience based on observations and impressions.

It is also interesting to note how such writers are operating in the framework of *aims* which can be explored within the communication triangle (Kinneavy, 1971; Beard, 1984) (Fig. 22.3).

They are in the business of *persuasion* and so they used the hallmarks of persuasive writing: emotional appeals – 'an organic book . . . is a natural, wholefood approach to writing' (Waterland, 1985, p. 35); compelling 'logic' – 'Literature makes readers in a way that reading schemes never can' (Meek, cited in Waterland, 1985, p. 35); a dismissive approach to a caricature of the opposition – 'it can no longer be argued that content is unimportant so long as skills are learnt' (Moon, 1986, p. 36).

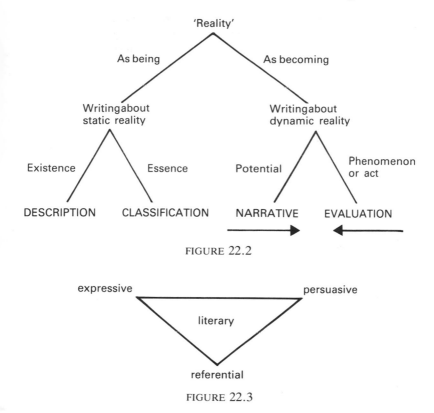

FIGURE 22.2

FIGURE 22.3

It could be chastening for those who are caught up in such zealotry to consider the gains from pursuing more *referential* aims. Here the world is seen as available for investigation, providing information and sources of evidence to validate it. This perspective could confront the zealots with some evidence which could prove uncomfortable. For instances, laudable and ambitious research into the effects of increasing the supply of literature in schools, the Bradford Book Flood Project (Ingham, 1982), provided inconclusive results, highlighting instead the complex influences on attainment and patterns of voluntary reading from the knowledge and attitudes of parents and teachers, from how books are made available and from the reactions of family and friends. Similarly, the misleadingly titled book *Achieving Literacy* (Meek *et al.*, 1983) provides inconclusive results on the use of children's literature with adolescents experiencing difficulties in learning to read. It might well be that even a total abolition of reading schemes would provide little more than 'no score draw' of results and outcomes in this rather over-polarised debate. Meanwhile, it seems overoptimistic and misleading for anyone to assume that there is something called an 'apprenticeship approach' which *guarantees* literacy. A sense of realistic proportion is crucial here. Is there *really* a school in Cambridgeshire in which *all* children, whatever their background and abilities, could learn to read? This would surely be a breakthrough on a world scale . . .

Besides which, any talk of 'real' begs questions about the 'real world' for which we are mandated to prepare children. This world is full of unsuspecting reading demands, many of which are certainly non-narrative, for instance demands to locate information quickly and efficiently, often information of a technical and context-dependent nature (Torbe, 1982). The world of advertising is probably even more subtle and intensive than it was when Alma Williams (1976) published her pioneering book *Reading and the Consumer*; the national press seems more biased and vituperative than ever before (Butler and Kavanagh, 1984) and non-fiction is purchased by men just as much as fiction (Euromonitor, 1984), confirming Clark's (1976) findings that boys who were young fluent readers not only often learned to read *silently* but also in many cases did this by using functional 'environmental' print. This is a further indication that the topical apprenticeship approach as it is conceived by Waterland is not the catch-all that some have suggested it might be. The approach is thrown into further critical light by the finding from the Haringey research (Tizard *et al.*, 1982) that children improved their reading performance even when regularly reading aloud to their illiterate or non-English speaking parents.

A communicating curriculum

If there is anything resembling a catch-all framework, I would be inclined to look at the nature of written communication, providing that its relation to the 'reality of the world' is also kept firmly in mind. It is important to recognise that there are other parallel debates going on in primary education, such as that over the *consistency* of curriculum provision, set in motion by the HMI survey of primary schools (DES, 1978). A quarter of the schools in a nationally representative sample undertook no form of history or geography either as separate subjects or as part of topic work. Among the curriculum areas *not* found in the 'base-line' of 80 per cent of observed classes were the teaching of drama, spelling, science and environmental studies. Commentators such as Colin Richards (1982) have argued that such curriculum inconsistency is incompatible with a genuinely comprehensive education system in which children and parents can be assured of the provision of a similar set of curriculum elements to all pupils at a particular stage of education, whether or not they are in the same class.

Alexander (1984) has gone further and identified an unfortunate and probably unintentional distinction between what he calls curriculum I and curriculum II; put simply, 'the basics' and 'the rest'. 'The rest' receive less time, less priority, less appraisal and are open to *ad hoc* and even whimsical planning. It seems to me that we need to work towards a merger of curriculum I and curriculum II, so that the development of children's language and literacy can be considered as part of what knowledge, ideas, skills and attitudes children need to develop and in which reading can be seen in its most relevant and significant light, one which focuses not just on texts or making sense of print but on its role as part, and only part, of written communication.

References

ALEXANDER, R.J. (1984) *Primary Teaching* (London: Holt, Rinehart and Winston).

BEARD, R. (1984) *Children's Writing in the Primary School* (Sevenoaks: Hodder and Stoughton).

BEARD, R. (1986) 'Reading Resources and Children's Writing', in Root, B. (ed) *Resources for Reading: Does Quality Count?*' (London: Macmillan/ United Kingdom Reading Association).

BEARD, R. (1987a) 'Behind the lines', *The Times Educational Supplement*, 2 May.

BEARD, R. (1987b) *Developing Reading 3–13* (Sevenoaks: Hodder and Stoughton).

BENNETT, J. (1982) *Learning to Read with Picture Books* (Second edition; third edition, 1985) (Stroud: The Thimble Press).

BENNETT, N., DESFORGES, C., COCKBURN, A. and WILKINSON, B. (1984) *The Quality of Pupil Learning Experiences* (London: Erlbaum).

BEREITER, C. and SCARDAMALIA, M. (1987) *The Psychology of Written Composition* (London: Erlbaum).

BRYANT, P. and BRADLEY, L. (1985) *Children's Reading Problems* (Oxford: Basil Blackwell).

BUTLER, D. and KAVANAGH, H. (1984) *The British General Election of 1983* (Basingstoke: Macmillan).

CARPENTER, H. (1985) *Secret Gardens* (London: Allen and Unwin).

CLARK, M.M. (1976) *Young Fluent Readers: What Can They Teach Us?* (London: Heinemann).

DAHL, R. (1985) 'Mystery Man' (Interview with Polly Toynbee), *The Guardian*, 23 December.

DES (1978) *Primary Education in England* (London: HMSO).

DES (1982 *Education 5 to 9: an illustrative survey of 80 first schools in England* (London: HMSO).

DES (1984) *Education Observed 2* (London: HMSO).

DES (1985) *Education 8 to 12 in Combined and Middle Schools* (London: HMSO).

ELLIS, A.W. (1984) *Reading, Writing and Dyslexia: A Cognitive Analysis* (London: Erlbaum).

EUROMONITOR (1984) *Buying and Reading Books in Great Britain* (London: Euromonitor Publications Ltd).

FRANCIS, H. (1982) *Learning to Read: Literate behaviour and orthographic knowledge* (London: Allen and Unwin).

GRAVES, D.H. (1983) *Writing: Teachers and Children at Work* (Exeter, New Hampshire: Heinemann).

HADLEY, E. (1980) 'The Scrubbed Pine World of English Children's Fiction', *Use of English* 31, 2, pp. 56–65.

HALL, N. (1987) *The Emergence of Literacy* (Sevenoaks: Hodder and Stoughton).

INGHAM, J. (1982) *Books and Reading Development* (second edition) (London: Heinemann).

KINNEAVY, J.L. (1971) *A Theory of Discourse* (Englewood Cliffs, New Jersey: Prentice Hall).

KINNEAVY, J.L., COPE, J.Q. and CAMPBELL, J.W. (1976) *Writing: Basic Modes of Organisation* (Dubuque, Iowa: Kendall Hunt Pub. Co).

KRESS, G. (1982) *Learning to Write* (London: Routledge and Kegan Paul).

LEESON, R. (1985) *Reading and Righting* (London: Collins).

MACKAY, D. THOMPSON, B. and SCHAUB, P. (1979) *Breakthrough to Literacy: Teacher's Manual* (second edition) (London: Longman for the Schools Council).

MEEK, M. *et al.*(1983) *Achieving Literacy* (London: Routledge and Kegan Paul).

MONEY, J. (ed) (1962) *Reading Disability* (Baltimore: Johns Hopkins Press).

MOON, C. (1986) 'Spoit and Pat: Living in the Best Company When You Read', in Root, B. (ed) *Resources for Reading: Does Quality Count?* (Basingstoke: Macmillan/United Kingdom Reading Association).

PETERS, R.S. (1964) *Education As Initiation: Inaugural lecture* (London: University of London Press).

REID, J.F. (1974) *Breakthrough in Action* (London: Longman for the Schools Council).

RICHARDS, C. (ed) (1982) *New Directions in Primary Education* (Lewes: The Falmer Press).

TIZARD, J., SCHOFIELD, W.N. and HEWISON, J. (1982) 'Collaboration Between Teachers and Parents in Assisting Children's Reading', *British Journal of Educational Psychology*, 52, pp. 1–15.

TORBE, M. (1982) 'Communication skills in employment and the young school leaver', in C.R.A.C. (Careers Research and Advisory Centre) *English Communication Skills and the Needs of People in Industry* (Cambridge: Hobsons Press).

WATERLAND, L. (1985) *Read With Me: An Apprenticeship Approach to Reading* (Stroud: The Thimble Press).

WATERLAND, L. (1987) 'Taking their time', correspondence in *Child Education*, August, p. 5.

WILLIAMS, A. (1976) *Reading and the Consumer* (London: Hodder and Stoughton).

Chapter 23

Alphabets, Books and Computers: Past, Present and Future

Jonathan Anderson

Alphabets, books and computers signal quantum leaps in human communication. Each of these 'a b c' technologies was to change for ever the shape of people's lives, the way they thought, and how they communicated. This paper traces these evolutionary milestones – the development of writing (when alphabets were created), the invention of printing (leading to the mass production of books) and, most recently, developments in telecommunications (ushering in computers) – and their effects particularly on concepts of literacy and learning. How the present has evolved from the past is one way of looking to the future. The paper concludes by examining likely developments in computer-based technologies in the decade ahead, and asking what these mean for reading and language teachers.

Before the alphabet

According to archaeologists, crude bone, pebble and stone tools have been found in the fossil record dating back to more than two million years. These are the earliest record we have of human life. The kinds of tools used did not change very much until about 34000 BC (give or take a few thousand years), when a wider range and more sophisticated tools began to appear. Up until this time, for uncounted millennia, change had been glacially slow (Davies and Shane, 1986), but then the first of four world-shattering breakthroughs in communication took place. Each was to change the human species for ever.

The first of these events, which coincided with more standardised tool forms, may have been brought about, suggests Leakey (1981, p.135), because humans had developed another tool – the tool of language. From tool-using animals, humans had evolved to become talking animals as well.

Alphabets and writing

The second revolutionary milestone to have had a profound effect on human evolution was the development of writing, which Arthur C. Clarke in *Profiles of the Future* describes as 'perhaps the most important single invention that mankind ever made or ever will make' (Clarke 1982, p.138).

We can be a little more precise about the advent of writing. Although early forms – rock drawings and cave paintings – may have been precursors, developed writing systems date to approximately 3000 BC when inhabitants of the Nile region devised a system described later by the Greeks as hieroglyphs (that is sacred carvings). According to Breasted's account in *Ancient Times* (1944), the great contribution of the ancient Egyptians, beyond which some tribes in different parts of the world never passed, was twofold. First, was the pictograph stage where pictures of, say, a leaf or the sun always represented specific words (say 'leaf' and 'sun' respectively) rather than ideas as formerly (perhaps 'foliage', 'leaf' or 'greenery' in the one case; 'rise' or 'shine' in the other). Second, was the phonogram stage when signs of, say, a bee or a leaf now stood for particular sounds or syllables. This meant that the bee and the leaf sounds could be put together to represent a word like 'belief', and so abstract ideas could begin to be communicated.

> This possession of *phonetic* signs was what made real writing for the first time. It arose among these Nile dwellers earlier than anywhere else in the ancient world.
>
> (Breasted 1944, p.63).

The Egyptians also developed certain signs denoting consonants (they had no vowels), which the Phoenicians, the Greeks and, later still, the Romans were to refine to the alphabet used in publications such as this where there are signs for consonants and vowels. The Roman alphabet which we inherit is only one of many alphabets, and nor is it particularly well suited to English since there are many more sounds in the language than letters. Other alphabets, like ITA for example, have been tried in recent times for teaching reading.

Another significant contribution from Egypt was the invention of writing materials – sharpened reeds, ink and papyrus. Breasted echoes Clarke's sentiments:

> The invention of writing and of a convenient system of records on paper has had a greater influence in uplifting the human race than any other achievement in the life of man.
>
> (Breasted 1944, p.66)

With the invention of the alphabet, man became not only a tool-using talking animal, but also a writing animal.

Books and the printing press

The third evolutionary milestone in human history was the invention of the printing press, attributed to Gutenberg in the German town of Mainz in about 1440. It is one of the ironies of history that, although print provides a permanent record, precisely who first assembled a machine to print on paper with movable metal type, and exactly when, cannot be ascertained with absolute certainty.

As often happens with new technologies, printers initially imitated earlier book styles with their choice of type; the content of early printed books, too, reflected the religious themes of the past (most readers were clerics) and books on grammar were also popular; and, initially, the language used was almost invariably Latin. But more than any other single event, printing ushered in a new epoch. It led to the gradual demise of Latin; it promoted the growth of the vernacular, leading to standardisation of language and the emergence of national literatures; it made the Reformation the world's first mass media event; and it extended the skill of reading, formerly confined to the cleric and privileged classes, to the reach of all. 'An elite society gave way to a mass society' (Febvre and Martin, 1976, p. 11)

Some changes brought about by printing would have seemed quite incredulous had they been predicted at the time. Prior to the fifteenth century, for instance, among the most respected occupations was to be a manuscript copyist or illuminator. A rhyming couplet of the day foretells the disappearance of the prestigious position of scribe:

> In one dayes time a Printer will Print more
> Than one man could Write in a year before

Manuscripts themselves, prized possessions in the Middle Ages, would soon become museum pieces, still prized but not objects for everyday use. Febvre and Martin comment:

> The printed book could be said to have 'arrived' between 1500 and 1510. Little by little it displaced the manuscript in library collections, relegating it to second place, and by 1550 the latter was hardly used, except by scholars for special purposes.
> (Febvre and Martin, 1976 p.262)

The development of formal education and improvement in levels of literacy are closely related to the growth in printing and changes in society generally. Each development fuelled the other. A few key dates, some within living memory, serve to remind us of these parallel developments:

1840: Penny Post was introduced.

1850: The Public Libraries Act was passed leading to the establishment of municipal libraries and museums. Within forty years it was estimated that 26 million books were borrowed in the UK annually.

1870: The Education Act specified certain minimum periods of education for all. This was followed by further Acts in 1902 and 1944 extending the range of education.

1886 The linotype machine was invented to mechanise type setting. This heralded the first of the mass communication media, the newspaper.

1940: The paperback revolution commenced (Penguin Books was founded just five years earlier).

Growth in the printing industry is thus seen to parallel closely the diffusion of knowledge. Changes were effected in people's daily lives with consequences for both the content and nature of learning. Man had evolved to become a tool-using, writing and reading animal.

Computers and the information explosion

We are currently experiencing possibly the most revolutionary milestone of all, the development of telecommunications, which might be said to have commenced in 1837 when Samuel Morse sent information by electricity with his invention of the telegraph.

The chief characteristics of current developments in communications technology are the breaking of both time and distance barriers: the developments of writing and printing broke the time barrier and developments in telecommunications, the distance barrier. We are travelling along an 'informational superhighway', as one writer put it, 'spanning the globe and transmitting knowledge and data at the speed of light' (quoted in Adams and Jones, 1983 p.20). Consequently, Plato's *Dialogues* or Homer's *Iliad* and *Odyssey*, need no longer be memorised but can be simultaneously transmitted to, and accessed from, every corner of the globe, and beyond.

History records that at each major milestone, such as those we have been describing, there were periods of adjustment, a questioning of current practices, and a looking back at some supposedly golden era. With the development of writing, for instance, Socrates (in Plato's *Phaedrus*) argues that students would become lazy and fail to develop their memories; with the development of printing, there were some who bitterly resisted the printing press as an invention of the devil because it produced identical copies of works like the Gutenberg Bible; and, at the end of the last century, one headmaster in Scotland (Spence, 1899) complained that young people no longer listened, as in previous times, but merely read.

The difference between today's world and any preceding time is the vastly greater amount of data and information gathered. In terms of evolution, people are now bombarded by all kinds of information to the extent that they might be termed multisensory animals. All of this has been made possible largely by the ubiquitous computer. As a single example, it has been estimated that every flight of a jet airliner involves the sending of at least 30,000 messages (plane bookings and inquiries, weather information, staffing, catering, fuelling, and so on). A veritable explosion of information fills the air waves, and it is available to all those who know how to access it – for proper or improper ends.

Extended notions of literacy

There seems little doubt that, as in previous evolutionary milestones of human communication, the new computer-based technologies will bring about changed concepts of literacy with resultant consequences for reading teachers. In the foreword to a series of reports on computers and literacy (Chandler and Marcus, 1985), Adams writes:

> The evidence is very clear that the impact of microelectronics and computing generally will make more rather than fewer demands upon literacy, and that the definition of literacy will have to be extended to include screen reading and writing if it is to be adequate to the needs of those growing up in present-day society.

Geoffrion and Geoffrion (1985) echo similar sentiments in their account of computerised dynamic books, which the new technologies can be expected to make a reality in the not-too-distant future. The harbingers of such books, where readers can request additional information such as the meaning or sounding of words, are already here.

Reading of computerised screen displays is similarly a demand already made on increasing numbers in the work force. Public and private information databases such as Prestel, Viatel, Captain and others, require readers to take in information by 'screenfuls'; and moving backwards and forwards with screen-based texts calls for somewhat different literacy skills compared to book reading. The display of text on computer monitors is usually much more dynamic than book text.

However, the major new demand upon literacy is for students to learn how to access the new world storehouses of information. These new storehouses of information are an inevitable consequence of today's vastly increased supply of information and the new modes of storing this information on computer media. Throughout history, literacy has given power to those who have mastered the necessary skills required by society at the particular stage of social and political development reached. Dillon's conclusion, therefore, that 'computer literacy will be the new access to power in a high technology and information processing society' (Dillon, 1985, p. 98), seems inescapable.

Looking ahead

If one looks back at forecasts made ten to fifteen years ago about the use of computers in education, there is not a close match with current practices (O'Shea and Self, 1983). In the United States, for example, there were many predictions made in the early days of computers that routine computerised drill and practice in schools and colleges would be in almost universal use by 1979 and that more sophisticated learning programs would supersede these over the next ten-year period. In Britain, by contrast, the Council for Educational Technology in 1977 did not foresee any revolution in computer education, since computers would 'remain obstinately expensive'. Even Toffler, author of that best seller of the 70s, *Future Shock*, not only failed to predict the impact the microprocessor would have on society but failed to mention microprocessors at all. The simple explanation – the date of his manuscript (Toffler, 1970) predated by a year the invention of the first chip by Intel in 1971. O'Shea and Self conclude that most predictions about educational computing in the past ten years have been 'either wildly over-optimistic or over-pessimistic' (1983, p.260).

With caution, then, we look forward to the next decade. Developments that perhaps can be foreshadowed with some degree of certainty are:
* smaller, more powerful personal microcomputers,
* software incorporating speech,
* the advent of fifth generation computers,
* the coming of age of artificial intelligence and the increasing sophistication of expert systems.

These anticipated developments are discussed very briefly.

Dramatic breakthroughs in new superconductors which no longer need to be cooled with liquid helium, together with increasingly large-scale integration for memory chips, seem certain to lead to even smaller, more powerful computers. A hand-held computer has already been released with a 2-in microdisk, which may become in time a new standard for auxiliary storage. Because human fingers are not getting smaller, the computer keyboard is the one component unlikely to decrease in size though its shape and function may well change. The biggest impact as far as schools are concerned, is likely to be in truly portable, battery-powered microcomputers, which students carry from class to class and from home to school.

Along with more powerful computers, we might expect more powerful software, that is software that is generally easier to use and incorporating more features. One feature already present in certain programs is synthesised speech (for example 'Talking TextWriter' and 'Reading Comprehension'). In the same way that silent movies gave way to the 'talkies', it seems reasonable to suppose that today's largely silent software will similarly give way to programs incorporating sound (including speech) and graphics. One computer company has labelled its latest educational computer GS (for graphics and sound) thereby indicating its views on future directions.

The 'fifth generation computer' is a concept: it is the name given to a national project of the Japanese, the main goals of which are to develop machines that are many times more powerful than today's supercomputers but, more importantly, machines that have almost human qualities of hearing, speaking, seeing and problem solving (Feigenbaum and McCorduck, 1983). This Japanese project, announced at the beginning of the present decade with a life-span of ten years, although reportedly on target, may fall short of its ambitious aims.

Artificial intelligence (AI) includes the development of programs that are designed to make machines behave intelligently, like speaking and hearing, for example. The Fifth Generation Computer Project in Japan, and similar projects in other parts of the world, have given enormous impetus to research on artificial intelligence since the two are closely entwined. Research in AI, in turn, has led to the development of what are called expert systems, which are programs for solving problems in narrowly

defined fields where a degree of human expertise is well established.
There are some who might question the relevance to classroom practice
of a dream for a new generation of computers, as yet not realised; others,
like Weizenbaum (1984), have seriously questioned whether research should
even be undertaken in developing programs to make what are essentially
human decisions. It is significant though, that the Director of the Fifth
Generation Project, Dr Kazuhiro Fuchi, expects the results of the Japanese
research will have its greatest impact on personal computers:

> The real impact will be on the computers that are readily available
> to people—personal computers—rather than mainframes or supercom-
> puters. The purpose of this project is to develop basic technology.
> Then, using this technology, you can make big computers and you
> can make small computers. But it is more important for the world
> to apply it to the personal type.
>
> (Quoted in Ahl, 1984, p.113)

If Dr Fuchi is right, that the impact of this national research effort will be
felt on personal computers similar to the kind currently in schools, colleges
and universities, then there are obvious implications for education.

Artificial intelligence is no longer regarded with the same suspicion as in
earlier years (perhaps Weizenbaum excepted); and some quite sophisticated
expert systems have already been developed. In some fields, such as medical
diagnosis, the performance of expert systems is as good as the very best
human experts. Similar embryo systems are under development for
diagnosing reading difficulties (Colbourne and McLeod, 1986) and research
into correction of English essays is yet another application that is well
advanced.

These, then, are some predictions about future computing developments.
The introduction of the printing press saw in the course of time the demise
of the position of scribe. Will the computer lead to redundancies in the
teaching force? Will reading teachers be displaced, or will their role become
more central in the educational process? And what about the school itself?
Is its position as an institution for compulsory attendance under threat?

Printed books soon completely replaced manuscripts. Is it possible to
imagine books in their turn being replaced? Is the rate of increase of
knowledge and the need for up-to-date information such, that in our
lifetime, technical and reference material (manuals, journals, directories,
encyclopedias) will be accessible primarily via computers, video or optical
disks?

Printing saw the pre-eminent role of Latin as the international language
challenged. As printing spread across the world, the use of vernacular
languages like French, Italian and English became more acceptable. Certain
vernaculars gained precedence over others and written language became
more standardised. Will telecommunications (computers, television, satel-
lites) reverse the process, making English dominant over all languages as
Latin had formerly been?

Printing saw the change from restricted to mass literacy. Is it at all likely that advances in computer speech recognition and speech synthesis will cause reading as a skill to decrease in importance? With such computer aids as calculators, spelling and grammatical checkers, will the teaching of certain basic skills be rendered unnecessary?

Each of the previous evolutionary milestones discussed in this paper brought about major changes in the human condition. What are the changes that can be expected from the widespread introduction of computers in society? Are schools ready for the changes? Can teachers and schools play a more positive role in directing these changes?

References

ADAMS, A. and JONES, E. (1983) *Teaching Humanities in the Microelectronic Age* (Milton Keynes: Open University Press).

ADAMS, A. (1985) General editor's introduction, in D. Chandler and S. Marcus (eds) *Computers and Literacy* (Milton Keynes: Open University Press).

AHL, D.H. (1984) 'Progress on the project: an inverview with Dr Kazuhiro Fuchi, *Creative Computing*, 10(8), pp. 113–114.

BREASTED, J.H. (1944) *Ancient Times: A History of the Early World* (2nd ed.) (Boston: Ginn).

CHANDLER, D. and MARCUS, S. (eds) (1985) *Computers and Literacy* (Milton Keynes: Open University Press).

CLARKE, A.C. (1982) *Profiles of the Future* (2nd rev. ed.) (London: Victor Gollancz).

COLBOURNE, M.J. and MCLEOD, J. (1986) 'The potential and feasibility of computer-guided educational diagnosis', special joint issue of *Remedial Education* 18(4) and of *COM 3* 12(4) on Computing and Special Education, pp.21–25.

DAVIES, I.K. and SHANE, H.G. (1986) 'Computers and the educational program', In J.A. Culbertson and L.L. Cunningham (eds) *Microcomputers and Education* (Eighty-fifth Yearbook of The National Society for the Study of Education, Part 1) (Chicago: The National Society for the Study of Education).

DILLON, D. (1985) 'The dangers of computers in literacy education: Who's in charge here?' in D. Chandler and S. Marcus (eds) *Computers and Literacy* (Milton Keynes: Open University Press).

FEBVRE, L. and MARTIN, H.J. (1976) *The Coming of the Book: The Impact of Printing 1450–1800* (Translated by Gerard, D.) (London: NLB).

FEIGENBAUM, E.A. and McCORDUCK, P. (1983) *The Fifth Generation* (Reading, Mass.: Addison-Wesley).

GEOFFRION, L.D. and GEOFFRION, O.P. (1985) 'Beyond the electronic workbook', paper presented at the 1985 Meeting of the International Reading Association, New Orleans.

LEAKEY, R.E. (1981) *The Making of Mankind* (London: Michael Joseph).
O'SHEA, T. and SELF, J. (1983) *Learning and Teaching with Computers: Artificial Intelligence in Education.* (Brighton, Sussex: Harvester Press).
SPENCE, J. (1899) *Shetland Folk-lore* (Lerwick: Johnson and Greig).
TOFFLER, A. (1970) *Future Shock* (London: Pan Books).
WEIZENBAUM, J. (1984) *Computer Power and Human Reasoning* (2nd ed.) (Harmondsworth, Middlesex: Penguin).

Chapter 24

Reading and the Scottish Tradition

W.A. Gatherer

There is a long-established tradition of pride in Scottish education. For centuries it has been widely accepted that the Scottish educational system is among the best in the world. Recent scholars have thrown some doubt on these assumptions, challenging the claim that Scottish education made for democratic independence and equality, and especially that it produced universal literacy and a high degree of culture. This paper discusses these views, arguing that reading was always given high priority for religious and social reasons, and that for that reason reading was taught with exceptional skill and devotion.

Reading and the Scottish Tradition

In this paper I propose to discuss some of the contradictions, myths and realities that lie at the heart of the educational history of Scotland. One of the most important of our anxieties as a nation is our centuries-long struggle to assert ourselves as a nation – to prove our national identity in the world, and even in that part of the world known as the United Kingdom. All of us who live in the UK are conscious of many real differences between the indigenous nations. As R.L. Stevenson put it, 'England and Scotland differ, indeed, in law, in history, in religion, in education, and in the very look of nature and men's faces, not always widely, but always trenchantly'.

One of our most salient characteristics is national pride — less of a deadly sin because it goes hand in hand with a propensity to hate ourselves! And of all our national institutions the one that gives us most reason to boast is our education system. Since the seventeenth century the Scottish education system has been renowned throughout the world. Praise has been lavished on the universality and efficiency of our schooling. There is ample evidence. Impartial academic studies galore have confirmed it. Listen, for example, to Henry Barnard (1854), an American scholar who, in the 1830s, went around Europe examining and describing the different national education systems.

> The parochial schools of Scotland have been the pride of her own people and the admiration of enlightened men in all countries . . . It has been usually expected that a Scotch parish schoolmaster, besides being a person of unexceptionable character, should be able to instruct his pupils in the reading of English, in the arts of writing and

arithmetic, the more common and useful branches of practical mathematics, and that he should be possessed of such classical attainments as might qualify him for teaching Latin and the rudiments of Greek.

Barnard goes on to aver that this superlative education system has produced superlative persons:

'It would be no easy matter,' he says, 'to exaggerate the beneficial effects of the elementary instruction obtained at parish schools, on the habits and industry of the people of Scotland. It has given to that part of the Empire an importance to which it has no claim, either from fertility of soil or amount of population. The universal diffusion of schools, and the consequent education of the people, have opened to all classes paths to wealth, honour and distinction. Persons of the humblest origin have raised themselves to the highest eminence in every walk of ambition, and a spirit of forethought and energy has been widely disseminated.'

(Barnard, 1854, p.652)

This is a classic statement of the great myth of Scottish education as a prime source of the nation's energy and genius. It is echoed in a thousand volumes of history, reminiscences and letters to the newspapers. The world's progress, it is claimed, owes a great deal to the Scottish lad o'pairts – the poor, hardworking, intellectually gifted boy who is made into a scholar, or a great engineer, or a pioneer of empire, or a philosopher or statesman by the free and thorough schooling he got at the local parish school. We have a folk picture of the lad o'pairts, sitting on a rudely fashioned bench in the wee school in the glen, his hamespun breeks carefully darned by his reverend, frugal mother back in the humble croft. He sits beside the son of the laird, and both get the same learning and the same stern but kindly admonishment from the village dominie, himself a worthy product of another parish school in another glen. And so it is that many a parish school in Scotland can boast of a galaxy of distinguished alumni, lads o'pairts to a man. Let me quote from the memoirs of John Kerr, Her Majesty's Inspector of Schools, floreat 1860 to 1896. His book is called *Memories Grave and Gay.*

Since the Reformation we had theoretically in every parish, and frequently in point of fact, schools which in respect of quality and cost the sons of the poorest in the land could make, and did make, stepping stones to the university. There is no county in Scotland that cannot furnish examples of this kind. One of the most remarkable cases – though there are many others of similar type – is the parish school of Udny in Aberdeenshire, from which, under the management of Mr. Bisset, there went direct to the university during the twelve years before 1826 a number of lads destined to earn name and fame in a considerable variety of directions. Among these were Sir James Outram, Lieutenant-General of the Indian Army, distinguished for both military and literary ability; Joseph Robertson, an antiquary of almost unsurpassed reputation and a historical scholar of whom Dean Stanley said that, though he had known all the eminent historians of his time, he never met one who walked in the past with such completeness of knowledge. To these may be added John Hill Burton [he was one of Scotland's leading historians in the Victorian period] . . . James Craigie Robertson, Canon of Canterbury, a scholar and historian of repute; George Smith of Chicago, one of the founders of that city, and the first white man who slept in Milwaukee.

(Kerr, 1903, p.78)

Let me also quote a letter written to the *Scotsman* newspaper in September of last year. It was an answer to a speech made by one of Scotland's living lads o'pairts, Lord Thomson of Monifieth, a leading British and European politician. Lord Thomson had said that Britain's relative economic decline since the Second World War is the result of an anti-industrial culture that has discouraged the most talented students from entering manufacturing. 'How right he is,' said the letter writer, Mr Hamish MacKinven, and he goes on to say that during the 1930s the anti-industrial culture was clearly in evidence,

when, at home and at school, every boy was under intense pressure summed up in the warning 'Don't go to the tools'. This was repeatedly dinned into us year after year, because parents and teachers knew 'going to the tools' almost certainly meant long spells of unemployment, low wages and poor working conditions with little chance of gaining a better way of life. Pressure to don a white collar was unremitting and naturally the route followed by many. Recalling my days at Campbeltown Grammar School in the 1930s I can count among those lost to the tools two surgeons, two master mariners, one member of Edinburgh's financial hierarchy, Mr James Gulliver, Argyll Foods, the Chaplain-in-Ordinary to the Queen in Scotland, an international airline pilot, one Civil Service mandarin and the professor of Geography at a Canadian university. A reasonably impressive list. Many others reached less exalted ranks among the white collars, but perhaps no more impressive than that gained at similar Scottish schools, including Grove Academy, Dundee, where Lord Thomson himself, a white collar achiever in the 1930s, was educated.

These are instances of the mythic power of our pride in our education system; but they are also examples of a deeper aspect of that pride: they show our high esteem for the culture, and the cultural achievements, that education brings; and, along with that, a strong pragmatic respect for the rewards that a good education can bring, both to the individual and to the nation. This mixture of hardheaded relish for worldly success and esteem for scholarship was implicit in the Book of Discipline, the great manifesto of the Scottish Reformation. The Reformation and the founding of the Kirk of Scotland was one of the crucial events in our history. The Reformation was a great popular revolution, as much a political uprising as a religious reform movement. Like all revolutionaries, the Scots Reformers knew that their movement required to be strengthened through time by the education of the people. They were convinced that poverty and ignorance were their chief enemies, and that systematic instruction in the Christian truths of the Bible must be the mainstay of the new reformed society. Of these twin foes, ignorance could be the more successfully fought. The new society they were building would be the more akin to the kingdom of God if people could read the Bible for themselves. The primacy of education for the strengthening of the revolution demanded the provision of schools for the citizens. John Knox and his associates set out to create an intellectual and political elite in the body of the kirk's ministry, insisting that the parish ministers should be well educated and also financially secure as well as godly. 'It is not to be supposed,' they wrote in the *Book of Discipline*.

'that all men will dedicate themselves and children so to God, and to serve his Kirk, that they look for no worldly commodity. But this cankered nature, which we bear, is provoked to follow virtue when it seeth honour and profit annexed to the same... And sorry would we be that poverty should discourage men from study, and from following the way of virtue . . .

(*The First Book of Discipline*, p. 289)

The Reformers respected education as a good in itself; they described wisdom and learning as 'a treasure more to be esteemed than any earthly treasures'; but they were conscious also that schooling was an essential instrument of public control and progress. What they called 'the Necessity of Schools' was a carefully worked out plan for a universal scheme of education, and it grew out of their intention that the doctrines and principles of the reformed faith should be handed down through the generations.

For as the youth must succeed to us, so ought we to be careful that they have the knowledge and erudition to profit and comfort that which ought to be most dear to us, to wit, the Church and Spouse of the Lord Jesus.

(*The First Book of Discipline*, p.295)

The Reformers were also convinced of the immediacy of religious experience, and the direct personal relationship that must exist between each individual and God. So they asserted the primacy of the parish in the governance of the kirk, and created arrangements that allowed ordinary people a strong measure of participation in the affairs of the kirk. They decreed that every parish must appoint a schoolmaster, and that every child must be taught 'their first rudiments' and the Catechism. The 'first rudiments' were the skills of reading: not just the basic skills of word recognition, but the ability to read with understanding and to reflect upon their reading. In the Book of Discipline, in fact, they say 'two years, we think, more than sufficient to read perfectly': the kirk required a much more mature understanding in its people than could be got through initial reading ability.

The Scots Reformers profoundly believed that their preaching must appeal to the intelligence, that preachers should expound the teachings of the Bible and their listeners should absorb these teachings rationally and reflectively; the prime object of religious attention was interpretation of God's written Word. They erected knowledge into a supreme desideratum for the nation's well-being. Thus everyone must learn to 'read perfectly'–to read well beyond the a b c. For these reasons schooling must be universal, compulsory and comprehensive. They insisted that when boys were found to be able to continue study—"apt to letters and learning' as they put it—they must be compelled to go on: 'then may they not (we mean neither the sons of the rich, nor yet the sons of the poor) be permitted to reject learning; but must be charged to continue their study, so that the Commonwealth may have some comfort by them.' The 'rich and potent' must educate their children 'of their own expenses, because they are able', but the capable boys of the poor should be able to go to the university by means of bursaries if necessary. Thus the national education system they devised had some of the characteristics of the modern, democratic society's provision: schooling was to be available to all; it was to be possible for the ablest to go on to study as far as they could, including university studies, which they expected to be accessible to the poorest of students. It was to be comprehensive education in the sense that every child, including girls, should have an education appropriate to their ability and needs. It was, however, to be uncompromisingly a theocratic education system, supervised by the church and serving the exoteric aims of the Reformation.

The Reformers' plans for universal elementary schooling were frustrated by lack of money; the expropriated wealth of the old church was mostly grabbed by the self-seeking aristocrats who led the political wing of the movement. But schools were set up here and there during the next hundred years; and by 1872, when compulsory free schooling was established, every Scottish town had its school, and schooling was nationally acknowledged as a social and cultural imperative. John Knox and his fellow reformers did not establish the parish school system; but they established the idea of universal, compulsory, free education, and they injected the love of learning, and the duty of study, into the conscience of the Scottish people.

In recent years certain revisionist historians have set out to challenge the complacency which is so characteristic of the standard 'Acts and facts' histories of Scottish education. These histories have promulgated the myth that the Scottish educational tradition has smoothly evolved through one progressive innovation after another through the centuries, each generation contributing toward the glorious near-perfection of today. A particular target of the new sceptics is the claim that Scottish education, with its strong motivation towards equality of educational opportunity, created an egalitarian, or democratic, social ethos. The poor lad o' pairts sitting beside the son of the laird in the parish school, and later tramping to the Varsity with his bag of oatmeal and few precious books, has been the symbol of a myth that has been damaging as well as false.

Our national history has, in fact, been one of continuous conflict and exploitation. Besides being historically the prey of successive imperialist English governments, the Scots have been continually impoverished by our own aristocracy. Our great Reformation was certainly in part a popular revolution, but it was also the cynical dispropriation of the Church by a pack of baronial magnates without a groat's worth of patriotic feeling. The aspirations of Knox and his associates did not even include the labouring poor, who were in actuality treated as non-persons. Scottish society in the seventeenth and eighteenth centuries was, if anything, even more class divided than most of those in Europe (Smout, 1969). There were men of gold, men of bronze and men of iron. The men of gold were the clan chieftains, the lowland earls and the country lairds, the rich Glasgow merchants and the affluent Edinburgh lawyers: they lived lives of comparative luxury while the men of iron slaved in the mines and saltpans of Lothian and Fife, and in the dirty factories of Lanark and Glasgow and Dundee, or half-starved in their tiny filthy highland clachans: poor, oppressed, ignorant, ruthlessly exploited, and hardly ever mentioned. We have an exceptional and horrifying testimony from Andrew Fletcher of Saltoun in 1698:

> There are at this day in Scotland (besides a great many poor families very meanly provided for by the church-boxes, with others, who by living upon bad food fall into various diseases) two hundred thousand people begging from door to door. These are not only no way advantageous, but a very grievous burden to so poor a country. And though the number of them be perhaps double to what it was formerly, by reason of this present great distress, yet in all times there have been about one hundred thousand of those vagabonds, who have lived without any regard or subjection either to the laws of the land, or even those of God or nature . . .

Henry Barnard in the nineteenth century was aware of this submerged Scottish population: he was told that the streets of Aberdeen were 'infested by little vagrants and beggars' and that there were 280 beggar children known to the police. The streets of Edinburgh and Glasgow were thronged by similar mobs of uneducated, badly fed, raggedy nuisances (Barnard, 1854, p. 512). Education was neither universal nor free.

The men of bronze, the ministers, dominies, tenant farmers and petty shopkeepers, were docile, subservient, pious, dourly industrious, deluded by such slogans as 'the rank is but the guinea stamp, the man's the gowd for a' that'. And the education system to a large extent reflected these divisions. Legislation through the eighteenth century may have assured the provision of a rate-supported school in every rural parish, but by the 1830s the population had doubled with no corresponding improvement in the structure of state schooling. The cities were especially badly provided (Withrington, 1983). By the 1930s Scottish education was still a grand egalitarian delusion: the men of gold sent their sons and daughters to

English public schools or Scottish imitations, the men of bronze cherished the anglified culture of private day-schools, while the children of the men of iron languished in the junior secondary slums. In our own day the iniquitous divisions persist even in our comprehensive schools in the form of covert streaming; and we are fighting a losing battle against the impending destruction of our six-year secondary schools, the imposition by bribery of T V E I with all its connotations—sending the poor to the tools, the better-off to the Varsity—the starvation of cultural and recreational activities, and above all the cruel, complacent acceptance of youth unemployment as an alternative to schooling.

Another target for our revisionist historians is the so-called myth of universal literacy in Scotland. Dr Rab Houston's research has seriously challenged the claim that we Scots have enjoyed a higher rate of popular literacy than most European peoples, especially (and importantly) the English. Using the ability to sign one's name as the most evident criterion of literacy, he has demonstrated that the degree of illiteracy in Scotland during the seventeenth and eighteenth centuries was at least as high as that in England and much of the rest of Europe. 'Scotland's achievements in literacy, he says, 'were among the best in Europe, but they were not unique,' (Houston, 1985). However, it must be said that Dr. Houston's reliance on sign-literacy rates renders his conclusions dubious (Stocks, 1987). Writing, even writing one's own name, was always subordinate to reading. It seems incredible to us now that people could have learned to read without being able to write even their own names; but such was the case. Throughout Europe, the incidence of writing ability was always much lower than that of reading ability. In Scotland, reading was always considered to be the prime accomplishment.

In the sixteenth century elementary schools were often called 'Lecture schools' because their main duty was to teach reading; and in the eighteenth century many were called 'English schools' for the same reason: 'English' meant *reading* (Law, 1965). By 1800 nearly all the inhabitants of rural Ayrshire, for example, learned to read, but only half the readers learned to write. 54 per cent of the pupils took reading only, and 32 per cent took both reading and writing; and the fees for reading lessons were much lower than for writing lessons (Boyd, 1961). In the advertisements for dame schools writing usually came well down the list of accomplishments offered, especially for young ladies. Generally, it was usual for girls to be taught reading, sewing and knitting, but not writing. Writing instruction was not considered necessary for the sons of men of iron, and even less for their daughters. Since the graphemes for the classical longhand script bore little resemblance to those of print, it is not surprising that sign illiteracy could coexist with reading ability. Writing was a difficult accomplishment even for well-educated Scots; as the poet James Beattie wrote in the eighteenth century: 'We who live in Scotland are obliged to study English from books like a dead language. Accordingly, when we write we write it like a dead language, which we understand but cannot speak' (Miller, 1912). Beattie actually followed David Hume the philosopher in compiling a list of

Scotticisms to be avoided: it includes 'feeling a smell', paying a tailor's 'account' instead of his 'bill', and speaking of 'coarse weather'.

But reading was always perceived as an essential social and personal accomplishment, to be learned, ideally, by all. It was, as we have seen, regarded as the key to open God's Word, and the Bible and Catechism formed the main texts used in schools. The Shorter Catechism has, indeed, entered the soul of Scottish educational tradition. To know the Catechism was, for many generations, a *sine qua non* of schooling. Robert Louis Stevenson has written: 'The happiest lot on earth is to be born a Scotchman. You must pay for it in many ways, as for all other advantages on earth. You have to learn the Paraphrases and the Shorter Catechism.' In his essay on 'The Foreigner at Home' R.L.S. said that the differences between the first questions of the English and Scottish Catechisms summed up the difference of our national temperaments: the English Catechism tritely inquires 'What is your name?' but the Scottish Catechism strikes at the very roots of life with 'What is the chief end of man?'

The catechetical examination by the minister was an essential ordeal for every lad and lass in the Scottish congregation. It was called 'Getting their questions', and our comic literature has many stories about it. Dean Ramsay tells us that in answer to the question 'Why did the Israelites make a golden calf?' one 'shrewd and reflective' little girl answered 'they hadna as muckle siller as wad mak' a coo.' Another lad, asked how many commandments there were, answered cautiously 'Aiblins a hunner'. On his way home from the manse with a flea in his ear, he met a friend who was on his way to 'get his questions', and asked him what he would say if the minister asked him the number of the commandments. His friend replied, 'I shall say ten, to be sure'. To which the other rejoined, with great triumph, 'Ten! I tried him wi' a hunner, and he wasna satisfeed' (Ramsay, 1926). The Shorter Catechism was published in a version authorised by the Church of Scotland in 1644 especially as a primer for young children learning to read; the little book includes the a b c in capital letters, lower case letters and gothic type, with illustrations of vowels and consonants. Later editions included the numbers up to 1000 in letters and figures, and more recent editions had the multiplication tables on the back cover (Law, 1965, p.153).

Mid-Victorian Scottish schools were still using biblical texts as standard readers. The New Testament was used for the eight and nine year olds and pupils were promoted to the Old Testament when they were ten or eleven. Children would refer to the class they were in by saying 'I'm in the Testament' or 'I'm in the Bible'. Reading the Bible aloud could be hard going for the pupils. John Kerr (1903) tells the story: 'when a little girl reading in a portion of the Old Testament which bristled with proper names of great difficulty, came to a dead stop, the old mistress, probably herself puzzled, said to her, "Jeannie, just read ye straucht on. Dinna mind hoo ye miscaa them, they're a' deid".'

By 1800 Scottish teachers were famed for teaching the 'New Method' in reading. This was placing emphasis on the pupils' understanding of what they read as opposed to what we now call 'barking at print'. Teachers qualified to use the New Method were much sought after by parish boards. New Method teachers used passages from profane literature as well as biblical texts, and they made much of grammar and rhetoric. Reading aloud and reciting with 'gracefulness' and 'propriety' were prominent activities. Pleasure in literature, interest in language and precision of speech were explicit objectives in this new approach (Law, 1965, p.196). There is ample evidence in the many textbooks about teaching that were written and published in Scotland that reading beyond the a b c was an important educational principle long before the introduction of universal schooling.

When universal literacy became a political objective for British government in the second half of the last century, widescale testing of basal reading was conducted by Her Majesty's Inspectors, and during the notorious period of the Revised Code, and 'payment by results', schools and teachers depended for their very existence on the numbers of pupils who could demonstrate their attainment in the 'three Rs in their barest form'. This is what the Scottish inspectors called 'the beggarly elements', and they deprecated the 'educational pabulum' required in English schools (Kerr, 1903, p.57). It had long been the case that Scottish schools went far beyond basal reading instruction. Reading was commonly used as a vehicle for the development of intelligence, and even as a moral force. To be able to read with ease and pleasure and to *need* reading as a necessary condition of the good life were attributes handed down through the generations.

The association of reading and religious power is graphically illustrated in Victorian reminiscences. For example, here is a story about a Banffshire teacher:

> After I had learned the 'A B C', not only on the card but by heart and memory, and was able to name every letter promiscuously through the whole 26, one day Janet seemed to be in a serious mood, and took me close beside her, and said—'Now you've learned the 'A B C', go to the door and bring ben the key to me.' I did so. She took the key, and held it up before my face, and said—'What is that?' I said—'It is a key'. 'What is it for doing?' 'For opening the door and locking the door.' She said, 'That is right.' She then laid the key on the corner of the hearth beside her tobacco pipe, took the 'A B C' card and held it up, and asked—'Do you know what the tod and the lambs mean?' [This is a game played on a chess board.] I said I did. 'What are they for doing?' 'We shift the lammies and gar'd them tak' the tod.' 'That's right,' said she. 'Now, the letters of the 'A B C' are the key, and by shifting them you can make words. By placing the words in position you make sentences; and in that way you open the door to knowledge and shut it to ignorance. You open the door to wisdom, and shut the door to folly. You open the door to truth and righteousness, and shut the door to falsehood and superstition. Now you see that the 'A B C' is just a key; and if you use that key rightly, you will do great and manly things. It was this kind of key that Jesus gave to Peter, and Peter handed it down to

others, and everyone that has got this key and uses it rightly can open the door of heaven and shut the door of hell. But only for themselves.'

('A Herd Loon', 1903)

Reading is a Scottish tradition, and today, when the facile notion that reading may be obsolescent is beginning to gain some currency, when the TV and the cassette and the computer seem to be supplanting the book, let us remember the tradition with gratitude and renewed faith, that we might all continue to work, with something of the moral fervour of our ancestors, for the better teaching of reading beyond the a b c.

References

BARNARD, H. (1854) *National Education in Europe* (New York: Charles B. Norton).

BOYD, W. 1961 *Education in Ayrshire Through Seven Centuries* (London: University of London Press)

DICKINSON, W.C. (ed) (1949) *The First Book of Discipline*, in *Knox's History of the Reformation* (London: Nelson).

FLETCHER, A., (1979) 'The Second Discourse Concerning the Affairs of Scotland'. in Daiches, D. (ed) *Selected Political Writings and Speeches* (Edinburgh: Scottish Academic Press) p. 55.

'A HERD LOON' (1903) *The Kingdom of Forgue* (Aberdeen: G. and W. Fraser) p. 21

HOUSTON, R.A. (1985) *Scottish Literacy and the Scottish Identity 1600–1800* (Cambridge: Cambridge University Press) p.22.

KERR, J. (1903) *Memories Grave and Gay* (London: Blackwood).

LAW, A. (1965) *Education in Edinburgh in the Eighteenth Century* (London: University of London Press)

MACKINVEN, H. (1986) Letter to the *Scotsman*, 5 September.

MILLAR, J.H. (1912) *Scottish Prose of the Seventeenth and Eighteenth Centuries* (Glasgow: James Maclehose and Sons) p. 180.

RAMSAY, DEAN (1926) *Reminiscences of Scottish Life and Character* (London: Peter Davies Ltd) p.51.

SMOUT, T.C. (1969) *A History of the Scottish People, 1560–1830.* (London: Fontana).

STEVENSON, R.L. (1911) The Forcigner at Home', in *Memories and Portraits* (London: Chatto and Windus) p.10.

STOCKS, J. in *Scottish Educational Review*, Vol 19, No. 1, May 1987.

WITHRINGTON, D. (1983) '"Scotland a Half Educated Nation" in 1834', in Humes, W.M. and Paterson, H.M., (eds) *Scottish Culture and Scottish Education* (Edinburgh: John Donald).

Chapter 25

Early Teachers of Reading: Their Struggles and Methods from the Sixteenth Century

Ian Michael

There is much evidence, mainly from spelling books and elementary readers, about the teaching of reading between the sixteenth and nineteenth centuries. The work of most early teachers was conditioned by their own limited education; by a view of pedagogy which assumed that short things were easier to learn than long ones; by a strong reliance on memorisation; by uncertainty concerning the relations between speech and writing and between reading and spelling. Nevertheless some textbooks contain important and little-known information about teaching methods. The struggles of our early colleagues are full of variety and are worthy of our respect.

What we know about early methods of teaching reading comes almost entirely from textbooks which have survived from the late-sixteenth century onwards. But only a few teachers wrote textbooks: those who were particularly thoughtful, particularly ambitious, or particularly philanthropic. The ordinary teacher of reading was not a regular teacher working in a school. He taught reading in his home or in his shop. His sole qualification was that he could himself read. We must envisage two kinds of teacher: a large number of men and women, unsophisticated and little educated, who were helping out; a small number of (more or less) educated regular teachers, some of whom, from various motives, wrote textbooks. The two groups shared the same assumptions about how children learnt and about how language worked. They differed in that the textbook writers were more aware of questions of method. Because our evidence comes from the textbooks we tend to forget the silent majority, and to marvel that so many teachers, three hundred and fifty years ago, were wrestling so actively with some of our present difficulties.

Notions of learning

Teachers' methods were determined principally by their views about children and about language. Children were thought to be unformed, empty; the characteristics which were distinctive of childhood were considered of little

226

value in themselves and as having little desirable connection with adult life. Children should be receptive, but passive. Learning was thought of more as the acquisition of items than as a training in skills. Small items were easier to acquire than large ones, so learning was the accumulation of items of increasing size, and therefore, it was assumed, of increasing difficulty. It followed that the teacher's approach was severely analytical. Only occasionally is there evidence that impression, wholeness, gestalt, is considered significant. It followed also that learning was equated with memorisation. The teacher could not know that the items had been accumulated unless she knew that they had been remembered.

On the basis of these assumptions children learnt first the *letters*; then they learnt *syllables*; then they learnt *words*. Only in the final stage did the pupil meet *sentences*. He had, of course, met sentences when he was first reading words, because the words were normally, but not always, presented in sentences. But in the early stages the sentences were not offered as meaningful wholes: they were syntactically coherent, but often nonsensical and usually trivial, concatenations of words: 'Both cow and calf; you know not yet half . . . A cap and a belt, with a hog that is gelt' (Coote, 1596, p. 11). One seventeenth-century textbook, after its syllable drill, continues with a long list of 'Certaine words devised Alphabetically, without sense, which whosoever will take the paines to learne, he may read at the first sight any English booke' (*A Newe Booke*, 1601, p.25). Another seventeenth-century teacher went so far as to exclude from his book any continuous reading matter, on the grounds that as he provided 'only words, not continued sentences, it enforceth the learner to rely wholly upon the sound of the Letters' (Evans, 1621, preface).

Letters

Learning the letters raised more questions for the teacher than we might suppose. The simplest questions were: in what order should the letters be learnt? Should they be learnt all together, or in groups? How long should it take? Most teachers, of course, took the letters as they appeared on the hornbook or in the alphabets prefixed to the catechism or primer, but as early as 1570 a teaching order had been suggested: first the vowels; then *l*, *m*, *n*, *r*, *h* and *sh*; then the remaining consonants grouped in pairs, 'brother and sister', phonetically: *b* and *p*, *d* and *t*, and so on (Hart, 1570, p.245). One writer recommended first the vowels, then the nine consonants whose shape does not extend above or below the line – 'the short ones'; then the downward long ones; then the upward long ones (*The Needful Attempt*, 1711, pp. 4, 15).

Many kinds of grouping are suggested over the years. In nearly all of them the vowels are learnt first; the consonants are then grouped by similarity of shape, by similarity of sound or, which comes to nearly the same, according to the speech organ dominant in their formation. By the early nineteenth century simplicity of shape is the main criterion, applied to both vowels and consonants. The best known system derives from Pestalozzi, whereby I, L, T and O were taught first. But there were other systems, the most interesting of which is Bartholomew Dillon's. Dillon made a fivefold classification of capital letters: those formed by straight lines only; those by oblique lines only; those by straight and oblique (Z K Y N M); those by curves only; those by lines and curves (Dillon, 1830, preface).

How long were children expected to take in learning the letters? Varied statements are made, both gloomy and hopeful. Hoole says that children 'of a slower apprehension', if they were set to learn the alphabet as a whole, would have learned only six of the letters by the end of a year (Hoole, 1660, pp. 4–5). On the other hand J.Sims, a London schoolmaster, reported to the SPCK in 1700 that he had evolved a secret method by which he could teach the whole alphabet in a day. His secret was never revealed (Jones, 1964, p.106). Another teacher, in 1728, says that as it takes a year to teach the alphabet taking it all together, he teaches one letter at a time, and one each day (*Instructions*, 1728, preface). As late as 1860 a Glasgow school required four letters to be learnt each week, and the whole alphabet to be known before the pupils began to read words (Scotland, 1969, p.201). There are similar variations in statements about how long it takes children to learn to read. Reading competence is not clearly defined, and there is seldom any reference to the time given to instruction. A sixteenth-century teacher claims, on the title-page of his book, that it will enable children to read perfectly in one month (Clement, 1587), and a few later teachers give the same promotional promise. An ABC of about 1555 says six weeks, but John Knox, in 1560, says it takes two years to read perfectly, to answer the catechism, and to know some elementary (Latin) grammar (1895, 2, 212). Most seventeenth-century teachers allow twelve months or less, but Charles Hoole, a grammar school headmaster, says it takes two to three years to attain perfect reading (1660, p.23). Thomas Tryon says it takes nine or ten weeks at three hours a day (1700, p.97) and at the end of the eighteenth century Maria Edgeworth says twenty-six weeks at four or five minutes a day (1798, p. 47). One of the most careful accounts is that of a Bristol teacher in 1709 who analyses the performance of fifty-eight boys entering his school between the ages of seven and ten. Of the twenty-eight who could read 'indifferently or ordinarily' the average progress (there were wide variations) was: learning the letters and spelling took three to six months; indifferent reading took another six months; good reading took a further six to nine months and was achieved about the age of ten (Jonathan Barry, current research).

Out of many methods of training recognition the picture alphabets were the most common, but they were criticised because the children remembered the picture, not the letter, or because a picture might confusingly be associated with different words, as when Thomas Lye shows an animal looking to the right as M for *monkey*, and a similar animal looking to the left as long A as in *Ape* (1671, plates 2 and 3). In books which did not contain pictures a similar effect is attempted in words, as by Richard Lloyd, who describes M as 'the great Rakes head with the teeth downward' (1654, p.3)

The most difficult question about the letters was: what should they be called? It had always been felt that in an ideal alphabet the name of a letter should be its sound, and that a letter should represent only one sound. There seems to have been a tacit agreement that the vowels, although they each represented a number of sounds, should be uncontroversially named from only one sound. The vowels were not thought to be difficult. The consonants, however, had always been defined as making no sound on their own. A consonant was said to have 'power' or 'force', that is, the effect it had on any group of sounds with which it was associated. As vowels also clearly affected the sounds with which they were combined it seemed that they too must have force. Name, sound and force were regularly confused.

To read a syllable aloud was to join together the *sounds* of its letters. To spell a syllable was to join together the *names* of its letters. If the names and sounds of the vowels were often the same, and if the names of the consonants expressed their force, and if force and sound were often identified, it is not surprising that the two processes of reading and spelling were knocking up against each other all the time.

A main reason for the teachers' difficulties was, of course, their inherited assumption that the letter was the basic unit on which the accumulative process of reading must be built. A number of easements were attempted for this undiagnosed difficulty.

The commonest easement was to give uniform types of name to the consonants, either all on the pattern of *b, c, d,* so that *h* was called *he, l le, w we, z ze,* etc., or all on the pattern of *l, m, n,* so that *b* was *eb, c ec, t et, z ez.*

The second easement drew on the first, but was discussed by only a handful of writers at the end of the seventeenth century and early in the eighteenth. They believed that children found it easier, in a spelling method of reading, to make the transition from a vowel to another vowel than from a vowel to a consonant. All the consonants, therefore, except *y* and *w,* were given both kinds of name. B, for example, was called both *be* and *eb*. In reading the word *bib* the pupil would call the first letter *be*, but the last letter *eb*, so that the movement through the word was always from one vowel to another: *be-i-eb*.

A third easement was the notion of what was later called 'incipient sound'. William Bullokar illustrates the name of one of his new letter symbols by saying that it has the sound of *th* in *thief*, 'the vowel of that syllable being left unsounded, and leaving out *eef*' (1580, p.2). Suggestions of this kind occur during the seventeenth and eighteenth centuries and are common in the middle of the nineteenth century. The name 'incipient sound' was introduced by J.F. Denham, who says, of his representative example *b*, 'The only sound which should be uttered in pronouncing this letter, is that which peculiarly belongs to the consonant itself, suppressing the *vowel* associated with it *as much as possible*. . . As nearly as it can be *written*, however, it should be like the word *ub*, *u* being suppressed' (1834, pp. 8, 9).

The difficulty which we all have in discussing, in print, the sounds of speech affects our reading of these early authors. We often do not know just what they expect the children to say. When the children put each vowel after the consonants in turn it appears in print as *ba*, *be*, *bi*, etc. But what do the pupils actually say? Do they use the names of the vowels, which they have just learnt, saying, 'bay, bee, bye'? Do they say 'ba' as in *bat*, or 'ba' as in *bark*? Do they say 'bu' as in *but*, or 'boo' or be? When the children put the vowels in front of the consonants did they say 'ayb' or 'abb' or 'ahb'? What rule (in the practice of the times) would they have been following? This is only the most familiar example of an uncertainty which affects our understanding of the phonetic aspects of this analytical method: a method which kept the teachers' work rigid. Our uncertainty is real, because the sounds of the vowels were taught as a distinct part of learning to read. What sounds were taught varied greatly. The letter *a* is said by one teacher in 1763 to represent two sounds; many others assign it three or four; others give it five or six, or seven or eight. It is no wonder, perhaps, that in 1817 the governors of Ackworth School complained that too much time was being spent on 'learning the sound(s) of the vowels' (Thompson, 1879, p.145).

Syllables

When the pupils had learnt the letters they learnt syllables. The routine of *ba*, *be*, *bi* was never abandoned, but the more thoughtful teachers chose syllables which were also words. The two methods were discussed during the seventeenth century. The argument in favour of an all-embracing mechanical method was that if you had learnt all possible syllabic combinations you could then read any regular word, however long. The argument in favour of a selective method was that if the syllable had meaning the task was easier, because more interesting, and more or less meaningful sentences could be introduced at an early stage.

The syllable was considered the central element in learning to read and spell. Until the middle of the eighteenth century the less thoughtful teachers prescribed lists of syllables to be read, and probably learnt by heart. The lists were usually formed according to the number of letters in the syllable, from one to eight (*strength* was the standard example of the longest syllable). The least thoughtful lists were mechanically formed, by increasing the number of letters without caring whether the resulting 'syllable' was a combination which occurred in English. John Brooksbank, an eccentric minister and teacher in Fleet Street, published in 1654 *An English Syllabary*, where his mechanical methods produced 'syllables' such as *poomd*, *rewnk*, *schairkld* (1654, pp. 26, 28). In most cases the lists were formed in accordance with another teaching consideration of great importance during the sixteenth and seventeenth centuries: the combination of consonants which could begin, or end, a word. There are many English words beginning *tr-*, but none beginning *mr-*. Combinations of consonants which were 'proper' to begin or end a word were listed and had to be learnt by heart. A teacher in 1596 lists thirty beginning combinations of two consonants; initial combinations of three consonants, such as *spl-* or *thr-*, might number between six and fourteen. Proper final combinations, all to be memorised, were more numerous. One teacher, about 1681, lists more than seventy. In sensible hands the syllable lists became lists of one-syllable words arranged according to the vowel and its combination with a 'proper' initial or final group of consonants. Against the combination *-uke*, for example, are listed *duke, Luke, puke*; against the combination *-aught* are listed *caught, naught, taught, draught, fraught*. Against the combination *mn-* is listed only the proper name *Mnason* (for whom see *Acts 21.16*) and the combination *bd-* is regularly given because the writers were so pleased with *bdellium*.

We have only now, after an incomplete and very sketchy account of the earlier stages, reached the reading of words of more than one syllable. The pupil had to know how to divide a word into its component syllables. This was a procedure standard in both reading and spelling, and it was governed by rules:

1. Every syllable except the final one should end in a vowel. Hence a word like *Babylonian* was easily divided into its five syllables; hence *honest* was to be divided *ho-nest*, not *hon-est*.
2. If two consonants came between two vowels, as in *master* or *tabernacle*, the pupil had to decide whether the two consonants formed a proper combination. *St* in *master* was proper; *rn* in *tabernacle* was not. The rule said that a proper initial combination should be kept together before the vowel; so *ma-ster*. If the combination was not proper it was split; hence *ta-ber-nacle*. If there were three consonants, as in *worship*, the same rule applied: *wor-ship*.
3. If the two consonants were the same, as in *potter*, they were to be separated: *pot-ter*.
4. If there were four consonants, as in *transgress*, considerations of propriety were superseded by a rule that compound and derivative forms were to be preserved. *Transgress* was divided *trans-gress*, which did obey the propriety rule (*gr-* being a proper initial combination) but in *boasted* the compound rule, which made *boast-ed*, overruled the propriety rule, which would have made *boa-sted*.
5. Another rule said that two vowels, not forming a diphthong, should be separated: *triumph* was a frequent example. A rarer example illustrates also the constant difficulty created for children by the importance attached to biblical proper names, however rare. This exchange, in question and answer, comes from a textbook of 1700:

> *Q.* Suppose, as in *Elioenai*, I have several Vowels together: How must I divide them exactly into Syllables?

A.　Let a Word have as many Vowels as possible, yet this Rule is infallible, viz. As many of them as are distinctly sounded, so many Syllables there are, and accordingly they must be divided.

Q.　Then how spell you *Elioenai?*

A.　It must be divided thus, *E-li-o-e-nai*, where both the *o* and the *e* are proper syllables, because they are distinctly sounded (Browne, 1700, p. 13).

It is noticeable in that exchange that the question 'How do you spell. . .?' is answered, 'It must be divided thus . . .'. The term *spelling* carried two meanings. To spell a syllable was to itemise its letters, in order; to spell a word was to divide it into its syllables.

Syllables were divided as part of two distinct processes. When a pupil was reading she met a word she was uncertain how to pronounce. What she was looking at was a sequence of printed letters. She had to group these into syllables, according to the rules. She had either to say each group as she formed it or, having formed all the groups first, she had to hold them in her mind's ear and then say them in sequence. When the pupil was writing, however, or spelling orally, she said the word to herself. Then she divided it, by ear, into its syllables, moderating the results by the appropriate rules. The rules were more helpful when applied to reading than when they were applied to writing. In reading the letters were already present, and the rules, which referred always to letters, could be applied easily to material which was visibly present. In writing the pupil had to provide the letters herself, mentally, before she could apply the rules. But providing the right groups of letters is precisely the task which the rules were meant to assist. Several teachers, therefore, including many who stated the rules, advised the learner just to spell as she pronounced. The teachers were not being inconsistent. They were providing precise rules for the reading technique and general advice for the writing technique.

Although the division of syllables was a standard technique in the teaching of both reading and spelling until well into the nineteenth century a thoughtful minority of teachers did not approve of it. They said, truly, that the rules had been taken over from the teaching of Latin, a language with a more consistent orthography than that of English, and that pupils who tried to follow them were regularly led into a wrong pronunciation. Bishop Lowth expressed the objection in words which were quoted by teachers for at least a century: 'The best and only sure rules for dividing the syllables in spelling is to divide them as they are naturally divided in a right pronunciation' (1762, p. 7).

Modern' Notions of Learning

The emphasis put by nearly all teachers on the aggregation of units of increasing size – letter, syllable, word, sentence – expressed common assumptions about the ways in which language was used and the ways in which children learned. There are, however, several signs and a few explicit statements of two contrary opinions, which we like to think of as comparatively modern. *First, that certain kinds of material should be learnt as wholes*, not analysed; *second, that most things are learnt better if they are learnt in a context.* These opinions occur in the teaching of the letters: Joseph Aickin, at the end of the seventeenth century, recommended that the letters should be learnt 'not in Alphabetical order altogether, but as they are mixed in Syllables, words and Sentences' (1693, p. 16), but the most important instances are those related to reading. Henry Edmundson emphasised context:

> '*Naked* and *bare* words without any *Analogy* to other Words, or to the things they signifie, have nothing to *fix* their observation, but are *loads* and *tortures* to the *Memory*; wheras *Analogy*. . . yeilds a *clearer* and *fuller* notice of them to the understanding'
>
> (1655, A4).

A few years earlier George Snell had put a similar emphasis on meaning, and extended it to a context in logic:

> 'First . . . teach them single names: as *father*, *mother*. . .*apple*, *sugar* . . . then bring them to propositional sentences; as, *the milk is hot* . . . thence to reasoning causal; as, *this broth will bite your tongue, becaus it hath pepper*. . .Lastly, let him read illative Reason: as, *My father is angry, therefore hee will chide*'.
>
> (1649, pp. 10–11).

A context of meaning was sometimes supplied in the spelling lists. Instead of being grouped according to the number of syllables, or the vowel sounds, words were also listed by meaning: names of toys, household implements, and by the beginning of the nineteenth century spelling lists were derived from a reading passage and learnt in its context. As a rather sarcastic author wrote:

> It is found by experience that a child will learn to spell the monosyllables when they occur in lessons which contain some meaning, much sooner than where the words are jumbled together, without conveying any ideas; therefore the charm of *dab, crab, grab*, etc. is, in this book, generally avoided'
>
> (*The Child's Instructor*, 1797, preface).

Comenius, in the words of his translator, Charles Hoole, maintained that children could learn to read merely by looking at the captions to the pictures in his text: 'without using any ordinary tedious spelling, that most troublesome torture of wits' (1659, preface). It is perhaps uncertain just how far Comenius advocated a whole-word approach, but he and later writers certainly wanted syllables to be treated as wholes. Francis Lodwick disapproved of 'the usual way of teaching to spell', which was 'to dismember every syllable . . . into many syllables, by expressing every letter apart'.

He wanted pupils 'to express every Syllable entire at first Sight' (1686, p.243). Philip Sproson quotes Lodwick and follows the same procedure: 'The child should be taught to speak every word or syllable at once without any distinction of the letters. By this means he will, by degrees, get an habitual certainty in the right pronunciation' (1740, pp. vi–vii). About the same time Sayer Rudd, master of an academy in Deal, bothered by the difficulty caused by *gh* in a spelling method, wanted all the words in the language which contain *g* and *h*, together or separately, to be listed so that the pupils 'may . . . learn *their use* by *frequent inspection* (reading such words and getting them *by heart*, without attempting to spell them) (1755, p. 47n.).

Richard Lovell Edgeworth is sometimes said to have been the first to propose look and say methods. He was in sympathy with them but, as we have seen, was not the first to advocate them, nor did he use the term *look and say*. The Edgeworths refer to whole-word methods in their *A rational primer*. 'Children,' they say, 'who soon become impatient of the labor of spelling every word as they go on, quickly attempt to spell *logographically*, and in this ambition they should be gradually encouraged' (1799, p.36, first pagination). The most interesting part of that comment is its recognition that a whole-word approach is what children naturally come to desire, and is not something forced on them by teachers. Logography was a system of printing by means of block words, not single letters, which had a vogue at the end of the eighteenth century, and was applied to language learning in *The logographical-emblematical English spelling book*. Its author, P.V. Lenoir, repudiates an alphabetical approach to reading: a boy, he says, who had been kept for two years on Dilworth's spelling book could not read a word of five letters. Lenoir's method postulates eighty-four basic sounds, represented by single letters or by groups of letters such as *ing*, *ision* and *cious*. Associated with each sound is the picture of an object whose name *ends* with that sound. The sound *sh* is accompanied by a picture of a fish; the sound *bl* by the picture of a table; the sound *a* by a picture of an umbrella. Each picture is printed on a separate counter, on the back of which is shown not only the particular group of letters with which it is associated but also the other letter combinations, perhaps four or five, which may make the same sound. The counters cost eighteen shillings a box. Lenoir seems to have been a little unsure of his method, as he promises that he will 'attend six or eight times, without any charge' on purchasers in town who do not understand his system; other purchasers 'may be supplied. . . with female teachers whom he has taken the trouble to qualify' (1800, passim).

Conclusion

The struggles of Lenoir and many other teachers suggest that it is more difficult for adults to *teach* children to read than it is for children to *learn* to read. But one does not study these pioneers in order to find a moral or some forgotten method which could be applied today. For some people such study is mere antiquarianism, but I think it is true of all professional and craft skills that some knowledge of their historical development stimulates the imagination in a way which may have present and practical value. More important, however, is the feeling of historical solidarity: that one belongs to a succession of colleagues who, even if (like one's present colleagues) they could hold the most extraordinary opinions, were fellow practitioners. It is always interesting to see someone else at work, and we can gain a deeper understanding of our own situation if we see it in its historical context. These early teachers are worth our interest and our respect. They are an important, and neglected, part of our social history (Michael, 1987, chaps.2 and 3).

References

AICKIN, JOSEPH (1693) *The English Grammar*, (Scolar Press facsimile edn., Menston, 1967).

BROOKSBANK, JOHN (1654) *An English Syllabary*.

BROWNE, RICHARD (1700) *The English School reformed*.

BULLOKAR, WILLIAM (1580) *A short Introduction or Guiding* in Danielsson, B. and Alston, R.C., eds. *The Works of William Bullokar* (1966) Vol. 1 (Leeds: University of Leeds School of English).

The Child's Instructor, 1797.

CLEMENT, FRANCIS (1587) *The petie Schole* (Scolar Press facsimile edn., Menston, 1967).

COMENIUS, J.A. (1659) *Orbis sensualium pictus*, tr. Charles Hoole (Scholar Press facsimile edn. Menston, 1970).

COOTE, EDMUND (1596) *The English Schoole-maister* (Scolar Press facsimile edn. Menston, 1968).

DENHAM, J.F. (1834) *A Spelling and Reading Book, upon new principles*.

DILLON, BARTHOLOMEW (1830) *A first Book for Infants*.

EDGEWORTH, MARIA and R.L. (1798) *Practical Education*.

EDGEWORTH, MARIA and R.L. (1799) *A rational Primer*.

EDMUNDSON, HENRY (1655) *Lingua Linguarum*.

EVANS, JOHN (1621) *The Palace of profitable Pleasure*.

HART, JOHN (1570) *A Methode or comfortable beginning*, ed. Danielsson (1955) (Bror: Stockholm).

HOOLE, CHARLES (1660) *A New Discovery of the old Art of teaching Schoole* (Scolar Press facsimile edn., Menston 1969).

Instructions for Beginners (1728).

JONES, M.G. (1964) *The Charity School Movement*, (London: Cass) (Cambridge: Cambridge University Press, 1938).

KNOX, JOHN (1560) *The first Book of Discipline*, in Laing, David, *The Works of John Knox*, 1895.

LENOIR, P.V. (1800) *The logographical-emblematical English spelling Book*.

LLOYD, RICHARD (1654) *The School-master's Auxiliaries*.

LODWICK, FRANCIS (1686) *A second Essay concerning the Universal Primer*, in Salmon, V. (1972) *The Works of Francis Lodwick* (London: Longman).

LOWTH, ROBERT (1762) *A short Introduction to English Grammar* (Scolar Press facsimile edn., Menson, 1967).

LYE, THOMAS (1671) *The Child's Delight* (Scolar Press facsimile edn., Menston, 1968).

MICHAEL, IAN (1987) *The Teaching of English, from the sixteenth century to 1870* (Cambridge: Cambridge University Press).

The Needful Attempt (1711) (Scolar Press facsimile edn., Menston, 1969) *A New Booke of Spelling with Syllables* (1601).

RUDD, SAYER (1755) *Prodromos* (Scolar Press facsimile edn., Menston, 1967).

SCOTLAND, JAMES (1969) *The History of Scottish Education*.

SNELL, GEORGE (1649) *The right Teaching of Useful Knowledge*.

SPROSON, PHILIP (1740) *The Art of Reading*.

THOMPSON, HENRY (1879) *A History of Ackworth School*.

TRYON, THOMAS (1700) *The Compleat School-master*.

Chapter 26

The Case for Fiction: The 1987 Muriel Spark Lecture

Allan Massie

The Scottish Post Office and the UKRA presented the 1987 Muriel Spark Lecture (first in a series) in James Gillespie's High School, Edinburgh, on 30 July.

With an Introduction by Ian Barr, Chairman, Scottish Post Office Board and Inaugural Remarks by Muriel Spark, the Lecture 'The Case for Fiction' was delivered by Allan Massie.

Allan Massie's most recent novel was Augustus, *the imaginary memoirs of The Roman Emperor, which, like an earlier novel,* The Death of Men, *won a Scottish Arts Council Book Award. He also won the Frederick Niven Prize for* The Last Peacock. *He has been principal fiction reviewer for* The Scotsman *since 1980, and is one of the judges for this year's Booker Prize. Herewith the transcript of his talk:*

Let me begin with an apology. You are not going to hear a lecture under the anounced title. There are two reasons for this, one respectable, which I shall keep till later, and one much less so. This is that I forgot the title I had given to Mrs Anderson, the President of the UKRA, or rather misremembered it. I thought I had told her I would speak on the Delight of Fiction. You are therefore going to hear a lecture on the Delight of Fiction, and my hope is that in the end the two subjects will not be far apart: the delight of fiction being indeed the strongest part of the case for fiction.

The Delight of Fiction

The famous Regency dandy, Brummell, wrote to Byron's friend, Scrope Davies, asking for £200: 'the banks are shut, and all my money is in the 3 per cents'. Scrope replied 'My dear George, 'tis very unfortunate, but all my money is in the 3 per cents'.

Why does this exchange, glinting through the dusts of time, make me think of the novels of Muriel Spark? Well, novels are – among other things – a matter of the tone of voice; and the tone is there. The dandies were later dismissed by Carlyle as 'clothes-wearing men', but the essence of dandyism was its insistence that life itself could be transformed into art by the exercise of the will. Now life is the novelist's raw material also, and when you add imagination to the exquisite precision and dispassionate detachment of the dandy, the result is these novels – seventeen of them now, I think, published over thirty years, which, while of remarkable variety, are yet all of a piece, a precious and unique jewel.

novels – seventeen of them now, I think, published over thirty years, which, while of remarkable variety, are yet all of a piece, a precious and unique jewel.

Muriel Spark has been admired by the best writers from the first. 'Read *Memento Mori*', Evelyn Waugh offered his friend Ann Fleming. And, a couple of years and novels later: 'How do you do it?' he asked her herself. 'I am dazzled by *The Bachelors*. Most novelists find there is one kind of book they can write (particularly humorous novelists) and go on doing it with variations until death. You seem to have an inexhaustible source.'

That was in 1960, and the source shows no sign of drying up. She described her last novel, *The Only Problem*, as 'a meditation on the Book of Job'. The meditation, you will remember, is set in the Vosges district of France; it concerns, among other matters, modern urban terrorism, one of the few miseries not exactly inflicted on Job; and it is simultaneously her deepest and airiest book. Job's problem was how to reconcile the existence of evil with that of a benevolent Creator. Muriel Spark has been looking this in the eye since she started writing, since – I imagine – her childhood in this divided city of Edinburgh, which so dramatically, in its architecture and nature, speaks of the duality of our nature, where every Jekyll Hydes his darker self.

At the end of the novel there is this exchange:

> – He says if you want to adopt Clara, you can. He doesn't want the daughter of a terrorist.
> – How much does he want for the deal?
> – Nothing. That amazed me.
> – It doesn't amaze me. He's a swine. Better he wanted money than the reason he gives.

Muriel Spark hasn't – I observe – any illusions about money. She might agree with Scott Fitzgerald that the rich are different. In *The Hothouse by the East River*, a novel that reeks of the callous irresponsibility of the rich, she has one character say, 'Money is how things are done' – which is certainly something we can see in the world around us. Yet she knows that the greed for money is not the root of all evil. There are other roots – self-obsession, and the will to cause pain and to destroy – which run deeper and more twisted.

I began where Waugh told Mrs Fleming to start, and read *Memento Mori*. At the beginning of a time which pretends that even the old are immortal, which would cheat death with magic, she is absolute for death. 'She could not let him lie in the grave and rot', we are told in *The Bachelors* of a woman who has taken up spiritualism. But she is absolute for life too, and against its distortion. Jean Brodie – in this school, we may say, though not in this building – 'thinks she is the God of Calvin, she sees the beginning

and the end' . . . 'Miss Brodie', Sandy senses, 'has elected herself to grace.'
Which makes her both evil and comic.

You have novelists, many of them admirable in their way, who reproduce
life. When you read them, you are pleased to find the novel correspond to
your experience But there are others who change the way you see things.
Muriel Spark belongs to this second, and rarer, company. She is airy and
concrete, light as a soufflé, and – if she will forgive me, tough as an old
boot – I speak only of her fiction. She shirks nothing. Graham Greene wrote
once that 'with the death of Henry James the sense of evil disappeared
from the English novel'. It came back in Muriel Spark. She is, as befits a
Scot, a metaphysical, in all senses of that difficult word; and yet, so exact
is her dandy's tone, so keen her eye for discrepancy, her novels are the
perfect expression of the Comic Spirit of our time.

Reviewing *Loitering with Intent*, I wrote 'No novelist so surely conjures
up delight, so unfailingly makes the spine tingle, the hairs on one's neck
stand on end. She is quite simply beyond compare.' And so she is: the
crème de la crème. And the spring, I must tell you, will bring a new novel.

It is a great honour to have been asked to give the first Muriel Spark
Lecture. I am grateful to you for asking me to do so, and to the Post
Office, and its Chairman in Scotland, Ian Barr, for making it possible. And
there could, of course, be nowhere more appropriate than James Gillespie's
School, for if it is not exactly the Marcia Blaine School where Jean Brodie
taught, it may yet be taken as a transfiguration of it.

When I was asked to give the lecture, I was also invited to choose my
own subject. I thought of considering the peculiarity that Edinburgh has
nurtured three novelists of the first order, whose names all begin with the
letter S – Scott, Stevenson and Spark – but then, mindful of the delight I
have received from Muriel Spark's novels, and confident that delight is the
first quality one seeks in art, I chose the title which has been announced.
Since then, I may say, I have been invited to act as one of the judges for
this year's Booker Prize, as a result of which I am now about half-way
through a shelf of almost a hundred novels – I haven't actually dared to
count – and I must say that, had I known this was to occupy my summer,
I might have chosen a different title; for you will not be surprised to know
that the delight of fiction is not exactly uppermost in my mind.

And yet I'm not sure. Even the experience of reading these novels
submitted by their optimistic publishers – many of which, I must tell you,
seem to me about as exhilarating as a field of sugar beet on a grey
November day – can be held to justify my theme; and there are two reasons
for this.

First, there is, of course, the enormous reward of seeing the real thing
surface from the depths. You won't, of course, expect me to say just which
novels offer the real thing. And second, there is the salutary and chastening
reminder – no doubt to be brought still more forcibly home when I meet
my fellow judges for discussion – that tastes differ, that others feel delight
where I may feel none. One assumes that the optimistic publishers have,
for I am not so cynical as really to suppose that no one in a publisher's
office has read the novels they publish. And this does seem an appropriate

occasion to remind you of the variation in taste that must exist. There are keen, even devoted readers of novels who see no great merit in even some of the greatest writers.

Now, some of you may have found something familiar in the phrases I quoted from my review of *Loitering with Intent*. That one, for instance about the hair on one's neck standing on end – that's from Housman, of course, from his lecture on *The Name and Nature of Poetry* – in which he said that there were certain lines of poetry he couldn't let himself remember while shaving – or he would cut himself. I'm not quoting exactly. He put it, being Housman, in more elegant and lapidary fashion. And that other – about the tingle in the spine – that's from Nabokov, from his priceless *Lectures on Literature*, which offer the best course in reading that I know.

Nabokov used to give his students a little quiz at the start of the academic year, Ten Definitions of a Reader, and from these ten the student had to select four which would combine to make a good reader.
The ten were:

1. The reader should belong to a book club.
2. The reader should identify himself or herself with the hero or heroine.
3. The reader should concentrate on the socioeconomic angle.
4. The reader should prefer a story with action and dialogue to one with none.
5. The reader should have seen the book in a movie.
6. The reader should be a budding author.
7. The reader should have imagination.
8. The reader should have memory.
9. The reader should have a dictionary.
10. The reader should have some artistic sense.

Well, of course, the kindly old scoundrel had actually loaded the dice. Even so, many of his students contrived to throw them wrong, and went, for instance, for the socioeconomic angle, refusing to see that the requirements of a good reader are imagination, memory, a dictionary, and some artistic sense – which last – I admit – begs a big question. But if we accept that these are indeed the requirements of a good reader, we are some way towards understanding the delights of fiction; for we may observe also that they are precisely the requirements of a good writer.

I would like first to approach fiction from the standpoint of the writer. Why do we write fiction? Why do we choose to spend hours, days, weeks, months, even years of our life in recounting the adventures of imaginary people and inventing imaginary tragedies and so on. Well, let me quote Nabokov again. 'The art of writing', he says,

> 'is a very futile business if it does not imply first of all the art of seeing the world as the potentiality of fiction. The material of this world may be real enough (as far as reality goes) but does not exist at all as an accepted entirety; it is chaos and to this chaos, the author says 'Go', allowing the world to flicker and to fuse. . .

This is rather like Stevenson's observation that

the novel exists, not by its resemblances to life, which are forced and material, as a shoe must still consist of leather but by its immeasurable difference from life, which is designed and significant, and is both the method and the meaning of the work.

'The life of man,' he goes on to say, 'is not the subject of novels, but the inexhaustible magazine from which subjects are to be selected. . .' Life, I think we can go on to say, is merely the raw material of fiction. You can't take life and put it straight into a novel. Each of us in the course of a day receives and transmits innumerable impressions, many of which we are consciously unaware; the artist's business is to select from them those which seem significant. When we take a character, we make him of so many lines of dialogue, so many touches of description, so many significant acts; and that is all. He is not a real person; but he has, if the job is done right, an urgent reality.

For the writer, this is the first delight of fiction: to catch the glimmer of an idea and see it take shape. I don't know how other writers work, though, of course, many have accounted for their methods, especially since the interview became a popular form of journalism, but I do know, in my own case, how vague and unformed my ideas of characters generally are till I see them begin to take shape in prose. The writer really does have the sensation of making something out of nothing. He starts with a blank – even literally a blank sheet of paper. He or she has the germ of an idea, often no more. There is perhaps some scene, some place that has been lurking in the back of his mind. Stevenson again says that

certain dank gardens cry aloud for a murder; certain old houses demand to be haunted; certain coasts are set apart for shipwreck . . . The old Hawes Inn, at the Queen's Ferry makes a similar call upon the fancy. There it stands apart from the town, beside the pier, in a climate of its own, half inland, half marine – in front, the ferry bubbling with the tide, and the guardship swinging to her anchor; behind, the old garden with the trees. Americans seek it already for the sake of Lovel and Oldbuck who dined there at the beginning of *The Antiquary*. But you need not tell me – that is not all; there is some story, unrecorded or not yet complete, which must express the meaning of that inn more fully . . .

What is this but 'the art of seeing the world as the potentiality of fiction'? And Stevenson himself later tried to launch the boat with his own hands in *Kidnapped*, adding 'some day perhaps I may try a rattle at the shutters . . .'

Let me stay with Stevenson a moment, remarking that few men have thought more deeply about fiction, and that it is curious that he has been so neglected by academic critics. He also said 'fiction is to a grown man what play is to a child'. And this, I think, has been held against him. It has been interpreted as lacking in a certain seriousness. After all, novelists are supposed to agonise over their creations – and some of them, such as Conrad, have made us fully aware of their novel's growing pains; and here we have Stevenson – another dandy writer, you may observe – comparing this mightly wrestling with intractable truths to 'a child's play'.

Yet nowadays 'we know more about the functions of play' for the child than the Victorians generally did – though no more than Stevenson. Play is more highly regarded than when it was seen as frivolous and even dangerous. No one would think of play now as schoolmasters in Dickens, or Mr Murdstone did. On the contrary, we are agreed, aren't we, that play is a valuable activity, even a necessary one. And not merely as recreation. If I have it right, play is valued because it exercises the child's imaginative and inventive faculties, and because it represents a means of coming to an understanding of the world beyond the child's immediate experience. And this seems to me precisely what Stevenson meant by his comparison.

A novel is – among other things – a means of making sense of life. Life sweeps before us, surges round us, confused, contradictory, violent, absurd, heroic and ignoble. It is the writer's business and his delight to seize on some aspect of this confusion, and give it shape. This is difficult, as all matters of measure are. The shape must not be too neat, or the distance from life will be too great. If so, the pleasure afforded will be a tepid one – this is the criticism that one can level – fairly – at the classic detective novel. It must not, on the other hand, be too loose. If it is, we may get pleasure from the novel, but it will not be an aesthetic one. This, I may say, because you may object, is itself a vague measure, therefore an unsatisfactory one. What is the measure of looseness? It can't simply be plot, can it?

It's well-known that Henry James objected to the novels of his Victorian predecessors and dismissed them as 'loose baggy monsters'. One sees what he meant, and why he objected. Yet his judgement leaves most readers uneasy. After all, Dickens, Thackeray, Trollope, Emily and Charlotte Bronte, and going a little further back, Sir Walter Scott, have such vitality – a vitality missing, some may think, from James himself. And yet they are, by his standards, despite their intricate theatrical plots, apparently shapeless. How can they satisfy our artistic sense?

I don't think the answer is too difficult. James looked for line in the novel, and they may lack that. But they have their own unity, the thing which holds these apparently rambling books together. It is first a unity of tone. No fiction – I think – pleases unless it possesses a distinctive, even unmistakable tone of voice. This is for me one of the chief pleasures of James's own fiction, to listen to that tireless and consequential American voice, endlessly refining his meaning, exploring sensibility and moral questions. The voices we hear may be very different – Thackeray's clubman tones, Kipling's man-in-the-know, Jane Austen's judicious, Emily Bronte's impassioned; it may have a wide range and different registers like Scott's and of course Dickens' too; but it is there. 'You know how it is early in the morning in Havana,' Hemingway begins *To Have and Have Not*, and I at least murmur, yes indeed, and surrender. The true voice always has authority, and it is unmistakable. If I was to make a distinction between the novelists who last and those who don't or are unlikely to, I think it would come down in the end to this question of voice. Think of Scott

Fitzgerald. His novels are full of weaknesses, they are mostly ill-constructed, though he gave much thought to questions of construction. He knew very little about other people, and many of his guesses seem inadequate. Compared to many of his friends – Edmund Wilson, John Dos Passos – he was ill-read, ill-informed, and despite his efforts at self-education, ill-educated. His response to life was instinctive, his judgement of his characters unreliable, and – many would say – the people about whom he wrote largely worthless. Yet he survives and delights, because, ultimately, of his voice which invites you to suspend disbelief. I know Gore Vidal dismisses him as second-rate, but then Vidal, who is everything Fitzgerald is not, writes dull novels because in his fiction, he has no personal voice.

And closely allied to voice, there is mood. Mood can give unity too. I don't need to elaborate on this. We can all, I am sure, think of examples – some leap to the eye like the fog in *Bleak House*. But mood cannot successfully exist on its own; it works with character, situation, and events. Mood that is not yoked to something happening becomes inert; but when the mood and the event coalesce, you have art and delight. Graham Greene has expressed his dislike of the term Greeneland, used to describe his books, and one sees why. Nevertheless, it is precisely the mood that word represents, that makes his work so remarkable; and that mood, the atmosphere in which even the tender and admirable emotions invite more corruption, that atmosphere is produced both by the rhythm of the prose and the choice of detail.

A Greene character walks a tightrope between loyalty and betrayal, and can never be sure which is really which. The novelist walks a tightrope himself. His problem – to put it simply - is to fuse what goes on in his head with what he sees out of the window. The fiction in which I chiefly delight achieves just that fusion. It does not try to offer a transcription of the view from the window, because any attempt simply to imitate reality (as far as reality goes) is . . . quite simply . . . dull. It offers no tingle to the spine. Take, for example, the novels of C.P. Snow, a writer much admired in his time. And fairly enough. Snow has indeed much to offer. He has a distinctive tone of voice, not a very agreeable one perhaps, but certainly not lacking in authority. He does not lack moral seriousness, he writes about subjects we might all agree in thinking important, and he does so truthfully. He writes also about a world with which we may be unfamiliar, and he offers valuable information about the way things are done there. He is a very respectable novelist. But not an exhilarating one, not just because he lacks invention, but because he is content to reproduce and to judge. And that is not enough – for me at any rate.

At the other extreme, no one could accuse a novelist like Tolkien of lacking inventiveness. His world is all invented. There are no Hobbits and we all know it. His story of the Ring is mere taradiddle. Of course, it may be an allegory, and significant for that reason. But it is too remote from experience, too whimsical for my taste. Tolkien can do anything he likes, and it doesn't matter. He is making his own rules entirely. He has escaped the constraints of probability. Of course, you may say that his stories require an internal probability if they are to work, and I would accept that, while still finding it insufficient, and judging his work fanciful rather than imaginative. What I seek, and don't find there, are correspondences.

Before the days when English was studied in universities and when only English grammar was studied in school, critics, who were not employed to teach, were fond of a phrase which has fallen into disrepute. They said that a writer 'created a world of his own'. I suppose it was a lazy phrase, and yet it is not a bad one. Because this is – I think – what all real novelists do – not in the sense of pure or impure escapism – but in the sense of offering an alternative version of reality as the writer perceives it. Novelists, however pure their art, do interpret the world. I said, however pure their art, but, of course, we must admit that the novel is an impure art. There is no such thing as abstract fiction, and though a novel may aspire, as Schopenhauer said all art does, to the conditions of music, it can't really attain it. The novelist is tied to fact even while he creates fictions. If he puts leaves on an oak tree in January, he must be able to offer a convincing explanation if he is not to lose credibility. (If he writes with a fine dash, of course, such mistakes will be forgiven, as Scott was forgiven for having made the sun set over the sea as Lovel rode up the east coast of Scotland.) This sort of problem worries novelists – and quite right too. It means their imagination is at a low ebb – or was. If your heroine's eyes change from blue in chapter one to brown in chapter three it suggests that you haven't seen her very clearly or that she hasn't made a strong impression on your imagination. When I submitted the manuscript of my novel *Augustus* to my publisher, I had Augustus at one point wave a scrap of paper, and I am glad to say that that piece of paper does not appear in the novel because my publisher, more vigilant than I, remembered that there was no paper in Ancient Rome.

So novels may be aerial, but they are also earthy. And this is one of the delights of fiction, simply that it can be as pure as poetry and as impure as journalism. I don't know if you have noticed that supermarket chickens can stand an extraordinary variation in roasting times; consequently, in my family, we often say that they are very tolerant birds. Well, the novel is a tolerant bird too. It can accommodate an extraordinary variety of things, styles, moods and ambitions. You can use the novel to expose social evils, as Zola did, and you can use it to escape society altogether. It can be disguised autobiography, and it can be remote from anything the writer has himself experienced – gentle old ladies of both sexes writing chilling crime fiction.

Yet, for all that, certain requirements are constant, if the work is to be any good; and the chief of these is a sympathetic imagination. Without this, fiction is inert, dead, cold mutton.

Towards the end of his life, Eric Linklater, whom I regard as the best Scottish novelist between Robert Louis Stevenson and Muriel Spark, was interviewed on the radio. Linklater had led a full life – he had travelled widely, fought in both world wars, enjoyed a happy marriage and a fairly jolly social life, and he was asked what had been the best part of it all. And he replied: 'When I was working on a novel, and it was going well,' and he added – rather sadly – 'and I don't think I shall have that experience again.'

Yet I think any true novelist would agree with him. There is nothing like
it. There you are, all alone, and you are at the same time making a voyage
of exploration and constructing something, forcing it into a pleasing form,
and making it so that it will give pleasure to others, and, you hope, will
last. You are playing, if not God, at least God's shadow. Of course, the
final result is never what you hoped it would be. The novel which you were
going to write was more perfectly formed than the one you have finished.
If you are God's shadow, then the novel you write is the shadow of the one
that lurks in the depths of the imagination. This accounts for the feeling of
flatness novelists feel when they are finished. It is not just that you have
parted with an old friend, as Gibbon called the *Decline and Fall*; it is also
that the job, even when you have done it to the best of your ability, must
disappoint you. I think this is why few of us really enjoy reading our own
books. It is not just that they belong to a part of your life that you have
outgrown, but that, in the reading you see where you have gone wrong,
where you have fallen short. Evelyn Waugh once expressed regret that
novelists, unlike painters, were not permitted to touch up their works. I
know what he means, and it is perhaps their freedom from the demands of
professional authorship that accounts for the peculiar radiance of the
occasional one-novel writer, someone like Lampedusa who had brooded on
The Leopard for twenty years before he wrote it.

Yet, if this disappointment exists, it doesn't cancel out the joy of creation.
Nothing can. Nothing can destroy that moment when a scene suddenly
takes shape, when you realise that you have hit, by some unaccountable
miracle, on precisely the right gesture, the right line of dialogue. Or from
the slow satisfaction that envelops you when you feel the raw material
falling into place, and the whole book achieve its form. And of course
there are times when we may read a few pages again. As Hemingway said,
'I read them sometimes to cheer me up when it is hard to write and then
I remember that it was always difficult and how nearly impossible it was
always'. That is a good saying.

I have been talking mostly from the point of view of the writer. You
may say, it's easy to see what he gets out of fiction, how he obtains delight
and so forth. What of the reader?

Well, in fact, the reader's case seems to me to be not so very different.
If we go back to that lazy phrase 'the writer creates a world of his own'
and look more closely at it, we can see that this is just what the reader
may get out of fiction: the writer offers an enlargement of experience, sets
up a parallel or alternative world as a means, for the reader, of living more
fully by living with a wider and deeper appreciation of the way the world
is constituted, and of how people behave, and should behave. This is, of
course, a form of vicarious living to invite us to share in the adventures of
Alan Breck and David Balfour, for example, but in as much as the novel
also offers a criticism of life, we may finish even a novel of adventure like
Kidnapped with a fuller understanding, such as David himself achieves.

The desire to attain this is why so many young people read novels, and
the disappearance of that desire is why so many older ones stop doing so.

Of course, I won't pretend that we always read novels, any of us, for such a weighty reason. We also read them for pleasure pure and simple, and for relaxation. I confess that when I have done a day's work, I don't often pick up a new novel – part of my day's work may have been reviewing one – or turn to Dostoevski or Flaubert. Instead I pick up old favourites – Wodehouse or Buchan or Conan Doyle or Chandler or Simenon–I was delighted when Muriel told me last night that Madame Maigret was almost her favourite female character in fiction – or I read the new Dick Francis. Such reading is like a conversation with an old friend, and I have always had sympathy with the Bishop who said on the wireless that for relaxation he liked nothing better than to curl up in bed with his favourite Trollope.

Yet in the end I insist that the principal reason for reading fiction and the chief reward one gets from it, is aesthetic delight. And this is something which does not have to be justified. It is good in itself. Of course, plenty of people may seem to do without it, and it is tempting to agree with Plato that such live like swine and go down good for nothing to the world below; but I am not sure. Most people have some source of aesthetic delight; fiction is only one – though a rich and copious and versatile one.

I seem to be ending by reverting to my announced title. The second reason for abandoning that was that the case for fiction has been made by a greater authority and more skilful advocate that I:

> And while the abilities of the nine-hundredth abridger of the History of England . . . eulogized by a thousand pens, there seems almost a general wish of decrying the capacity and undervaluing the labour of the novelist and of slighting the performances which have only genius, wit and taste to recommend them.
>
> 'I am no novel reader' – 'I seldom look into novels' – 'Do not imagine that I often read novels' – 'It is really very well, for a novel. . . ' Such is the common cant – 'And what are you reading, Miss?' – 'Oh it is only a novel', replies the young lady, while she lays down her book with affected indifference or momentary shame – 'It is only Cecilia, or Camilla or Belinda' or, in short, only some work in which the greatest powers of the mind are displayed, in which the most thorough knowledge of human nature, the happiest delineation of its varieties, the liveliest effusions of wit and humour are conveyed to the world in the best chosen language . . .

With an advocate like Jane Austen, ladies and gentlemen, I may fall silent. The case for fiction rests.

List of Contributors

Professor Jonathan Anderson
Flinders University of South Australia

Roger Beard
Lecturer in Education
School of Education
University of Leeds

Peter Brinton
Deputy Head
St Columb Minor C.P. School
Cornwall

Carol M. Butzow
Reading Consultant
Pennsylvania
USA

John W.Butzow
Associate Dean
College of Education
Indiana University of Pennsylvania
USA

Asher Cashdan *et al*
Communication and Information Research Group
Department of Communications Studies
Sheffield City Polytechnic

Professor Margaret M.Clark
Faculty of Education
University of Birmingham

Doug Dennis
Worcester College of Higher Education

Dr Rona Flippo
Fitchberg State College
Massachussetts
USA

Sheila Flower
Headteacher
Fallin Primary School
Scotland

Ronald Fyfe
Northern College of Education
(Aberdeen Campus)

Keith Gardner
Formerly Senior Lecturer
School of Education
Nottingham University

William A. Gatherer
Formerly Chief Advisor
Lothian Region

Professor Christian Gerhard
George Washington University
Washington D.C.
USA

Nigel Hall
School of Education
Manchester Polytechnic

William Jackson
Foundation of Writing Project
Scottish Curriculum Development Centre
Moray House College of Education
Edinburgh

Joyce Kilpatrick
Assistant Principal Teacher of English
Inveralmond Community High School
Livingston

Susan Lehr
Department of Education
Skidmore College
Saratoga Springs
New York
USA

Joy A. Leitch
Senior Lecturer in Education
Department of Management and Education in the Public Sector
North East London Polytechnic

Allan Massie
Writer
Selkirk
Scotland

Professor John E. Merritt
Emeritus Professor
The Open University
The Leverholme Trust
Charlotte Mason College of Education
Ambleside

Ian Michael CBE
Visiting Professor
Institute of Education
London University

Evelyn Mitchell
Kettybrewster Primary School
Aberdeen

Mary Neville
Director
Scottish Education Department
Language Monitoring Project 1982–86

Sue Palmer
Writer and Teacher
Cornwall

Bridie Raban
Department of Education
University of Reading

Anne Robinson
Senior Lecturer in Education
Community Studies in Education
Manchester Polytechnic

Betty Stirling
Headteacher
St Margarets Primary School
Polmont
Scotland

Professor Marian J. Tonjes
Western Washington University
Washington
USA

David Wray
Department of Education
University College
Cardiff